AN OASIS UNDER SOUTHERN SKIES

"Don't die with the music in you"

GD Editions

Copyright © Gordon Derbyshire 2016 - All Rights Reserved

Photography by Dave Williams rlphotos/Jean Roig, Andrew Varley Agency
Michel Clementz, Hélène Tarbes-Ribière, Perpignan Museum Archives
Gérard Barrau Tourouzelle-Lézignan and Catalans Dragons

The author of this book has made every effort to avoid breaching copyright, and to acknowledge (and pay for) the use of any photographs not already covenanted

Layout, design and type setting by Fabienne Acquaviva

Printed in France 2016 by Copymedia - 33693 Mérignac-Bordeaux

ISBN 978-2-9555267-0-5

No part of this book may be reproduced or transmitted in any form or by any means without prior written permission from the author.

CONTINENTAL LIGHTS
A CATALANS DRAGONS STORY

EL SEGADORS .... p. 5
FOREWORD .... p. 7
ACKNOWLEDEGMENTS .... p. 9
PREFACE .... p. 11

Chapter 1 - GUASCH .... p. 21
Chapter 2 - STACEY'S COMING .... p. 27
Chapter 3 - WEMBLEY .... p. 47
Chapter 4 - LE PADRE .... p. 65
Chapter 5 - BARCELONA .... p. 79
Chapter 6 - BOAR LANE .... p. 97
Chapter 7 - ACT 2 .... p. 117
Chapter 8 - FORTRESS BRUTUS .... p. 139
Chapter 9 - A FRENCH CLUB .... p. 163
Chapter 10 - HEADINGLEY FALLS .... p. 181
Chapter 11 - WILL CARNEY PLAY .... p. 209
Chapter 12 - WHERE NOW .... p. 237

POSTSCRIPTS .... p. 245
WORLD CUPS 2008-2013 .... p. 245
FRENCH ELITE 1 COMPETITION .... p. 260

APPENDICES .... p. 267
FACTS & FIGURES .... p. 267
POT-POURRI .... p. 275

PROFILE – GORDON DERBYSHIRE

Born and raised in Widnes
Attended Simms Cross Primary School, Fairfield Secondary Modern, Edge Hill College and Liverpool Polytechnic
Played on the wing for Widnes RLFC 1969-71
PE Teacher and later Leisure Services Officer in Gloucestershire
Lived in Carcassonne in the South of France since 2000
League Weekly correspondent covering Catalans Dragons home games since 2007

ELS SEGADORS

Els Segadors («The Reapers») is the official anthem of Catalonia both sides of the border and sang before all the clubs home matches. The Spanish Catalan government adopted «Els Segadors» as the anthem of all Catalonia in 1993.

Catalonia triumphant
shall again be rich and bountiful.
Drive away these people
Who are so conceited and so contemptful.

Strike with your sickle!
Strike with your sickle, defenders of the land!
Strike with your sickle!

Now is the time, reapers.
Now is the time to stand alert.
For when another June comes
Let us sharpen well our tools.

May the enemy tremble.
upon seeing our symbol
Just as we cut golden ears of wheat
when the time calls we cut off chains.

FOREWORD

By Ray French

Gordon……. It is not often that an ex English teacher is asked to put pen to paper on one of his former pupils' books. And I would suggest that it is an even rarer occasion to be able to write a foreword on one of the great passions of my life – Rugby League!

There might be those who consider that to write a history of a club which has only been in existence for ten years is somewhat premature. Not so, for the Catalans Dragons and their famous Stade Gilbert Brutus in Perpignan have been the catalyst for the surge of interest in the 13 a side code not only in France but throughout Europe. The style of rugby played, their success on and off the pitch – already recognised with an appearance at Wembley Stadium in the Challenge Cup Final of 2007 – the impact on the production of French born players and the leadership given to every other league club throughout France cannot be praised too highly. Via TV, Radio and the written media rugby league has been placed once again before millions throughout France and the rest of Europe. And indeed, the Dragons have never been afraid to further interest in our game and help with the expansion of it as can be seen by the record 18,150 crowd attracted to their clash with Warrington in Spain in Barcelona in 2009.

As a young lad I well recall watching an experimental Italian rugby league team from Turin playing against my hometown club, St.Helens, at their Knowsley Road ground in August 1950. And I recall the excitement of reading about the tour across the Channel by the "Saints" at the end of the 1951/52 season to play matches in Toulouse, Tarascon and Figeac. I was enthused by such international activity and I still am today. When one considers the amazing development of the game throughout Europe and its impact again on its traditional and new French supporters then the ten years in the history of the Perpignan club has truly been extraordinary.

The work off the field by the likes of the Catalans' chairman, Bernard Guasch and his colleagues, the drive and spirit of coaches of the calibre of Laurent Frayssinous,and the pride and support on the pitch from the likes of Grégory Mounis, Rémi Casty, Thomas Bosc, Olivier Elima, Eloi Pelissier and company have proved that there is once again a rightful place for Frenchmen in rugby league. Not only in France but throughout Europe were they have revived the hope that our code might once again return to being at the forefront of international sport.

A history which covers just ten years of a club's fortunes is not a lengthy account but the impact of those ten years in Perpignan, in France, and elsewhere internationally has been far greater than that of many clubs over a hundred years. Long may that history continue!

Acknowledgements

Frank Jackson for proof reading and encouragement
Tom Twentyman, Patricia Stevenson, Veronica Fondin
David and Rosie Callinan, Vincent Béja
Jean Nohet, Arthur Whimperley
Magalie Bardin *L'Indépendant* Carcassonne
Yannick Rey Media Manager Catalans Dragons

Preface

The continental thing had always caught this scribbler's imagination from childhood. Since the grainy speckled images on Grandada Television from Molyneux of Wolverhampton Wanderers playing Moscow Dynamo more than half a century ago. It all appeared exotic and exciting back then to a kid growing up in downtown Widnes with war time rationing not a distant memory. Matt Busby at Old Trafford had his say too. His 'Babes' were on the rise and he was a dreamer. The United manager fought the feet draggers and doubters at the FA and placed his Manchester club into the heart of the European game. Soon Di Stefano and Eusebio of Madrid and Lisbon respectively too became part of our staple sporting diet through the wonders of the Eurovision link. In the end the round ball game never looked back.

Elsewhere rugby league was as northern as you could get. Lancashire and Yorkshire the centre of the universe with Cumberland as it was then a moon journey away. What memories, watching the "Chemics" in those classic black and white hoops with the great Frank Myler in his pomp. Making one's way down to Lowerhouse Lane traversing the Ditton Uplands, the industrial chemical waste tip painted the picture perfectly – not that it mattered one iota as long as our emblematic stand-off got the winning try. There was a wander lust too though. If Widnes weren't at home, heading for Wilderspool or Knowsley Road was always an option. The train from Farnworth Station to Warrington Central then dodging in and out of the crowd as it headed down Bridge Street, vainly trying to imitate Brian Bevan's footwork as we all swarmed over the Causeway. Loved it all, including often getting to St Helens on the bike, leaving it at the corner house in Dunriding Lane next to the training pitch, all for a penny.

It was in that part of Lancashire that one experienced something distinctly different on a grey damp day in November 1958. An international match for the first time played between a Rugby League Select – featuring an all Yorkshire pack with a prop named Vic Yorke and two great wings in Brian Bevan and the local's favourite the Springbok Tom Van Vollenhoven – and France. The first impression was how the two sides presented themselves. The home side appeared in plain green shirt with stiff starched white collar, white shorts, green socks and the customary heavy footwear. The strangers opposite on the other hand looked like royalty. Distinctive blue jumpers with red and white chevron with laced tie up and resplendent woven cockerel badge! With white ankle length socks and low cut boots they could have arrived from some Parisian haute couture cat-walk.

11

But could they play! Months before at the holy grail that was Naughton Park, Ces Thompson and Workington Town had broken our Challenge Cup hearts and dreams with a stick-it-up-you're jumpers performance par excellence. For Jean Rouqueirol's lads that day though it was more like the Harlem Globe Trotters stuff but with a sharper and tougher edge. Their passing and dexterity of movement was a sight to behold as the likes of Andre Savonne, Maurice Voron, Gilbert Benausse, Andre Carrere and Antoine Jiminez regaled us all. Game set and match to the Tricolours 26-8 and a memory for life.

Roll forward four decades and it was racing underneath the Channel on the Eurostar from Waterloo heading for gay Paris for the first ever Super League match between Paris Saint-Germain and Sheffield Eagles at the Charlety Stadium. It was the metamorphosis of all one's earlier sporting childhood dreams. A continental dimension at last for a peoples' game which although radical by nature never truly had the courage and confidence of its convictions. For that memorable night at least with 17,873 in attendance to see Jacques Fouroux PSG lads triumphed (30-24) against the Yorkshiremen at the dawn of a new professional era, the dreamers and innovators had their day in the limelight at last. Of course it didn't last like lots of things put together at that time in haste. The French contingent were run ragged, exhausted by doubling up for their local clubs in the south. By year two with by then nearly an all Australian formation living in hotels on visitors vistas, the writing was on the wall.

At the dawn of the new century and by then living in Carcassonne with rugby league once again at the front door. The local "Canaris" were moribund, languishing in the second tier and everything around the game seemed depressingly down beat. The demise of Paris Saint-Germain was a huge disappointment to the French followers this side of the Channel. By 2015 the PSG brand after its take over by Qatari money was on the verge of joining the biggest names in European sport along side Real Madrid and FC Barcelona. If only.

The only ray of light was further west up towards Bordeaux at Villeneuve-sur-Lot. The local USV club was one of the founder clubs set up by the legendary Jean Galia back in 1934. At the dawn of the new century the 'Leopards' had a more than handy side. The Australian player-coach Grant Doorey led an impressive side including two refugees from Paris in Kiwi Vincent Wulf and Fred Banquet plus three promising local youngsters in Julian Rinaldi, Laurent Frayssinous and Jamal Fakir.

Their domination of the French league was so complete – half a dozen national titles behind them – that by the time they beat the newly formed Perpignan based UTC at Beziers in the 2001 Championship Final the Aquitaine club had started already to gaze seriously across the Channel for fresh challenges and a hope of infiltrating the English competitions. By then Villeneuve, who had already appeared in the Challenge Cup, reaching the quarter-finals in 2001 before going down to Warrington at Wilderspool. They felt, that playing outside of France and against better opposition regularly was the only way for them to continue to grow and develop.

The Toulouse Olympique club under the tutelage of the Welsh-Australian coach Justin Morgan and emblematic President Carlos Zalduendo had also started to make their mark winning the Championship Final in Paris in 2000 under the Spacers moniker. Elsewhere things had started to stir down in Perpignan. A wholesale meat trader Bernard Guasch had rekindled his passion for the sport; forming a new entity the Union Treize Catalan with the sole intention of joining the cream of European rugby league.

After the Paris debacle the RFL were bruised, and after an equally catastrophic 2000 World Cup, bust financially. The arrival of a former Davis Cup Tennis player Richard Lewis as the game's leading figure at the game's Leeds headquarters promised a new beginning especially for expansion and a fresh approach to France's involvement at the top table. For Villeneuve, Toulouse and the Catalans the race was on for the ultimate prize and they knew they were pushing against an open door.

And eventually open it did. The French after a lapse of eight years would once again be eating at the top table of the European game. For some of us it was a world turned upside down; a world of colour and light. The northern game metamorphosed at the side of the Mediterranean! Gliding south on the elegant TGV train passing the inland lagoons frequented by pink flamingos. Who would have believed it?

Gilbert Brutus
1887-1944

Member of the French Resistance. Died at the hands of the Nazis aged 56. Played for ASP union club in Perpignan. Later associated with Jean Galia at nearby Quillan XV.

1962 Stade Gilbert Brutus new home of XIII Catalan. Included an athletics track. tennis courts and indoor swimming pool. It seated about 6,000 with a total capacity of around 12,000 accommodated in two covered stands. The smaller fully cantilevered stand housed the changing rooms and press box with the larger Tribune Henri Bonzoms opposite a propped cantilevered version. The far end was a semi-circular open terraced area. Brutus hosted nine internationals in the first deacade against all the major nations. By the 1980s however the game was struggling and XIII Catalan, with gates in the hundreds, decided to re-locate to their former base across town at Stade Jean-Laffon.

2016 Stade Gilbert Brutus welcomed back rugby league with the arrival of Catalans Dragons in 2007. The municipal authorities invested heavily to accommodate the new Super League club with a complete overhaul of the tired facility. All the seating was re-newed including the open terrace behind the goals. Two open mobile seating structures were introduced either side of the smaller stand now renamed Guasch-Laborde while Bonzoms became a proper cantilever stand with stanchions removed. By 2011 the ground became fully rectangular with a new swimming pool complex at the score board end and the impressive Puig Aubert cantilever stand behind the posts at the opposite end. This structure with it bars, boutique, panoramic lounge and administrative accommodation would take the club to another level. The total upgrade amounted to €10M.

José Guasch the fiery XIII Catalan hooker on the charge at Stade Jean-Laffon in 1953, the original home of the club. His son Bernard would lead the Catalans Dragons into the Super League half a century later. Photo: Jean Ribière

The Boss was emotive, expressive and some. But without Bernard Guasch the edifice built unimaginable. Catalans Dragons was his creation. He was the initiator, the believer and the force behind the project. Passionate, fiery and determined but a mental strength aligned with innate savoir faire. It had to be for this to succeed against all the odds. He knew the game and he knew about commerce too running a successful wholesale meat business in the Roussillon region.

Guasch would know when to let-rip with the players – à la Alex Ferguson – but the intelligence too when not to. One of his strengths also has been to build a decent back room staff around him which has enabled the club to progress especially off the field. He would want to make clear to everybody associated with the organisation of the importance of the club in relation to the game not just in Perpignan and its surrounds but to France in general. After PSG in 2006-7 there was no going back; the Dragons had not only to survive but to be successful and become a major player eating at the top of the Super League table. But the journey would be long, after just ten years they're still in the foothills.

Bernard Guasch has become in the last decade an important, recognised sporting figure in South West France way ahead of the game's profile. In the code's pantheon this side of the Channel his standing rising all the time – the likes of Jean Galia founder, another Catalan and Paul Barriere, in charge during the glory years of the 1950s would have approved.

Chapter 1
– GUASCH –

Villeneuve-sur-Lot, after having their application for entry into the English second tier refused, then set their aspirations on a Super League bid. They had made a good job of organising an international match for the Federation at nearby Agen, against Great Britain, which attracted a decent five figure crowd in 2001. Although the town only had a population of around 25,000 the club represented the whole of the Aquitaine region. Their President talked of a Super League of a real European dimension, with up to three French participants and sides from Wales and Italy too.

Toulouse on the other hand represented the 4th biggest city in France with huge potential corporate support from the hub of the regions prosperous commercial and industrial base as well as the municipal authorities. Although the local club had a long, rich history and the city hosted internationals and Championship Finals, the game structurally had not developed as well as other areas. Rugby union, soccer and handball – played locally at the top level provided a tough competitive sports market to negotiate.

XIII Catalan was formed on the 24th August 1934 at the Café de La Poste in Perpignan and were, along with Carcassonne, the most decorated clubs in the history of the French game. Jean Galia, considered the father of the French game was born at nearby Ille-sur-Tet and although he played rugby union locally at Quillan, it was to Villeneuve where he would found the sport. Marcel Laborde, an energetic lawyer, was the spark plug to get the game up and running after he fell out with the newly formed USAP union club. Laborde had initially helped to set up another union club, the Association Sportive Perpignanaise in the summer of 1934 but they never played a game. A few months later they were seduced and joined Galia's band and the *neo-rugby* (new). The white *maillot* with the distinctive *sang-et-or* (blood & gold) chevron was born.

The club played its early games at Stade Jean Laffon out near the railway station. In their first five years they won the championship twice and the cup once. In 1948 a Catalan Selection scored a famous 20-5 victory over the Australians in a side which included three of Catalans greatest ever players Paul

Dejean, Gaston Comes and Elie Brousse. This feat was repeated in 1964 when Reg Gasnier's Kangaroos went down 15-11 to XIII Catalan but by then the club had transferred over to Stade Gilbert Brutus on the other side of town. In 1981 the club were involved in the infamous brawling Championship Final with Villeneuve which tarnished the game terribly. Their so-called "temperament of fire" got the better of them and they were suspended by the Federation only to bounce back later to win a record four championship titles successively. The media back lash from this abandoned Final, seen on public television nationwide, was considerable. The dramatic decline of the French game was in contrast to that across the Channel where David Oxley's new regime was in the ascendency. Soon, the local game reached absurd levels of support with some games crowds not even into three figures and that less than a decade since France had won a Test series against the mighty Kangaroos in 1979. XIII Catalan deserted their mythical 'Temple' home of Brutus to return to former base at a run-down Stade Jean Laffon. Even if crowds had melted away in France the game in Roussillon still had a discernable presence. By the turn of the century, four of the region's clubs; XIII Catalan, St Estève, Pia and St Cyprien were members of a twelve team Elite competition. Each of the clubs were well structured running with age group sides of U21s, U16s, U14 as well as schools of rugby for primary age children. The region would represent around 1,500 licenses including players, coaches and administrators.

Bernard Guasch's father José was a rough house front rower for XIII Catalan in the 1950's after 'crossing the rubicon' from USAP. The family originated from the Spanish side of the border with José carried on his fathers shoulders as the family tracked across the Pyrenean peaks with bare possessions escaping the Spanish Civil War. Bernard himself became a successful, combative half-back playing for both XIII Catalan and their near neighbours St Estève who had joined the domestic competition in 1965.

It was a 40th birthday celebration in the environs of Perpignan that the seed corn that was to be the Dragons was planted. Guasch, by then running a thriving wholesale meat business in the region was wining, dining and serenading eighty or so friends. After the Gitan orchestra had done their bit the talk got around eventually to rugby. With the local USAP union club on the rise, following the introduction of legitimate professionalism, rugby league in the area if it had a real future, simply had to meet that challenge. Around that dining table their unanimous opinion was that something drastic had to happen. In 2000 both Perpignan clubs had lost Finals; St Estève to Toulouse Olympique up in Paris and XIII Catalan the Lord Derby Cup to Villeneuve at Beziers. The two Catalan clubs where tired of pinching players from each other in an endless, futile merry-go-round. By the end of Guasch's birthday do' at eight o'clock the following morning Bernard had convinced guests the brothers Philippe and Thierry Arcens, both involved at XIII Catalan and in the other camp at St Estève, Jean-Michel Gau to look at a possible 'fusion' of the two arch rivals. 1 + 1 = 3 was to be the desired aim.

Within 24 hours Arcens and Gau where in discussions and the movement was launched. Just four days later it was near a done deal with Guasch to become a leading player. The first ever meeting of the Union Treize Catalan (UTC) was held in the club house at St Estève only a week after the Guasch's birthday party had concluded. Bernard thought he might be best used as the *directeur sportive* leaving the presidency with the tandem of Rene Durand-Georges Font but others were convinced that Guasch sitting in the armchair was the way to go. The French Federation had only requested that UTC would put a team in the Elite 2. The new entity opened up its gates at Stade Jean Laffon in the September against Lézignan with coaches Mathieu Khedimi and Marc Guasch at the helm. In 2002 St Cyprien who had been promoted the previous season and had defeated the UTC at St Estève also joined the party as the new *entente* started to grow and flourish. Each entity brought with it the public *subventions* with 500,000 francs for Perpignan, 700,000 francs for St Estève and 400,000 francs for St Cyprien that guaranteed a firm financial foundation.

Elsewhere a sympathetic ear from a new administration across the Channel for the French game to re-engage with the top of the European game was starting to emerge. Ray French, lobbying relentlessly had the ear of the likes of Greg McCallum at the RFL. At the time Guasch anticipated initially a European Club competition incorporating English clubs at Championship level playing against the likes of Villeneuve, Toulouse and UTC and to use that as a future springboard to Super League entry. He was perceptive as well as assertive. Guasch believed that a club representing the whole Catalan region would be the way forward and in time, maybe others would follow.

Although on the field the new UTC configuration were behind Toulouse and Villeneuve they quickly established themselves winning the Lord Derby Cup at the end of their first campaign beating Limoux. In 2002 they reached the Championship Final going down to Villenueve at Bezier and also played in the Challenge Cup for the first time beating Chorley away before drawing Wigan at home. They lost heavily (6-72) to the cherry and whites but drew an impressive 7,000 crowd to the union club's ground at Amie-Giral. By this time Richard Lewis head at the RFL had started to look seriously again about French participation in the Super League competition. Entry to the Challenge Cup had opened up in 2000 and on 10th February 2002 Halifax became the first British side to play a tie on French soil at St Gaudens.

Toulouse had won the Championship as the Spacers in 2000 and Villeneuve were Champions by the time candidates were asked to submit their applications in autumn of 2002. It was however the informed team of Guasch that got the nod of acceptance on 16th January 2003 for admission into the Super League for the season 2005. There was still a huge amount of work to do. With no structure, ground to play on, they still hadn't developed themselves as a credible force on the field, as St Helens starkly confirmed with a Cup thrashing in Perpignan (6-70) only weeks after their acceptance. The UTC were still finding their feet under the direction of coaches Marc Guasch, the club's Presidents younger brother, and Mathieu Khedimi. Villenueve, however would still go on to win another cup and league double that year.

The following season Bernard Guasch knew that a big push forward on his playing roster had to be made. He approached players from rival club Villeneuve signing their three biggest names Jamel Fakir, Julian Rinaldi and Laurent Frayssinous. On top of that he brought Englishmen Steve Deakin (assistant at Huddersfield) back to France after his earlier coaching spell at Cannes. These changes had the required immediate effect and by the end of the year UTC were joint top of the league along with neighbours Pia. Guasch and his team had a set-back however in November when the RFL deferred their 2005 Super League entry by a further twelve months. The other Super League clubs had voted not to expand the competition to fourteen and the RFL still thought their application needed further strengthening particularly with regards to the on field performances and lack of progress with the redevelopment of the stadium at Gilbert Brutus.

In essence, the Villeneuve signings were the start of putting a quality Super League team together. In 2004 they lost to St Gaudens in the Championship Final but had their best Challenge Cup run to date winning at Hull KR and more importantly pushing Super League Castleford all the way at Wheldon Road, going down honourably (20-32). In the close season the club signed three Australians of note, who would give them excellent service in subsequent seasons (Sean Rudder, Justin Murphy and Chris Beattie). The year before their eventual entry into Super League, UTC would remain undefeated in the domestic competitions winning both the cup and league titles in style. In 2005 they once again beat Hull KR in the Challenge Cup and gave Wigan a run for their money over in Lancashire losing respectively (10-16).

The RFL had recognised how the French side had reacted favourably to the two earlier seventy points Cup hammerings against St. Helens and Wigan. Now, the sentiment was that the time was right to give the Catalan club its place at top table of the European game without further delay. By the commencement of the 2005 Super League season the existing twelve clubs already knew that two sides would be relegated to allow the French club its place in 2006. UTC would be awarded a three year license exempt from relegation.

However the Catalans would have to go into their debut season with Stade Gilbert Brutus still a building site as the major renovation had slipped behind schedule and they had to look at alternative venues in Perpignan and around the region. The clubs new 'Dragons' moniker would be adopted from St Jordi (St George); symbolic of Catalan culture since the 17th century. A decade after English clubs still couldn't accept mergers, France adopted the concept willingly and saw it as their salvation.

The RFL had by now truly tied their colours to the Catalans mast. The Australian coaching co-ordinator David Waite was seconded to the embryonic French club. The task of making the new entity a success was paramount to the "movers and shakers" in Leeds. There was going to be no repeat of the Paris fiasco whereby players doubled up each weekend turning out for both their clubs in the South as well as in Super League when the competitions overlapped and when in year two, by then an Australian dominated group, playing on tourist visas and boarded up in hotels.

Waite's involvement centred on building strong administrative and coaching structures at the Perpignan based club. The Australian, Grant Mayer, would soon arrive to become the club's first Chief Executive Officer to oversee the new arrivals baptism season in 2006. It would prove a bumpy ride. David Waite's knowledge of the Australian game would be crucial in helping to put together a competitive squad. Although the club's last game was in May 2005, the time was still pressing to get everything shipshape for the grand finale opener in February the following year. UTC itself would continue to play in the French competition, a requirement stipulated by the French Federation. They would become the Dragons reserve team in everything but name and would base themselves at St Estève on the outskirts of the town.

Chapter 2
– STACEY'S COMING –

By the autumn of 2005 it soon became evident that the building work at Stade Gilbert Brutus was way behind schedule and the first real hurdle to overcome had already reared its head. Brutus had a special place in the hearts of all French rugby league fans and especially for the Catalans. It was opened in 1960 and was a regular Test match venue in its early days. By the end of that first decade Great Britain had only won one Test match in six encounters there. Alas twenty years later, Test football was only pulling average crowds of 4,000 to Brutus with the French game on its knees. By the time XIII Catalan relocated to the old Stade Jean Laffond it was looking worse for wear and given over to the local soccer club.

There was only one solution, the use of Stade Amie-Giral just down the road. Although municipality owned like most sports grounds on the continent Amie-Giral, had been commandeered by the USAP union club over a long period of time as the main sports club in the town. The seating coloured sky blue like its jerseys and the clubs insignia omnipresent. However when USAP where not playing their games at home, they had in principle no right to deny other users, although that wouldn't mean that all the amenities present would be freely available as the Dragons in due course would find out.

So the Catalans Dragons would play the majority of their games there in their debut season and where fixtures clashed with the union club they would have to relocate to venues further a field. This was not entirely a problem as the club wanted to show case Super League as widely as possible at the same time as respecting the wishes of local supporters and sponsors, particularly the public authorities who where investing heavily in the Dragon's project. It cannot be understated the extent of this level of support and why the Catalans wanted from the off a wider regional remit. From that perspective they could access public funding from regional, area and town council governing bodies.

Stacey Jones's signature though was the one that got tongues wagging. The Kiwi international scrum half was widely regarded as the best New Zealand player of his generation with 238 NRL games to his name and a true legend of the game.

It was a stellar signature for sure and showed the club's intent. Waite's connections back in Australia would further facilitate the arrivals of Ian Hindmarsh an experienced back row forward from Canberra, Alex Chan a 31 year old Kiwi prop from Melbourne and two three-quarters, John Wilson from West Tigers and Mark Hughes a former State of Origin representative from Newcastle. With the three Australians who had played for UTC in their last season prop Chris Beattie, winger Justin Murphy and stand off Sean Rudder retained, it brought to eight the number of antipodeans in the Catalans Dragons inaugural squad for 2006. The RFL gave the new franchise dispensation in its allocation of overseas players with the intention that over subsequent seasons the number would drop.

New faces in the French contingent would be the promising young prop from Lézignan, Rémi Casty and wing Fred Zitter who had been playing across the Channel at Barrow. Since their Super League nomination the Catalans had been like bees around the honey pot to French players. All the best bar the odd one or two were in Perpignan by the new year of 2006. The anticipation was that it was a squad which would make a fist of it driven on by the likes of Beattie and Chan up front and guided around by the maestro Jones with the French membership more than willing followers behind.

It would be as you would imagine a campaign of ups and downs but the decision on the eve of the season to dispense with the services of coach Steve Deakin was a bit of a bombshell. David Waite took the reins temporary assisted by Peter Donkin with a third Australian Matt Adamson a former Kangaroo international as fitness conditioner. The excitement was palpable as the kick off to the Dragons Super League era approached more so when it was announced that a club of Wigan's standing would visit Perpignan on the opening weekend in February. The clubs colours of blood red and gold ('sang-et-or') were as a given, replicating the Catalan national flag and the chevron matching that of the old XIII Catalan club. There was just a touch of blue in there to represent St Estève but that was gone by the following year. The size of the impending operation was overwhelming in a way from a UTC club who twelve months before sold maybe a dozen replica shirts and barely more season tickets.

Harlequins RL arrived after Christmas for a pre-season training camp and would become the first side to play against the brand new formation at the

Municipal Stadium in St Estève on Saturday 21st January in a pre-season game. Two new entities in fact after the Londoners fusion with their union neighbours was about to lift-off. Around 2,500 turned up which was encouraging on a sunny, mild winters afternoon. Phil Bentham the man in charge began early doors as the pantomime villain in the eyes of the French fans, dishing out his first yellow card inside half an hour to Chan. On a serious note the pace and precision of the Super League opposition led by the spring heeled McLinden and a thrusting Leuluai was timely reminder about what was to come. The new boys minus Jones put in cotton wool awaiting the Wigan opener a week later, took nine tries in a (6-46) walloping.

**STAR GAME 2006 SUPER LEAGUE XI ROUND 1 WIGAN WARRIORS
at Aime-Giral on Saturday 11th February**

Three weeks later it was the grand opener par excellence in front the Sky and Canal Plus cameras. Bernard Guasch's six year dream had become a reality and the French had got back her precious Super League place eight years after the Paris demise. Sitting high up in the Desclaux stand that evening was a special place to be with the glistening snow covered slopes of Pic de Canigou as a back cloth while pitch side the razzle-dazzle of AC/DC 's "Highway to Hell" merged with "Els Segadors". With 11,000 present mixing the curious with lapsed treiziste support and a sizable Lancashire presence too. The local team that night carrying the sang-et-or represented not just Perpignan or even French Catalonia but the whole of the rugby league community of France.

And what an uplifting start we got with Australian Hughes making history going over for their first ever points inside the opening five minutes; a try from Jones long looping pass. Wigan though responded in style with two tries from Dallas and Palea'aesina to put the cherry & whites a converted try in front. In a free flowing opening it was soon level though as Frayssinous latched onto a delicate chip into the in goal from Jones and then Fakir charged over to put the newcomers back ahead. The latter had the ignominy though of becoming the first Dragons player to be sin-binned and they dually paid the penalty as Wigan crossed twice to put them ahead 22-16 at the break.

The French newcomers didn't hang around on the restart with an unconverted Renaud Guigue score created by Hughes and Jones. The Catalans were ready to seize their chance now and with Beattie and Fakir to the fore, bit by bit, took the ascendency against their illustrious opponents. A delightful flowing movement saw a superb Murphy try converted with aplomb by Frayssinous from the side line as the lead changed hands yet again with the captivated crowd lapping it up. After O'Loughlin bombed a chance in the in-goal Richards forced his way past Guigue for a converted try followed soon after by a Tickle penalty leaving it at 30-26 to the visitors with less than 10 minutes remaining of a palpitating encounter.

The destiny was though with the sang-et-or on this their special opening night and they weren't going to be denied. Back they came with a winning salvo as first Hindmarsh barged his way over to edge them ahead and then Murphy crowned it all with his second try and the *'cerise sur le gâteau'*. Twelve tries recorded and the lead changing hands seven times (38-30). *Magnifique!* The fireworks exploded and the champagne began to flow. A new and exciting continental venture was well and truly launched.

Catalans 38-30 Wigan. HT: 16-22. Weather: Fine. Referee: Ashley Kline
Attendance: 11,122
For Catalans 7 tries from Hughes (2), Frayssinous (14), Fakir (30), Guigue (46) Murphy (53,77), Hindmarsh (75) & 5 goals from Frayssinous. For Wigan 5 tries from Dallas (6), Palea'aesina (12), Moran (35), Seuseu (40), Richards (70) & 5 goals from Tickle.
Sin-bin: Fakir (30-40)
Catalans: Frayssinous, Murphy, Wilson, Sadaoui, Hughes, Rudder, Jones ©, Beattie Rinaldi, Fellous, Guisset, Fakir, Hindmarsh Substitutes: Chan, Mounis, Jampy Guigue
Wigan: Ashton, Calderwood, Richards, Vaealiki, Dallas, Orr, Moran, Logan, Higham Palea'aesina, Hansen, Tickle, O'Loughlin © Substitutes: Godwin, Seuseu, J Tomkins Brown

The match got top billing in the following mornings popular regional newspaper *L'Indépendant* with the whole of the front page of its Sports Section dedicated to the opening game leading with *"Les Dragons au pinacle"* as their mast heading. This was a rarity for the game even when the Roussillon region had a surplus of clubs in the top echelon of the French league so dominated was the press coverage with most things USAP. The union club was the biggest name in town by half and the arrival of the Dragons would create a fresh new dynamism to the Catalan sporting landscape. A particular rivalry welcomed by some and not by others as subsequent events would reveal.

The local papers sports editor, Thierry Bouldoire summed up the previous evenings events succinctly: "Yes great spectacle and fabulous win but the hard work starts now. Long trips to England in the heart of winter will not be welcoming. Not all visitors to Perpignan will have the allure of Wigan. *'Le combat'* will not be won in the opening round. After five years of graft Bernard Guasch knows that better than anyone," was the editor's play on things.

What a difference a week makes. Bouldoire clairvoyant as Salford's Willows on a dark dank Lowry filled night revealed. If losing their coach on the eve of a fresh new dawn wasn't inconvenient enough, losing your marquee player and the one everything would centre around, captain and talisman Jones with a broken arm inside quarter of an hour, was catastrophic. It knocked the stuffing out of them from the second hurdle long before the water-jump complicated even further when half-back replacement Rinaldi also struggled to go the distance. Welcome to the real world. The neon lights of the entertainment venue behind the posts could have flashed as the French visitors lost the arm wrestle (0-16).

The Frayssinous-Rudder half-back pairing would be their third in as many weeks for the next away trip the week after in Yorkshire against Castleford. A difficult start at the old Wheldon Road had them chasing the score from the outset with two early converted tries conceded. They hit back before the break though with an outstanding score of their own from 70 metres out created by Beattie, Rinaldi and Bruno Verges and concluded by Thomas Bosc for his first Dragons try. Amazingly they pulled back a sixteen point deficit to go ahead late in the second period only to be pipped on the bell by two late Tigers touchdowns (28-34). Stand in coach Waite reasonably satisfied concurred, "Each match is a discovery of sorts for our players having never reached this level before. It was again a different challenge to that of Salford last week."

With Jones a long term injury Waite hadn't wasted time in recruiting a young Australian replacement from Canberra Michael Dobson to fill the void. At the same time he was to announce that one of the assistant coaches at his old St George Illawarra club in Sydney, Mick Potter, would take the reins of the Perpignan club in the coming weeks. The opening weeks in their new Super League adventure had been reasonably satisfactory but two of the sides faced so far had finished in the lower half of the competition the season before whilst Castleford had just been promoted. What lay ahead in the immediate future would be something else with the arrival at Stade Aime-Giral over successive weekends of the Yorkshire juggernauts Bradford and Leeds. This would offer a challenge of another dimension. It would test the mettle of the newcomers to the limit both on and off the field.

The whirlwind that was the Bulls back then roared through the Dragon's den on a mild winter's evening wrecking everything in its wake and leaving the near five figure crowd gawping in disbelief. Two converted scores inside the first ten minutes and thirty on the board by the break as Vangana, Harris and Hape et al did the business. Bradford were to prove just too big, too fast and too powerful as the locals would take their first ever heavy beating (18-50). It was an early reminder if need be of the size of the challenge which faced the new French entity and it was to be re-enforced seven days later with interest.

Leeds arrived as title holders on a cold, late winter's night beside the Mediterranean promising more of the same and they didn't disappoint. The fresh faced Dobson making his debut must have wondered what he had let himself in for as in no time the speedy and proficient Yorkshire heavyweights squeezed the living day lights out of the locals. The first ten minutes saw three converted tries rattled off with McGuire and Burrow at half-back untouchable. Dobson got a try back on his debut and Chan would be the first Dragons player to be sent-off on the half-time siren after a set to with Walker. It didn't get much better after the break as the Catalans took their first ten-try walloping (10-58) before a slightly disappointing crowd of less than 6,000 against one of the draw-cards. Had some locals already seen enough?

There was a distinct feeling within the camp that a definite reaction after the two previous defeats, and more particularly the manner of them, was a priority and the first away game to be televised against Warrington would be as good a time as any. To shake them out their stupor the trainer Adamson dragged them out of their beds at the crack of dawn the day after for a wake up dip in the sea at Canet Plage in the lead up and it did the trick. Before the watching eyes of their new coach Potter sitting in the stands the sang-et-or sprung to life inspired by Jérôme Guisset returning to the Lancashire club where he had spent four enjoyable seasons previously. In a see-sawing thrilling encounter with the lead changing hands four times the visitors just had enough in them with late tries from Murphy and Adel Fellous the key to their first ever success (28-26) and that achieved across the Channel to boot.

Salford had been the early surprise packet of the campaign so far with five wins out seven and sitting well in the top four. They would provide a stern test for the Catalans in Round 7 the following weekend. For once the Dragons got the ideal start with Wilson getting a try in the opening minute of play but then had to wait to the last minute of the half to cross again through Chan. In the mean time Karl Harrison's boys had shown their mettle and responded with four tries including a brace from lively full-back Fitzpatrick. There was a good feel about this contest with both sides showing up well. Catalans got back level after the break with a couple of touchdowns from centre Hughes only for the Lancastrians to forge a head yet again with two unconverted tries and a score line of (22-28) going into the final stages. The sang-et-or threw everything into the fray and were only deprived of a possible draw when wing Verges was pushed into touch a metre from the line seconds before the final bell. Exhilarating finale.

The crowd of 6,547 was nearly a thousand up on the last home fixture against the title holders Leeds. It felt as if the club had crossed a barrier and made a point. They had taken a couple of thrashings at home and survived gate wise in these tentative days. The newcomers were warming to the entertainment on offer and the quality the sport displayed. The club had worked hard to sell two thousand season tickets pre-season from a near zero base but other parts of the operation were struggling. They were selling their merchandise from a couple of trestle tables behind one of the stands while the USAP club restricted use of parts of the ground which they considered their own.

After seven rounds of Super League action it was the Challenge Cup which brought a different dimension to the proceedings. The amateurs Thornhill were in town on the opening weekend of April for the Cup game transferred across the city to the XIII Catalans old ground at Stade Laffont. The Dewsbury based club travelled in numbers and they provided most of the noise and colour to the occasion. With barely a thousand or so present in such surroundings it felt like a standard UTC French league match of the season before. The Dragons struggled to cope in the early stages with the Yorkshire sides imposing centre Bostock causing them all sorts of problems. It was only 14-0 at the break before the locals gained any type of ascendency. They got the job done with a dozen tries clocked up but Thornhill still made sure that they enjoyed themselves in defeat (66-0). Beattie appreciated their efforts the most. The big Queensland farmer's boy was content to throw them his jersey at the end.

The Catalans from the start had wanted to take games on the road to spread the word but in year one it was always going to be a huge logistical challenge for them when the refurbishment of Stade Gilbert Brutus fell behind schedule. Going to Carcassonne late in the day caused some disruption to Castleford supporters who had booked accommodation down in Spain and would have to cover the extra mileage involved. It wasn't though the first Super League game to be played at Stade Domec in Carcassonne as London Broncos had played Warrington there in 2003. The Dragons confidence was on the up after their first away win at Warrington followed by the more than decent performance against Salford and the Thornill Cup success. Coach Potter was to land his first Super League win with the French sides first half century of points with local born Verges becoming their first player to grab a try hat-trick. But it was the Trojan work of Beattie and Chan which laid the platform and Dobson weighing in with seven goals and a drop goal (51-14).

The Easter period is always considered an early indicator for how the competition will spill out with its three games in eight days. After the two points garnished from Carcassonne against the Tigers the Catalans were placed eighth on the ladder with six points but their first ever tussle with this hectic playing schedule would not smile on them. A visit to London and Harlequins was first up on Good Friday and the French were never in it well beaten (14-36) by the second from bottom team, giving the hosts their first home win of the campaign.

The league leaders and undefeated St Helens arrived at Aime-Giral three days later to offer the sternest challenge yet. Coach Potter freshened up the line-up a bit giving first runs to forwards Aurélien Cologni and Sébastien Martins and it had the desired effect giving the Lancastrians a real run for their money. Saints had only a couple of points lead at the break but won the contest with three tries in a ten minute patch early in the second period. Encouragingly unlike the home games earlier against the other heavy weights, the Bulls and Rhinos, this time the Dragons knew how to resist and finished strongly with two late scores leaving a respectable score line of (20-34) before a satisfying holiday crowd of more than 8,000.

It didn't get any easier as five days later it was the Challenge Cup holders Hull FC who left their suit cases beside the Mediterranean coast. This was another positive effort from the locals showing they were not going to be blown away at the first sign of trouble. In a free flowing encounter remembered by a Dobson try the length of the pitch along the touchline the Catalans chased the Arlie Birds all the way to the finishing line, failing by just one converted try (28-34).

However the improved form if not the results could not be sustained as two heavy subsequent losses accrued. The Dragons had drawn the short straw in landing title holders Bradford three times in their opening campaign and yet another mauling ensued this time at Odsal a week after the Hull FC game (6-54). The French players in particular were finding it hard to keep up the consistency of effort week after week. Already the Bulls had clocked up over a century of points against the Catalans and still another Odsal visit was scheduled later in the summer.

Warrington followed a week later seeking revenge for that shock home defeat taken in Round 6. A huge following, possibly the largest away support assembled besides the Quai Vauban, with their replica shirts and banners primrose and blue everywhere. The local press made a big thing of it with a page of photographs and comments. It wasn't what USAP brought to their party for sure and President Guasch was not slow in publicising it.

On a rainy spring like evening, Warrington or more particularly lynch pin Briers, had all the aces. The locals competitive in the first half keeping the deficit to just a converted try, fell away after the break. Brier's precise kicking game pegged the Catalans back repeatedly. After Chan had been sin-binned on the hour mark the French resistance crumbled with three late converted Warrington tries blowing out the final score (16-44).

After five losses on the bounce the newcomers were now very much on the back foot resting one off the bottom on the league table. Castleford over in Yorkshire was next up for the third encounter. The Tigers had been promoted from the tier below and where mid table and wanting to consolidate after their fine win at Wigan the week before. The French side had the extra incentive of landing a winning double for the first time after their success at Carcassonne. Centre Wilson gave them an encouraging early converted try lead and they were to hold that till the break in what had been a tough opening spell. Although the Tigers hit back to level it up after the oranges, it was the visitors who would finish the stronger led by an imperial Wilson finishing with a try hat-trick being the key. The Catalans would runaway with it (40-18) with Dobson chiming in with a personal sixteen point haul of six goals and a try. Herve Girette covering the game for the Perpignan paper, *L'Indépendant* announced the much needed 2 points with, *"Les Catalans roi (king) de la jungle"*.

Dobson had been a real bonus after the club had lost the services of talisman Jones in only his second game. The Canberra youngster's enthusiasm, all round kicking game and lively running had been a main feature in the Dragons first half of their opening campaign. The Tigers match would be his last Super League game for the Dragons finishing up with a personal tally of 83 points in a dozen games before heading off to Wigan. His superb try against Hull FC possibly his finest memory. Another Australian to pull the Dragons through those early choppy waters was a Queenslander Murphy. The pint sized winger, had actually arrived unheralded in Perpignan to play for UTC in the local competition a few seasons earlier. By mid-season his try haul had already reached double figures. His personal season would go on to bloom impressively.

So the French newcomers had arrived at the half way stage in their baptism season lying one off the bottom not too unsurprisingly with four wins from fourteen starts. What was a bit surprising was that two of these successes had come from across the Channel. For the Dragons to gain credibility, it was better to win in front of their own established public in Perpignan, but so far had only the home win against Wigan to comfort them. It was a tad ironic that their next game was in the 5th round of the Challenge Cup away at Widnes. Of course, the Cup wasn't new to them because as UTC earlier, they had been playing Cup football since 2002. But going to the Halton Community Stadium as it was then, just months after Widnes had had to concede their place in the elite to the French men, raised the hackles once more.

What was new for the Catalans though was their first ever appearance on the BBC in the Cup. Wing Verges got them off to a flyer within a couple of minutes as the visitors decided to play an expansive game despite the wet conditions. The Catalans didn't hang around but took the contest by the scruff of the neck forcing the pace leading by fourteen points at the break with Dobson as ever to the fore with his exquisite kicking game. Hughes and that man Murphy again grabbed second half tries always keeping the Dragons comfortably in front against a battling Vikings outfit. All six tries scored from their backs in a (34-16) success.

The last week of May brought the club both good and bad news. Skipper Jones was at last fit again after his broken arm at Salford which had kept him off the terrains for fifteen weeks a gap admittedly well covered by the admirable Dobson. The Kiwi legend was in the starting line at home against Wakefield, desperate to make up for lost time.

Off the field the bomb shell was the resignation of the Australian Chief Executive Office Grant Mayer mid-season. Getting the team to the starting gate each week was possibly the easier task but establishing a Super League club from scratch in virgin territory with a different culture and language was always going to be a formidable task. And so it proved. After the earlier Castleford re-arranged venue, Mayer was embroiled with the Wakefield game which was originally planned for Narbonne but Bernard Guasch lobbied hard with the municipality to delay the scheduled pitch refurbishment at Amie-Giral so as to permit the Trinity match to be played back in Perpignan. The politics around the use of this ground with the constant battles with the authorities and USAP was a major feature of their opening campaign.Getting Stade Gilbert Brutus back up and running couldn't come soon enough.

The Australian foot print had been all over the Catalans project from the off. Waite had been seconded by the RFL to ease their entry while coach Potter a late arrival had no previous French involvement. English was the language of the training paddock and the French lads had to adjust. For a season too after Mayer's, departure the club appeared to stumble round to get their front office functioning properly. It was all part of the learning curve. They just had to keep their nerve.

With their marquee player Jones on board, the locals were looking for that extra lift against a Trinity side similarly placed on the league table with both teams needing to pull away from the bottom places. On a hot, sunny afternoon favouring the French, Potter's charges started the stronger. Skipper Jones didn't wait long to impose himself with an opening try on 20 minutes to be followed by a surging Jamal Fakir to land a second before half-time. With the defence holding up well keeping the visitors try-less by half-time. The Dragons where always in charge in this one, even when the Yorkshire men hit back with two tries around the hour mark. They led throughout winning it (28-20) and improving their league position in the process to 9th place.

It was short turn around for the Challenge Cup as they were to jet off again across to Merseyside but this time to meet the formidable Saints just two weeks after disposing of Widnes. There was going to be no replica here though at Knowsley Road even after Jones and Long had exchanged tries in the opening quarter. Once St Helens retook the lead there was only going to be one winner. The Lancastrians led comfortably at the break and roared away after racking up 10 tries in a landside win (10-56), with wing Ade Gardner grabbing a try hat-trick.

The Gardner clan from Barrow were not yet finished with the Catalans however, as a week later at Huddersfield it was turn of his brother Matt, also on the wing, who replicated the same feat but for the claret and gold. It was a breathless free flowing affair of fourteen tries with Murphy's twinkling toes on the wing sprinting in for the visitors five minutes from the end to give them a narrow two point lead but only to be undone by a two late responses in injury time to thwart the French men on the bell (34-42) .

High summer would not smile on the French debutants. During June and July just two wins both at home. After the credible loss at Huddersfield, the Catalans well resisted again at Wigan, keen to make up for that opening day loss at Aime-Giral (18-24). Some players made reference to the tough travel schedule after the trip to the JJB being the third in as many weeks across the Channel.

The Harlequins visit saw the Australian referee Michael Clark in charge giving the affair a total M62 cold shoulder. The home side struggled early on against the Londoners inspired by the effervescent McLinden, yet again, tearing the Catalans defence to pieces. Fortunately they managed to hold on just long enough for Jones to steady the ship and bring them home eventually (38-18) before what would be their lowest league crowd of the campaign 4,197. This period coincided with their Narbonne excursions to the Stade de L'Amitie for two games against Hull FC and Salford. The Airlie Birds riding high in the league table came away from France again with the spoils (16-24) after winning earlier at Aimie-Giral but on both occasions little more then a converted try had been the difference.

Another heavy loss (26-52) at Knowsley Road, this time in the league was cushioned by the flying Murphy becoming the second Dragons player after Verges to score a hat-trick of tries and in doing so reached the incredible total of twenty for the season for a team still bottom of the league table. A second loss at Odsal, came as expected (16-30) but the points deficit was noticeable reduced to the earlier jousts which was encouraging. July had drawn a blank so far and the hope was for a better result on the return up the coast to Narbonne a week later.

Salford had already put the Dragons to the sword twice so it was doubly satisfying that Potter's crew were able to turn this one around. Possibily the best opening 40 minutes of their season with Jones leading them around the field with aplomb orchestrating three first half tries and none conceded. Murphy as per usual came up with a brace of tries after the oranges to finally put the *cerise sur le gateau* and a convincing victory (26-6) which got them off the bottom of the league with six games remaining.

The home straight was now in sight and the Catalans although protected from relegation, wanted to give everything to avoid the last place so as to not give substance to their detractors across the Channel. After rolling over too easily at Wigan (4-40) on the opening weekend of August it would be Wakefield next up at Belle Vue then lying in the in unenviable 11th spot on points difference to the French men both on 14 competition points. On a rainy, wet afternoon the Dragons never got going as referee Steve Ganson penalised them heavily putting two players in the sin-bin early on contributing to a 20 point half-time deficit. They showed more resistance from the return but went home empty handed (14-34) and still stuck in last place .

What irritated the Dragons management was the apparent disregard USAP had for them. The Catalans fixture list would have been known to the union club well before there Top 14 programme was being put together in the early summer of 2006 but they still somehow managed to arrange games at Aime-Giral in the August and September when both St.Helens and Huddersfield were due in Perpignan. Little entente was evident between the parties that year. Such as the score board not being made available and the first team changing rooms out of bounds.

The Dragons biggest challenge of the season was without doubt staging what would be their fourth clash of the campaign against the mighty St.Helens who would go on in 2006 to win a unique Super League and Challenge Cup double. With Narbonne also ruled out as a possible venue somewhere in or around Perpignan had to be found for their penultimate game. In the end the only solution was to go to Canet Village just a drop kick away from the beach. The draw back was Stade St.Michel only had one small grandstand and nothing else even if situated in a country park environment. But to their credit they managed the dilemma in style.

Two huge mobile seating platforms were erected opposite the main stand and everything fell into place. A small winding country lane led to the picturesque scene possibly the most bizarre setting of the Super League era. With the internet boards across the Channel casting doubts again of the Catalans organising ability they yet again finished with egg on their faces as the whole thing passed off without a hitch. A crowd of 4,551 meandered their way out to the coast on a balmy August evening to see St Helens looking for their fourth straight win against the French men one week before their Twickenham Challenge Cup Final date with Huddersfield.

The Lancastrians arrived with a host of young untried replacements and hardly a handful of regulars in sight giving the Dragons their best chance yet of turning the tide of fortune their way. The Catalans thought they were in for an easy ride with four tries in the first half hour before the young Saints lads responded in style closing the gap to just four at the break. The visitors hit the front for the first time early in the second period and defended their line as if their lives depended on it. With Guisset becoming the second Dragons player to be sent-off in 2006 with not more than five minutes remaining it seemed the Catalans last chance of beating St Helens had gone. Then out of nowhere, up popped captain magic Jones to burrow his way over the line for the decisive score seconds before Ashley Klein blew for time and secure two competition points (26-22) which put the French men back level with Trinity but in 12th spot on points different.

Although guaranteed their place in the competition there was no lowering their regime and desire to scrap to the end. The third match against title chasers Hull FC away two weeks later further confirmed this sentiment. Jones got an early try for the sang-et-or and they doggedly defended for their lives to hold a 6-4 lead at the interval even with Fellous in the sin-bin. They couldn't however hold the line and the Airlie Birds took the spoils (12-26) but all three match-ups against the Humberside outfit, who were to go on to Old Trafford that year were close and hard fought indicating the French sides progress over the course of the campaign. Mentor Waite pitch side summed it up, "The referee had slowed the play too much and spoilt the spectacle in what was nevertheless a decent game. The Catalans have gained in experience from their debut. It's encouraging for next year".

If across the Channel Wakefield and Castleford were scrapping like mad to preserve their Super League status in Perpignan, the Dragons were battling away just to get their last home game against the Huddersfield played. USAP had commandeered Aime-Giral for their match against Stade Toulouse on the second weekend of September with the municipal authorities seemingly powerless to intervene in a public facility they owned. President Bernard Guasch the scrapper that he was dug in and pressed the council officials for a compromise and it worked. The Canal Plus Sports television were contracted to cover both matches on the same weekend and this could have been a factor. So what unfolded was that the union match took place on the same day followed by a two hour delay to facilitate the league game.

The palaver generated over putting this and the St Helens fixture on seemed to take some energy and focus away from the team. It was a muted last home performance against Huddersfield. There was an arrangement that supporters of the union clash earlier could watch both fixtures but few took up the option. There was a distinct end of term feel with a host of Dragons players bidding their farewell. The Giants fresh from their Challenge Cup Final loss had just about enough energy in the tank to get across the finishing line first (12-20). It just remained the last hurrah at Headingley the Friday after to bring down the curtain on a momentous first season. It was a disappointing way to go out as the Catalans caved in under the Rhinos onslaught taking three tries in the opening ten minutes. Only Murphy's 27th try of the season lifted their spirits momentarily. The damage at the end was sixty points taken and the last place on the ladder secured (12-60).

Coming from the French competition the Dragons had a Pyrenean peak to climb to expect more than they got if you further take into account the travelling across the Channel every other weekend. Their eight wins and 16 competition points was still the best haul of points for the last placed team since the inauguration of Super League. With their two Cup success it gave them a win record of 32% in their debut season.

Losing Jones injured for three months was a hard hit from Round 2 even if Dobson had been a fine replacement. Potter's late arrival after the campaign had already started wasn't the best preparation. Losing Mayor the CEO mid season wouldn't have helped. But in the main it generally held up. It was a monumental learning curve for everybody involved with the club. Being stuck at the bottom end of France a world away from the M62 put them on the outer rim which in some ways made it easier to cope and in others harder. They adapted well to both the travelling and the issues around stadia availability.

At the end of the day Catalans gave Super League debuts to twenty French men. Of the overseas contingent three would depart Hindmarsh, Hughes and Beattie. The two first named struggled to settle but Beattie who had played earlier for the UTC was a whole hearted and popular player who continued to play in France at Lézignan. While the unassuming wing Murphy, will-o'-the wisp character ran off with the competitions leading try scorer accolade and with it a place in the Dream Team selection. Some performance. Regarding the local players the two surprise departures were Rinaldi and Frayssinous who had been two of the main stays of the UTC after forming an outstanding half-back pairing previously with both Villeneuve and France. Rinaldi went on to successful stints at both Harlequins and Wakefield while Frayssinous became one of Potter's assistant coaches the following year.

Bernard Guasch at the end was up beat with it all, "The game has won twenty years in a matter of months," he announced even if the referees had tended to officiate, "every encounter as if its an France-England match!". From a virtual zero base the club sold two thousand season tickets and the first supporters clubs, *les penyas* saw the light of day. Thousands of English fans had descended on Perpignan creating a unique experience in the games' one hundred year history. But more particularly it was completely revitalising a French game in urgent need of a boost. It put a spring back in the step of all treizistes to see the crowds turning out again. In just one season the Dragons had already become arguably the biggest club name in the games entire history across the Channel.

You cannot have a dance too without music, neither a game without the fans and in 2006 more than 92,000 rallied to their cause. Knowing that Stade Gilbert Brutus, the games spiritual home would be ready for the start of their second season the club started to look forward with fresh hopes for their second campaign, building on the progress made in 2006 without ever anticipating what would eventually unfold.

( ) Denotes Challenge Cup game

2006 FIXTURES	RND	DATE	VENUE	RESULT	ATT
WIGAN	1	11/02	AIME-GIRAL	W 38-30	11,122
SALFORD	2	17/02	WILLOWS	L 0-16	
CASTLEFORD	3	26/02	WHELDON RD	L 28-34	
BRADFORD	4	4/03	AIME-GIRAL	L 18-50	9,373
LEEDS	5	11/03	AIME-GIRAL	L 10-58	5,783
WARRINGTON	6	18/03	HJ STADIUM	W 28-26	
SALFORD	7	25/03	AIME-GIRAL	L 22-28	6,547
THORNHILL	CCR4	01/04	STADE J-LAFFONT	W 66-0	(1,200)
CASTLEFORD	8	08/04	CARCASSONNE	W 51-14	6,109
HARLEQUINS	9	14/04	THE STOOP	L 14-36	
ST. HELENS	10	17/04	AIME-GIRAL	L 20-34	8,294
HULL FC	11	22/04	AIME-GIRAL	L 28-34	6,877
BRADFORD	12	28/04	ODSAL	L 6-54	
WARRINGTON	13	06/05	AIME-GIRAL	L 16-44	5,877
CASTLEFORD	14	14/05	WHELDON RD	W 40-18	
WIDNES	CCR5	21/05	HALTON STADIUM	W 34-16	
WAKEFIELD	15	27/05	AIME-GIRAL	W 28-20	6,852
ST.HELENS	CCQF	03/06	KNOWSLEY RD	L 10-56	
HUDDERSFIELD	16	11/06	GALPHARM	L 34-42	
WIGAN	17	18/06	JJB STADIUM	L 18-24	
HARLEQUINS	18	24/06	AIME-GIRAL	W 38-18	4,197
HULL FC	19	01/07	NARBONNE	L 16-24	4,479
ST.HELENS	20	07/07	KNOWSLEY RD	L 26-52	
BRADFORD	21	14/07	ODSAL	L 16-30	
SALFORD	22	22/07	NARBONNE	W 26-6	5,070
WIGAN	23	04/08	JJB STADIUM	L 4-40	
WAKEFIELD	24	13/08	BELLE VUE	L 14-34	
ST. HELENS	25	19/08	CANET VILLAGE	W 26-22	4,551
HULL FC	26	03/09	KC STADIUM	L 12-26	
HUDDERSFIELD	27	09/09	AIME-GIRAL	L 12-20	6,463
LEEDS	28	15/09	HEADINGLEY	L 12-60	
				Total	92,794
				Regular season median	6,547

SUPER LEAGUE: P28 W8 L20 PTS 16 PF 601 PA 894 POS. 12TH
CHALLENGE CUP: P3 W2 L1

2006	GAMES	TRIES	GOALS	POINTS
BEATTIE	29	4		12
BERTHEZENE	20			
BOSC	12	6	1	26
CASTY	9	2		8
CHAN	27	3		12
COLOGNI	5	3		12
DOBSON	12	5	31(1dg)	83
FAKIR	30	6		24
FELLOUS	29	2		8
FRAYSSINOUS	19	4	33	82
GOSSARD	1			
GRIFFI	7			
GUIGUE	22	3		12
GUISSET	29	2		
HINDMARSH	27	3		12
HUGHES	26	12		48
JAMPY	13			
JONES	17	7	20	68
KHATTABI	3			
MARTINS	1			
MOUNIS	27	7		28
MURPHY	30	27		108
RINALDI	25	2	1	10
RUDDER	26	7		28
SADAOUI	7			
TEIXIDO	9	3		12
TOUXAGAS	7			
VERGES	28	9		36
WILSON	28	8		32
ZITTER	2	2		8

(30)

Chapter 3
– WEMBLEY –

Some famous old clubs like Oldham and Swinton have been at it for more than a hundred years and still not reached a Wembley Cup Final. Then out of nowhere the spanking new upstarts from across the Channel, the Catalans Dragons manage it in only year two of their existence. The only sacred new ground the French side were really looking to as 2007 dawned was the revamped Stade Gilbert Brutus hardly a drop kick away from Aime-Giral where they had resided rather uncomfortably during their debut year. The public authorities put in nearly €3 million to upgrade the 'Auld Girl'.

The main grandstand – tribune Bonzoms was completely overhauled into an attractive cantilever structure while the smaller fixture opposite was re-seated as was the crescent shaped area behind one of the goals which previously had been an open standing terrace. The last remnants of the old running track were now disappearing from view. The three sided ground looked spick and span with its near 10,000 'sang-et-or' coloured seats resplendent. It's popularly recognised locally as 'Le Temple' of the Catalan treize movement. It was a huge statement going back there where once XIII Catalan played and a venue which hosted internationals and domestic Championship and Cup Finals going back nearly fifty years.

Mick Potter swept a broom through the squad after finishing bottom of the pile as expected in year 1. The Australian coach was a late replacement the year before so it was his first opportunity to bring on board his own selections. Nearly half of the squad departed including a raft of players who had been a big part of the Union Treize Catalan set up which was to be the template for the future Super League club. The Australians Beattie, Hindmarsh, Hughes and Rudder plus surprisingly Rinaldi and Frayssinous who had been considered major cogs at the out-set, left. Potter chose wisely. Adam Mogg, a fine athletic threequarter had recently played Origin, Casey McGuire a hooker of note from Brisbane Broncos, a contemporary legend Jason Croker from Canberra and a stylish, effervescent full-back from St George Clint Greenshields arrived in Roussillon. Aaron Gorrell a fine hooker from St George was part of the new contingent but after a promising debut suffered a serious leg injury which finished his season before it had really begun and was replaced by Newcastle Knights Luke Quigley.

Queenslander Casey McGuire gets an early bath as the heavens opened on the new era at the renovated Stade Gilbert Brutus in February 2007. Wigan were visitors once again as they were a year earlier at Aime-Giral but this time triumphant McGuire arrived after an NRL Grand Final victory with Brisbane as well as Origin appearances. He would play in the sang-et-or colours 99 times before heading home in 2010. He was one of those who laid the strong foundations from which the club prospered. He would come back to play a season in France at Limoux along side David Ferriol in 2013.

Frayssinous was not lost completely though as he was encouraged to take up one of the assistant coaching positions alongside the Australian Andrew McFadden with Andrew Howe the new man in charge of the fitness. New French arrivals included two of the best and experienced players from the local competition in the burly Limoux prop David Ferriol and Toulouse's international second rower Sébastien Raguin who had impressed in their Challenge Cup run of 2005. The New Caledonian wing Dimitri Pelo would provide cover too for the departed Verges and Fred Zitter.

Wembley and the French had a short history. Villeneuve-sur-Lot and St Gaudens had got the ball rolling in 2001 but it was Toulouse Olympique under the direction of Justin Morgan who first made a real impact reaching the Challenge Cup Semi-Finals in 2005 going out eventually to Leeds after knocking out Super League Widnes in the quarter-finals. As in all straight knock out competitions the luck of the draw is a significant factor and in 2007 Catalan got the flyer they were looking for. Featherstone Rovers at the time were a middling semi professional club and drawing them to Brutus for the first ever 3rd round tie on the last weekend of March was a perfect start for the Frenchmen. Potter decided to include thirteen French players in his line up including the two young Bentley brothers Kane and Andrew who were born in New Zealand and raised in France. With skipper Jones pulling the strings as a contest it was over by quarter time with four tries already clocked up. On a big dry track in perfect conditions the part-timers struggled valiantly to stay in touch. It was a 12 try runaway with Mogg in his element finishing with an emphatic (70-12) score line watched by a reported attendance of just 1,545 but looked twice as many.

Round 4 would see Catalans breaking new territory with a first ever trip up into Cumbria to face Whitehaven at the old Recreation Ground. Going up there in May was a bonus for the visitors rather than the middle of winter but it was still overcast, showery and cool with a playing surface described as soft and uneven. It would be a test and more challenging than the previous round. The visitors strengthened with Greenshields and McGuire returning put too much possession down and struggled to control the game early on. Chan was in his element here leading from the front when needed. Bosc and youngster Vincent Duport, who had arrived from Vedene up in Provence close season, got them on the score board by the break with a couple of tries nudging them ahead of the feisty hosts by 8 points. Mogg extended their lead soon after the restart with a timely score. The Dragons had that extra gear and even when the Cumbrians got a second try with ten minutes to go Kane Bentley replied more or less immediately for the visitors to maintain the difference and steer them home (24-14) in front of 3,856 spectators.

There was now a building sense of anticipation across the Channel with a quarter final now in view but the draw dampened their optimism somewhat when a daunting trip to Humberside and Hull FC was made known. The Airlie Birds had won the Cup two years earlier and only the previous autumn had reached Old Trafford losing to St Helens in the 2006 Grand Final. Catalan had lost all three league games also in their debut season to the black and whites but an opening day (10-10) draw at the KC Stadium in 2007 at least gave the French team something to build on.

The Dragons got off to a dream start on a near perfect June afternoon with a couple of decisive tries from the influential Mogg and a third from Wilson by the half hour mark with only a penalty goal in response. The home side hit back though with a converted try before half-time to reduce the deficit to eight points. A real battle royal unfolded after the break as the hosts threw everything at the Frenchmen. They held out until the 53rd minute when a Hull forward crashed over for a converted try. Just after the hour mark it was all square at 16-16 after a penalty goal was conceded and the East Yorkshire outfit edged in front for the first time by a drop goal with just a quarter of an hour to go. The visitors though held their nerve.

Guisset of all people came up with an equalising drop goal and then Bosc added a penalty to put the sang-et-or back in front with just nine minutes remaining but more poignantly Hull lost a player sin-binned for the infringement. It was edge of your seats stuff until Greenshields came up with a converted try with Bosc clipping over another drop goal 3 minutes from the end to more or less seal an engrossing, palpitating tie with the hosts leaving it just too late with a converted try on the final whistle. Phew!! (26-23) in front of a paying crowd of 7,441.

This was now all unchartered territory. A Challenge Cup semi-final a year after the wooden spoon on debut. Such was the novelty and enthusiasm of the supporters hundreds dragged themselves out à la Llanbanère at Riversalts for when the plane carrying them home on the Monday morning arrived. The last four now in regal company of Bradford, St Helens and Wigan who in July where all three occupying top 4 places in Super League while Catalan struggling at the back of the class in tenth. It was to be the cherry & whites who would face the French challenge just a drop kick away from home base at Warrington's Halliwell Jones Stadium on the last Sunday of the month. The form book offered scraps to the Dragons with that opening day loss under the deluge at Brutus back in February and a right drubbing away (30-0) at the DW a week after the Catalans success in the Cup quarter-finals.

Wigan had the Australian ace Trent Barrett leading their charge in 2007 and with the great majority of the 10,218 crowd carrying the cherry-white favours it was as near a home tie as you could wish for. It made you wonder back then how entrenched the game had become in its northern enclave. In 1999 London played Castleford at Leeds and eight years later a French side had to travel to play a Lancashire side at Warrington. Whatever had happened to the European Super League concept of expanding boundaries?

Just as at Hull in the quarters, the Dragons took the bull by the horns on that glorious summer's afternoon in front of the BBC cameras. Not caught in the glare of headlights and in awe of the illustrious favourites as Stacey and his men took the initiative from the off and by some. Incredibly scoring four tries inside the opening quarter through McGuire, Wilson, Mogg and Duport with Jones converting three and adding a penalty to give an astonishing half-time score line of 24-6 against the most decorated of Challenge Cup winners. That soon turned to 31-6 with Duport grabbing his second try with the little Kiwi maestro converting and taking a drop goal to boot. Wigan would have their strong time too and the French had to weather that particular storm as the cherry & whites crossed for three scores all converted by Richards in a wobbly thirteen minute spell which coincided with the sin-binning of skipper Jones to bring it to 31-24 with still more than ten minutes remaining. Fortunately for the sang-et-or Jones's return clinched it. The first time he touched the ball he slid a delicate kick behind the Wigan defensive wall for the old Canberra legend Croker to pick his line perfectly and ground the ball as it was spinning out of bounds for confirmation and the try of victory (37-24).

It was a stunned and silent Halliwell Jones as Steve Ganson brought the proceedings to a halt. Just several clusters of visiting fans to witness this most momentous of all Challenge Cup ties celebrated as the whole of the clubs pitch side contingent swarmed on to the pitch with the champagne corks already popping. Maybe John Kear's Sheffield started to loosen that M62 screw in 1997 as things drifted south a bit before London two years later arrived at the side of 'The Twin Towers'. Who would have possibly believed that within a decade a French club would have made history but there would be no towers of any sort to welcome them in 2007 but Norman Foster's extravagant new state of the art Stadium costing nearly £800 million with its 134 metre high steel Arch.

It's what dreams are made of. Catalans had stirred up the nest. This wasn't in the script. This was a northern sport after all occupying the interests of Lancastrians, Yorkshire folk and hardy Cumbrians. Now the French had gate crashed the party.

The Cup and the game would never be quite the same again. "Les Dragons à Wembley", screamed the headline on the front page of the popular regional daily *L'Indépendant*. A beaming President Bernard Guasch illuminated that the Catalans had just gained four years of advancement in a single exploit.

A four week break awaited the Dragons to their moment of destiny to the mythical Stadium in the capital across the Channel. This would be unchartered waters for everyone. None of the players or management knew what to expect. For the supporters too, the logistics of how to prepare the trip and northerly route for the first ever time in the competitions century old competition. A reported 4,000 treizistes from all over the country would make the journey. Three chartered planes would lead the exodus from *le Midi* plus lots of others travelling overnight by mini bus crossing *la Manche* in the early hours arriving on Wembley Way bedraggled but elated just to be there.

In reality, it was maybe all too early for the newcomers to fully appreciate and benefit from the occasion. The club was still very much in its infancy and still developing its structures both on and off the field. They had already gone through three CEO's in a relatively short period of time as they wrestled to get their organisation up to scratch. But Potter had been up to the task even through that helter-skelter debut year after arriving late. He was the man for the moment and would prove his pedigree over the subsequent years. The famous Challenge Cup would be displayed in and around Perpignan as the build-up commenced. Some dissenters had questioned whether the French presence would affect the gate but all that was pure speculation as the turn out proved. Lots of English followers put their own allegiance behind them to become Dragons for the day come Cup Final Day.

St Helens qualified to play Catalans on the last weekend of August beating Bradford in the other semi final. The Saints were the Cup holders having beaten Huddersfield the year before knocking out the Dragons in the process convincingly at Knowsley Road in the 4th Round. Interestingly the two sides met the year before a week before the Final when Daniel Anderson played a near second string at Canet Village giving the Catalans their first ever win against the Lancashire heavy weights. In 2007 the two sides would clash a fortnight before the big day in Perpignan on the 11th August. Back in Round 11 the French had taken another thumping at Knowsley Road (53-10) but this first ever visit to

Stade Gilbert Brutus saw the Dragons at their very best against a full strength St Helens only lacking Pryce. Mogg was on fire inspiring his charges to one of their best results to date with an emphatic win (21-0). This would have given the French some hopes for the grand rendez-vous awaiting them in London. At the same time the players were cautious of how the English side would react to the league loss too. They would be more respectful and motivated to re-dress the bar.

The magnitude of the occasion though would be the greatest challenge facing the Dragons as vice-captain Guisset alluded to at the time.

"To be honest, it's hard to believe it's happening. It wasn't even a goal, more a dream to play in a Grand Final or a Challenge Cup Final."

"When I was a kid I wanted to follow the in the footsteps of people like Shaun Edwards and now that is happening. I really want to make the most of it and enjoy the moment. It's all happened so quickly; the whole thing has taken everyone by storm. It's absolutely massive because we're not just representing the club, we're representing a culture."

"The players are very proud of what they've achieved so far and they know the importance of the club to the people here in Catalonia. This is a big occasion for rugby league in France because we're the first French side to make the final. And I think it's great for rugby league in general, it shows the Cup is unpredictable and that a side that's not necessarily doing so well in Super League can come all this way."

"I think everyone will be nervous. It's so big an occasion that if we weren't, I think there would be a problem. Only Alex Chan, Jason Crocker and Stacey Jones have played in Grand Finals but the rest haven't experienced one. But nerves can be a good thing. It's about taking that nervous energy and making the best use of it."

With everyone having their suits fitted and booking their accommodation everyone was swept along by Cup fever. Potter though wasn't content. He had a bee in his bonnet for sure because Catalans had a league fixture to be played at Warrington and this had been scheduled to be played on the Sunday evening to accommodate Sky Television while opponents St Helens played Salford away on Friday night – a two day turn around difference made more complicated with the additional flights across the Channel. At the time little was made of it as there was so much excitement and expectation was buzzing around. On reflection it was the state the club was in and how they saw themselves in relation to the RFL and their gratitude of accepting the club into the competition just the year before. In other circumstances it would have been difficult to imagine for example a Wigan-Leeds confrontation accepting such discrepancies.

Elsewhere the Catalans achievement had quietened their critics after they had made most of the Dragon's wooden spoon in their debut year. "It's not so much about proving people wrong, it's more just validating that there is a warrant for a French team in Super League," alluded coach Potter, "it shows it's good to be expanding rather than be insular and just concentrate on that little strip in the north of England. It shows we're right to actively grow the game and hopefully, in the future we can grow Super League into even more places. I'm just a fan of rugby league and I want to see more young people playing it and more top teams playing in more areas."

"The first Wembley for this scribbler had been forty or so years earlier when the two ends where open and standing. It was Wakefield versus Huddersfield with Trinity ruling the roost back then triumphant 12-6 with the great Neil Fox in his pomp, a worthy Lance Todd Trophy winner. Still at secondary school with brother in tow I left Widnes North station around 10 pm on Friday night heading to Liverpool Lime Street to catch the night train for the capital. It chugged away arriving at Euston at dawn and there we were two lads lost on Challenge Cup Final day. The only sign of life were other small knots of northerners carrying the favours of the two Yorkshire protagonists.

In 2007 it was a bit more leisurely leaving Carcassonne station on the streamlined TGV high speed train on the Friday afternoon at 3pm heading north for Lille and the Euro Star. No hold ups and the early evening train after passing under the Channel was deposited safely to Waterloo around 10pm. The day following was as much about the new look Wembley as the history making Frenchmen. It was a tight schedule getting back to the Waterloo terminus by early Saturday night though passing by the French Federation President Nicolas Larrat having a quick bite to eat before boarding the same 7pm train for Paris. Got chatting to a teenager and his dad both carrying the Catalans colours and flag on the return trip. The family originally from Perpignan but now lived in Paris and just wanted to be there at Wembley on this special historic day. After an overnight stay in the French capital spent a leisurely Parisian Sunday morning wandering the Bastille 'arrondissement' taking a coffee and browsing L'Équipe the national sporting daily keen to see what coverage they gave the game.

Completely underwhelmed with hardly a fifth of a page and postage stamp size picture hardly gave the event the distinction it deserved. It was certainly less prominent than the Paris St Germain-Sheffield opening game of Super League coverage a decade earlier. Maybe it revealed the geographical remoteness of Perpignan and the Catalan region – and similarly how much the game had lost ground and prominence following that momentous mishap. It didn't help of course when so much of the game across the Channel pays lip service to what was once announced the European Super League. Paris and the rest of the country hadn't noticed. Catalans Dragons knew their journey for recognition and respectability would have to be fought tooth and nail both sides of the Channel. It would be a long journey even with a Wembley visit already under their belt.

It was just left then to get over to the 'Gare de Lyon' for the afternoon train for Carcassonne arriving back by 8pm from a Challenge Cup Final thought unimaginable certainly back in 1962. What a contrast. The game has a glimmer of another dimension. Has it the courage, sense and the wherewithal to take it one asked?"

The New Wembley – they all look mesmerised here just trying to take it all in after barely two years old as a club. The enormity of it all. Except for Ferriol and Channy of course – fully focused, jaws primed!

STAR GAME 2007 CHALLENGE CUP FINAL ST HELENS
at Wembley Stadium London on Saturday 25th August

The loss through injury a fortnight before of organiser McGuire was a big loss for the French side. He had played stand off all season long and alongside Jones had masterminded that semi final success against Wigan. They needed that experience against St Helens. At Wembley the Dragons had three lads on the bench under 21 years including K.Bentley and Casty who between them had played only twenty or so games at this level. On the eve of the game a fax was received at the team's hotel from the management, staff & players of the USAP union club offering their support ahead of the final.

The singing of the Catalan national anthem 'Els Segadors' by a Welsh male voice choir in the build up raised the tempo and hairs on the backs of the French fans. It was a sweltering late summer's day for rugby league fans everywhere to at last be back home on the sacred turf after an eight year hiatus. From the off the French as at Warrington where not overwhelmed and took the game to the Cup holders for the opening half hour. Unfortunately they couldn't convert that pressure into points even if Croker was millimetres from grounding a Jones kick into the in-goal area.

The Saints patient as ever soaking up the pressure knew how to respond. Roby got the Lancastrians and score board moving with a typical powerful surge shrugging off what appeared half the Catalan side before planting the ball over the line for the opening score. With the conversion successful it was imperative that the French side responded moving towards the break. Long uncharacteristically came up with a fumble underneath his own uprights which enabled Bentley to feed quickly Mogg on his outside. The former Canberra man saw some space out wide and his timely pass created a corridor for Younes Khattabi to surge through and dive over in the corner. What a special moment for the young lad from. Entraigues up in Provence who just a year or so before was without a club when Marseille folded. It was crucial now to hold out and regroup at the break with just the one conversion separating the sides. Alas it wasn't to be as Gardner squeezed in at the corner for his sides second converted try just as referee Klein was about to whistle for the break with the Dragons complaining that the decisive pass was forward. It was a crucial score which the Wembley newcomers weren't to recover from. Their inexperience and naivety undid them as St Helens went for the jugular minutes after the restart with Wellens and then Clough adding

Justin Murphy scored more spectacular tries but this one at Wembley he will always treasure. The Australian had played in the NRL Grand Final of 2002 for the losing NZ Warriors and later cameo appearances for Widnes in the Super League. By 2004 he was playing in the French competition for UTC as they prepared for their Super League entrance two years later. A good footballer on the wing with pace to burn, turned to gold in Perpignan. A revelation in their opening year scoring 27 tries and was named in the Dream Team. He would play 66 games for the Dragons and racked up an impressive 53 tries before taking his leave in 2008. He would finish his playing career representing France later that year in the World Cup back in Australia.

further tries to blow the score out rapidly to 22-8 on 50 minutes. It was sealed from then on in. Long added a late penalty and Gardner a second try while will-o'-the-wisp Murphy got a late consolation for the French to wrap it up at 30-8.

"They were less tired than us and their game more flowing. The forward pass for the second try or not doesn't change anything", commented prop Chan. Saints wing Gardner concluded," *The problem for them was that they didn't score during their strong periods and after couldn't react when we opened up a gap."*

Catalans 8-30 St Helens HT: 4-12 .Weather: Sunny & hot. Attendance: 84,241
Referee: Ashley Klein. For Catalans 2 tries from Khattabi (37) & Murphy (58).
For St Helens 5 tries from Roby (34), Gardner (40,79), Wellens (46), Clough (49) & 5 goals from Long.
Catalans: Greenshields, Murphy, Wilson, Raguin, Khattabi, Mogg, Jones ©, Chan Quigley Guisset, Croker, Gossard, Mounis Substitutes: Ferriol, Casty, Bentley K Duport
St.Helens: Wellens, Gardner, Gidley, Talau, Meli, Pryce, Long, Cayless, Cunningham © Fozzard, Bennett, Gilmour, Wilkin Substitutes: Graham, Roby, Fa'asavalu, Clough
Lance Todd Trophy Winners: Sean Long and Leon Pryce.

The mast heading on the main section of the L'Indépendant the day after had it as: *"St-Helens a terrassé les Dragaons Catalans"* (have floored) and leading in their Sports Section with, *"Les Dragons ont coincé"*, (cornered and unable to respond). The club's President Guasch was upbeat, *Le terrain a parlé. La victoire de St.Helens est logique.* We have shown bravery, courage and moments of quality too. We have learnt a lot today. It's up to us now to work even more so as to continue as a club to grow. But this evening I'm proud of my players."

During their debut in Super League Catalans had taken some beatings conceding nearly 900 points in total. It would have been one of Potter's targets going into 2007 to reduce that. It was certainly a promising start against Hull FC away with that low scoring draw (10-10) and followed by two excellent home performances against the might of Wigan and Leeds over successive weekends in February. Wigan had started the Catalan journey a year earlier at Aime-Giral and they were to become the first side to play at the re-vamped Brutus too. On a howling night when the heavens opened the Lancastrian just took the spoils by a couple of points (16-18) but a week later the Dragons turned it all around beating Leeds for the first time with a four star performance (30-22). The template was set. This was a different Dragons already especially getting this early success with talisman Jones out injured. Although they lost away at Salford (0-10) and Wakefield (20-40) at the beginning of March they confirmed their new credentials beating Huddersfield at home by a single point in a cliff hanger (23-22) in front off more than 8,000 spectators but more importantly on the last weekend of the month won away at the then formidable Bradford (29-22). A year before the French had taken more than 130 points in three games against the Yorkshire powerhouse.

As spring dawned the quartet of Mogg, McGuire, Croker and Greenshields was really making a difference. The promoted Hull KR were dumped on their own midden convincingly on Good Friday (34-20) as the Dragons settled into a heady mid table position. 2007 though would find their bête noir in the London side starting with Easter Monday with Harlequins convincing winners (16-38) in front of a bumper 9,000 attendance. Although Warrington were then beaten at home for the first time (27-16) if the Dragons needed reminding of what the best sides were still all about, it was driven home

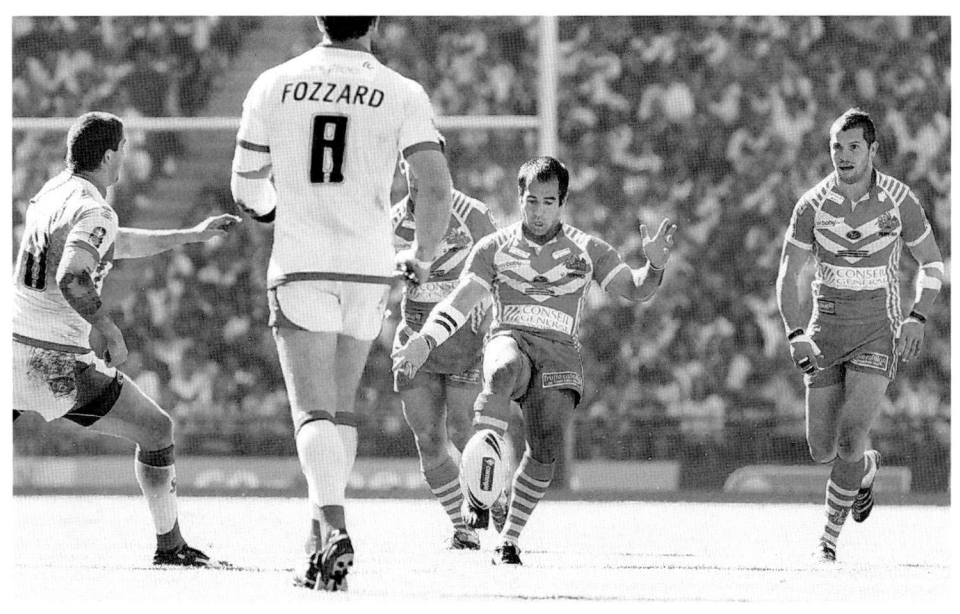

Stacey Jones after a stellar career with Auckland Warriors in the NRL became the first of many star players who would be attracted to the South of France. 29 years old when he arrived in Perpignan he had an inauspicious debut breaking his arm at Salford early on and would be absent for over three months. Played 45 games in total scoring 135 points. Captained the side and the following year led them all the way to Wembley and a Challenge Cup appearance in only their second year in the big-time. His leadership, passing and kicking game exemplary. Returned to Auckland and played an additional season with the re-branded New Zealand Warriors.

by two thumping losses at St Helens and Leeds (8-54) ; still revealing their vulnerability.

The RFL introduced the Magic Weekend concept in 2007 with all twelve sides reassembling at the magnificent Millenium Stadium in Cardiff on the opening weekend in May. Catalans was paired with the London side in the local derby format. The Dragons performed better in Wales than they had done in Perpignan on Easter Monday creating more scoring opportunities but not converting them in to points. It was a close one with both sides registering five tries but the Quins left with the competition points (28-32). The week after the Dragons took out their frustrations on a by then unravelling Salford side who had qualified for the play-offs the season before. The locals racked up a league record win (66-6) with Murphy in dazzling form on the wing with a hat-trick of tries and Bosc finishing with nine goals and a brace of tries.

Leading into the vital Challenge Cup quarter final at Hull the Catalans lost to both Yorkshire opposition Wakefield away (12-18) and Bradford at home (20-28) in close tussles. After the success at the KC Stadium and just one match away from a possible Wembley appearance it was a tad difficult for the young club to keep their focus. The height of summer saw them fall away some what with just a single success (24-22) at home to Warrington for the second time at Brutus on the last weekend of June. Being hammered at Wigan their future Cup semi final opponents was not a good omen with further defeats to Quins again (22-30) and home to both Humberside teams; (20-22) to the Robins and (18-34) to the Airlie Birds saw them drop to 10th on the ladder.

After the sensational exploit against the cherry and whites everything now centred on London and the 25th August rendez-vous. Huddersfield (22-42) and Warrington (18-22) took the spoils both away with the complicated visit of Anderson's Saints just a fortnight before the big day. The Dragons put on one of their best ever performances against a virtual full strength St Helens winning convincingly (21-0). Although they had won the year before at Canet Village in particular circumstances this success was really the first time they'd put the Super League Champions to the sword. It left the Lancastrians tied with Leeds at the top of the competition and the two points for the French kept them ahead of Hull KR back in 11th.

After the emotional draining Wembley weekend it was just a matter of wrapping up the league programme and bidding some farewells. September would see Catalans defeat both Wakefield and Quins at last (38-20) and (30-14) respectively with a loss at Bradford between them (8-40). It had been an extraordinary year by any stretch of imaginations. Obviously it was all about Wembley in just their 2nd campaign but wins in either cup or league against all of the top six sides that year really set out the template for what was to follow. They started to plug that defence too taking 23% less than in 2006. Skipper Jones was on his way home to Auckland after two injury plagued campaigns and stacks of memories. But everybody else was more or less settled. Mogg became after Murphy the second Dragons player to be nominated in the Super League Dream team and Potter had much to be pleased about and lots to look forward too.

Received at the mythical Nou Camp Stadium home of FC Barcelona before their Liga 1 game against Athletic Bilbao in front of 90,000 weeks after their Challenge Cup appearance at Wembley. "Quelle image!"

( ) Denotes Challenge Cup game

2007 FIXTURES	RND	DATE	VENUE	RESULT	ATT
HULL FC	1	11/02	KC STADIUM	D 10-10	
WIGAN	2	17/02	GILBERT BRUTUS	L 16-18	7,052
LEEDS	3	24/02	GILBERT BRUTUS	W 30-22	7,630
SALFORD	4	03/03	WILLOWS	L 0-10	
WAKEFIELD	5	11/03	BELLE VUE	L 20-40	
HUDDERSFIELD	6	17/03	GILBERT BRUTUS	W 23-20	8,120
BRADFORD	7	25/03	ODSAL	W 29-22	
FEATHERSTONES	CCR4	31/03	GILBERT BRUTUS	L 16-38	(1,545)
HULL KR	8	06/04	CRAVEN PARK	W 34-20	
HARLEQUINS	9	09/04	GILBERT BRUTUS	L 16-38	7,500
ST HELENS	10	13/04	KNOWLEYS RD	L 10-53	
WARRINGTON	11	21/04	GILBERT BRUTUS	W 27-16	9,050
LEEDS	12	27/04	HEADINGLEY	L 8-54	
HARLEQUINS	13	06/05	CARDIFF	L 28-32	
WHITEHAVEN	CCR5	13/05	RECREATION GROUND	W 24-14	
SALFORD	14	19/05	GILBERT BRUTUS	W 66-6	8,820
WAKEFILED	15	27/05	BELLE VUE	L 12-20	
HULL FC	CCQF	10/06	KC STADIUM	W 26-23	
WIGAN	17	14/06	JJB STADIUM	L 0-30	
WARRINGTON	18	30/06	GILBERT BRUTUS	W 24-22	8,850
HARLEQUINS	19	07/07	THE STOOP	L 22-30	
HULL KR	20	14/07	GIILBERT BRUTUS	L 20-22	7,830
HULL FC	21	21/07	GILBERT BRUTUS	L 18-34	7,560
WIGAN	CCSF	29/07	HJ STADIUM	W 37-24	
HUDDERSFIELD	22	05/08	GALPHARM STADIUM	L 22-42	
ST.HELENS	23	11/08	GILBERT BRUTUS	W 21-0	8,650
WARRINGTON	24	19/08	HJ STADIUM	L 18-22	
ST.HELENS	CCF	25/08	WEMBLEY	L 8-30	
WAKEFIELD	25	01/09	GILBERT BRUTUS	W 38-20	7,325
BRADFORD	26	09/09	ODSAL	L 8-40	
HARLEQUINS	27	15/09	GILBERT BRUTUS	W 30-14	8,420
				Total	105,907

Regular season median: 8,120

SUPER LEAGUE : P27 W10 D1 L16 PTS 21 PF570 PA 685 POS 10TH
CHALLENGE CUP: P5 W4 L 1

2007	GAMES	TRIES	GOALS	POINTS
GREENSHIELDS	31	13		52
MURPHY	18	10		40
MOGG	31	14		56
WILSON	25	9		36
PELO	13	4		16
MCGUIRE	24	7	1	30
JONES	28	5	22(3dg)	67
FERRIOL	28	4		16
BERTHEZENE	1			
GUISSET	29	1	(1dg)	5
CROKER	23	7	(1dg)	29
RAGUIN	18	1		4
MOUNIS	24			
BOSC	22	13	66(1dg)	185
GOSSARD	29	5		20
TEIXIDO	19	1		4
GRIFFI	19			
DUPORT	17	7		28
CHAN	31	5		20
FELLOUS	13	3		12
TOUXAGAS	20	1		4
FAKIR	2			
GORRELL	3		10	20
CASTY	12	2		8
KHATTABI	15	7		28
QUIGLEY	20	2		8
BENTLEY A	15	2		8
BENTLEY K	10	2		8
CHARLES	2	2		8
STACUL	2	1		4

(30)

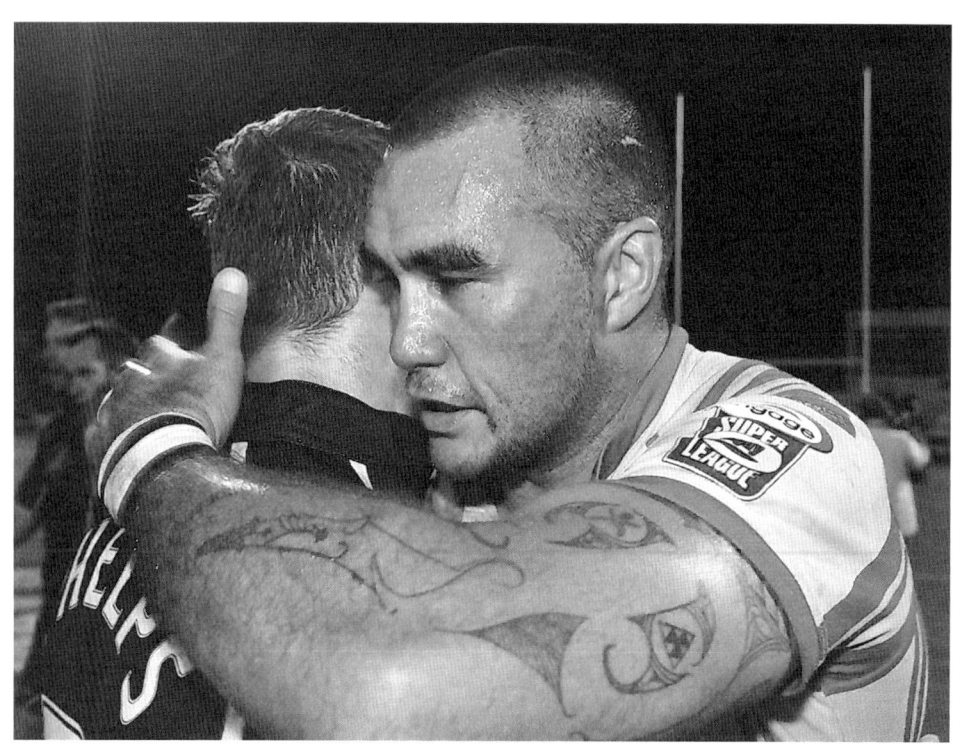

Alexandre Le Valeureux – alias Alex Chan 'Le Padre' who tended his flock in their tentative years. Would be the first Dragons player to see red. He would stand no nonsense or skullduggery against his team and by year 2 with Ferriol alongside, were fearsome. After his team had scored a try no show-boating for Chan. Marched back promptly into position behind the posts ready for the kick re-start with chin protruding. We go again! If others helped to dig the foundations Channy was the corner stone.

Chapter 4
– LE PADRE –

Bernard Guasch had said the club had acquired three sergeant stripes of recognition by reaching Wembley in only their second year in Super League and thus there was huge anticipation going into 2008 as well as the additional challenge of a World Cup for the Tricolours in Australia in the autumn. It had already been a fairy tale debut and by starting this their third campaign passed the PSG episode behind. Guasch was buoyant, announcing a budget of €5 million with sponsorship income up by 30% including a shirt signage with a nationally known construction company IDEC who also sponsored Toulouse FC in Ligue 1.The club who had barely got their feet back under the table at Brutus were already in discussions with the public authorities about building a third stand behind the posts at the airport end of the ground. For their second season at Brutus though, the club had the benefit of their own new fully fitted up weights gym under the Tribune Bonzoms, cutting the last link with St Estève where they were based in year 1.

With the progress of a much changed line-up to the previous year coach Potter made few additions. Dane Carlaw a forward from Brisbane with Kangaroo caps to his name was the marquee player engaged plus French man Olivier Elima signed from Wakefield. Elima had been at the Pole Espoirs in Carcassonne as a teenager but then went straight from there to Castleford and later to Trinity. Additionally three players who missed out on Wembley with season long injuries all returned healthy; Pelo, Fakir and Gorrell. With the latter at hooker, McGuire, who would captain the side, would move into the halves alongside Bosc.

As per 2007, the coach Potter chose to go with just a single preparation game and again against the same French President's Selection which was duly won (48-24). This permitted the players to stretch their legs before the grand kick off two weeks later at Wheldon Road Castleford. With first choice wings Murphy and Pelo still not quite apt, Jean Philippe Baile a new recruit from Carcassonne, got his debut alongside Cyril Stacul who had played a couple of times the year before. It was a good winning start too (21-14) before the Sky cameras on a cold February evening in the West Riding against the promoted Tigers after trailing by ten points at the break with Bosc impeccably leading the way.

Following that though they hit a sticky patch and a month passed without a single win. They stumbled at home against Hull KR (20-24) after leading at the break in front of 8,350 spectators. A week later the block that was Leeds at Headingley remained intact (6-34) even if they led early on and were only ten points in arrears at the break. *'Ils n'ont pas dansé avec les Loups'* (Wolves) either a week later in Lancashire submitting heavily (18-38) with Briers and Monaghan pulling the strings. Bradford undefeated so far in Perpignan remained so but by the tiniest of squeaks (18-20) with Finegan's last minute try sealing it. Even before spring had sprung, rumours began circulating that coach Potter was getting itchy feet and a possible move to St Helens was indicated.

If there was uncertainty in the Catalan camp it didn't show itself as the Saints arrived in the middle of March for a Challenge Cup re-match. After a titanic clash the 'sang-et-or' at last turned the corner with a super win sealed with talismanic prop Chan grabbing a late try to fend off any red-vee response (24-10). Little did we know then but the French side were about to set out on a journey of success which would catapult them from 9th on the Super League ladder up to the dizzy heights of 2nd by early May. Incredibly without a loss in all nine games including a Challenge Cup victory at Featherstone.

At the Stoop in the capital on Good Friday against the Harlequins without Mogg they had to dig deep into their resources coming from behind at the interval to claim it just (24-22). Easter Monday brought the holiday double with Wakefield going down (28-20) in a game, a reverse of the one in London, with the hosts this time in the ascendency early on taking more than a two score advantage with only an hour gone. The flamboyant Greenshields would bring his side home. Chan commented, "It's important winning these three matches back to back. We must win here before our own public after the two earlier losses."

The Airlie Birds were next up at Brutus the following Saturday. Hull FC had so far a 100% league success against the French club but were struggling towards the bottom of the competition table after a top 4 place the year before. All the scoring came early on with six tries registered in the first half with the locals just edging it. But with Khattabi in the sin-bin the home side wavered and Raynor's late try got his side a share of the points (28-28). With a third of the campaign completed the Dragons were half way up the league ladder and well placed to reach the play-offs for the first time in only their third season. As April beckoned, Catalans would be challenged by the prospect of gaining something away at both Wigan and Huddersfield, where they had yet to succeed. The Giants, who had made the play-offs the season before, were struggling to make an impact. The Dragons had taken a lot of points in their previous visits but this latest would be a much tighter affair. Bosc's two successful penalties just kept them ahead until a late Huddersfield converted score on the half-time bell changed things. The visitor's growing confidence though told after the oranges with three converted tries landing them the spoils (20-16). If happenings on the field were rosy, changes off it began to circulate, with the popular assistant coach McFadden looking to return home to Australia at seasons end. He of that magic half-back pairing at Canberra Raiders with Mark McLinden, had formed a capable back up team to coach Potter alongside Frayssinous after the duo of Adamson and Donkin in their debut year. Also mutterings around the future of the influential midfield dynamo Adam Mogg with arch enemies down the road USAP being mentioned.

Wigan though a week later would be the litmus test with the Warriors running 2nd. Catalans had taken some thrashings previously at the then JJB Stadium so would have to raise their game to maintain their winning run. It was close all the way with the visitors just two points clear at the break and at the end (24-22) with the former Kangaroo Carlaw scoring the winning try in the very last minute for a landmark victory. Sandwiched between Rounds 11 and 12 was a 4th round Challenge Cup tie at Featherstone Rovers which would prove a different kettle of fish to the clash in Perpignan a year earlier. On a cold, wet afternoon at Post Office Road, the French side just did enough (22-12) against the combative semi pro outfit. They got on top though early with three first half tries the key and managed the rest with Mogg in command mode. Elsewhere that weekend though French Cup hopes floundered with crushing losses, Toulouse Olympique at Odsal (6-98) against the Bulls and minnows Pia at Wigan (4-74).

Back on league duty six days later against the Rovers near neighbours Castleford, who were having a hard time of it down at the bottom. In more clement conditions, the locals sought to confirm and consolidate their present high standing. The Dragons roared away from the starting grid with 6 of their seven tries racked up in a palpitating opening period. The Tigers though where

Allez Julien Allez ! May 4th to the Millenium Stadium Cardiff and the annual clash with Harlequins. The second Magic Weekend and the Dragons flying high. The Londoners of Hill, Paul and Purdham had turned up and leading 16-6 with barely ten minutes remaining. Half-back Orr searching for the decisive score to put it to bed close to the Catalans line sending the French side packing. Suddenly though the Yorkshire man inexplicably coughs up possession, 10 metres out into the hands of the gleeful Dragons substitute Julien Touxagas, filling in at centre.

Touxagas foot soldier Catalan born played six terms at Brutus – 66 games in total, a lot from the bench, an unheralded back-rower. He would rack-up just five tries in the sang-et-or but on this particular day in Wales would see the lad from Palau claim his greatest He snapped up Orr's offering and headed into open field. Pinned his ears back, legs pumping like pistons and headed for glory. He just got there diving over, a stride a head of Sheriffe closing fast. Julien's effort would set up a late Catalan's revival with speedster Murphy winning it for them at the death 18-16.

promising to spoil the party; showed some real grit to get back into it in the second act narrowing the deficit to just a couple of points before Mounis's last minute converted try ushered in victory number twelve and a 2nd spot on the ladder for the French outfit. The local *L'Indépenant* had it : *"Rien n'arrête* (stop) *les Dragons!"* Heady days indeed.

By mid-season, coach Potter's departure appeared to be confirmed and the hunt for a replacement was on. Tony Rea of the Harlequins along with Brian Noble were mentioned in dispatches to be followed later by the former Kangaroo Kevin Walters the then present Queensland Cup coach of the Ipswich Jets. Regardless of all the conjecture around the coach, the team and group remained solid and confident behind the incumbent as the Dragons headed for Cardiff and the Millenium Weekend to tackle the Londoners. The year before in the Welsh capital the Quins had sneaked it but twelve months later the sang-et-or completed a right 'hold up' on the line. The French side not at their best and out played by a more composed opponent quicker in execution stayed in the contest till the end and pulled it out of the hat (18-16) with Julien Touxagas's famous interception and 90 metres gallop to the other end for his moment of glory.

The Challenge Cup 5th round followed with a trip to Bradford. There was to be no going back to Wembley though as the tie was decided (46-16) in quick time with Greenshields already in the sin-bin within just a few complete sweeps of the clock and down to twelve with four tries conceded in the first quarter of an hour. The Bulls wing Tadulala claimed a try hat-trick as they plundered thirty points by the break. Coach Potter was philosophical, "After the catastrophic decision by the referee to exclude Greenshields we could only defend in the heat. At the moment we're travelling a lot. In the last six weeks we've travelled away five times; with the flights and bus connections it's demanding and we've paid the price today".

After the first defeat in two months Catalans would dust themselves down and now make the Super League its priority. Yet another flight beckoned to take on the chasing St Helens. Knowsley Road would continue to be a bastion as the Saints continued where the Bulls left off. Potter's team again slow out of the blocks in recovery mould caught by the hosts early assaults bringing three rapid tries. 16-0 down at half-time told its tale. But this wasn't quite the febrile outfit of its infancy as the visitors showed commitment and resolve on the return making a game of it though still conceding the points (10-28).

Now in 3rd after the St Helens reverse and with the Cup exit at Odsal the Dragons wanted to show these two hiccups just transitory in their 2008 journey. A struggling Huddersfield back on terra firma would be ideal to pick up points in the march to a play off baptism. The locals blitzed the Giants with as commanding a performance as one could hope for (48-0) with eight tries racked-up at regular intervals. A week off for the Cup quarter-finals was a most welcome break before travelling again to Odsal for the league fixture. Same venue, different competition and more importantly a different result for the visitors as they turned the tables on the Yorkshiremen. The Dragons landed their sixth away win of the campaign with gusto turning over a six point interval deficit with a late Murphy try and Bosc penalty (24-16). They were starting on a roll again. The last two weeks of June shone on the Dragons more brightly than the Mediterranean sun.

A couple of home victories against two of Lancashire's best in Wigan and Warrington both in contention with the French club for end of season play off spots. For the cherry & whites visit, a club record attendance so far at Brutus of 9,125 assembled for what turned out a palpating tussle with the shirt sleeve crowd regaled by what was on offer. Thirteen sparking tries produced and the lead changing hands five times as the mini epic ebbed and flowed. Wigan led at the break by a couple of points but Catalan raised their game on the resumption with Greenshields in his element with a hat-trick of tries. The visitors wouldn't let go though and chased the home side all the way to the finishing line (45-38) with Mogg's late one point drop goal taking the strain.

It was announced that captain McGuire had extended his contract at the club for two further years and fellow Australian Croker to till the end of 2009. Going the other way this third year of the Catalans would see the departures of Chan, Wilson and hooker Gorrell. The old 'Wire' followed Wigan to Brutus seven days later desirous of making up for the home loss to the French men back in March. The visitors buoyed by their win the week before at home to Hull KR never looked like winners though and collapsed miserably before a large Warrington following who had made their way across the Channel. Thirty-eight unanswered points at the break the key as the locals ratcheted up a half century of points with wing flyer Murphy, also in his last term, claiming two of his sides 9 tries (52-14). Only Morley for the primrose and blue showed up and the only one to give his supporters some applause at the end. That Saturday night the Dragons really confirmed their standing as a top side in 3rd spot and five points clear of nearest chasers Wakefield as the finishing home straight came into view.

Trinity on the first day of July would have a chance to chase down the Frenchmen in their own Belle Vue lair after the mid season international the previous weekend. Coach Potter had set up camp across the Channel with Hull FC next up at the KC. The locals started like a house on fire with two early tries and in to double figures before the French men woke up. But as soon as Chan – *Alexandre Le Valeureux* – took the lead it would be a forgone conclusion. Catalan hit the front by the break and cruised after to a first ever victory in Trinity land (30-14) with a brace of tries each from McGuire and Khattabi.

A struggling Airlie Birds the Sunday after proved no different with the Dragons carrying on where they left off in the West Riding with two first half tries and blanketing out completely any offensive coming their way. It was nearly the hour before the hosts got anything tangible but by then the French where out of sight (30-18). Assistant coach Frayssinous commented, "Nine days ago on the night of our defeat against England the French lads were right at the bottom of the bucket. With the Dragons they've lifted their heads up in the best means possible". Back at the "Temple" that was Brutus, Harlequins shouldn't have proved problematic but in a game played out early on in a torrential thunder storm making conditions a lottery it turned into a fight to the finish. London had quality in Hill and Paul and they racked up five second half tries before the hosts woke up. It was tied as the end approached with a real dust up between Mogg and McCarthy-Scarsbrook which saw both dismissed and everybody thinking it was points shared. With the bell already sounded the Dragons kept the ball alive and gave it a mighty last fling. A kick high into the murky sky smiled on the chasing Greenshields to claim an incredible if fortuitous victory (32-26).

The winning run had stretched unbelievably to seven and also impressively nine victories picked up across the Channel in total as they as they built a fortress around their 3rd place ranking with a seven point gap opening up behind.

What a better way to welcome then the Leeds Rhinos to Brutus the following weekend. In contrast to the previous week a glorious July day presented itself for the visit of the Super League holders and World Club Challenge winners.

STAR GAME 2008 SUPER LEAGUE XIII ROUND 22 LEEDS RHINOS at Stade Gilbert Brutus on Saturday 19th July

What an ambiance for the protagonists with the summer sunshine and a new club record crowd of 9,880 gathered at Brutus. They were not to be disappointed with the fare put on show in a real ding-dong palpating encounter between two of the competitions best. The hosts missed Mogg's midfield direction and presence after his dismissal against the Quins and Ferriol's absence sorely missed too against the likes of Peacock and Ellis up front.

Although full-back Smith got the Yorkshire men off to a flyer with an early try it was the French side who had the better of the first half with tries from Stacul, Elima and Raguin giving them a half-time lead of 18-10. It turned into a real cat and mouse affair. Lauiti'iti's introduction proved the key though. He crossed from Sinfield's pass which put them in front again 26-20 on the hour mark a lead which they where not going to relinquish.

Burrow and McGuire played a major role in their teams triumph with each grabbing a try and their direction and footwork caused problems for the hosts through out. Pace was the ultimate difference in this clash epitomised by wing Donald's score, running through the heart of the Dragons defence from just outside his own 20 metre line for a sumptuous and decisive try. Skipper Sinfield put his troops more than one score ahead for the first time with less than 5 minutes on the clock. Flying wing Hall's second try at the death was just the *cerise sur le gâteau*.

"We showed a lot of character against a very tenacious side who are doing some terrific things over here," commented the Rhinos coach Brain McClennan." I have full respect for them and they made it very tough but we hung in there. Scotty Donald's brilliance on a kick return was a very good effort and we're extremely pleased with the outcome." Mick Potter in the opposite corner was not too disappointed despite the first loss since early March at home,"The guys are tired and I'm very proud of them; we were just on the wrong end of the score board. We're looking forward to a week off now and recharge our batteries."

Catalans 24-37 Leeds. H-T:18-10.Weather: Hot and sunny. Attendance: 9,880 Referee: Richard Silverwood. For Catalans 4 tries fom Stacul (7), Elima (14,50) & Raguin (25) & 4 goals from Bosc. For Leeds 7 tries from Smith (3), Hall (34,79) D McGuire (44,53), Lauiti'iti (60),Donald (74) & 4 goals, 1 drop goal from Sinfield. Catalans: Greenshields, Stacul,Wilson, Raguin, Pelo, Bosc, C McGuire ©, Elima Gorrell, Chan, Croker, Mounis, Carlaw Substitutes: Casty, Guisset, Touxagas Quintilla.

Leeds: Smith, Donald, Toopi, Senior, Hall, D McGuire, Burrow, Peacock, Diskin Leuluai, Jones-Buchanan, Ellis, Sinfield © Substitutes: Lauiti'iti, Scruton, Ablett Kirke.

Putting their feet up the weekend of the Challenge Cup Semi Final's provided a welcome break before heading to Humberside to take on the Robins in their nest. The home straight well and truly now in view; the Dragons 5 points ahead of their nearest rival with five to play. It was for them to lose. Hull KR were just too good on the opening weekend of August at the new Craven Park led home majestically by former Catalans favourite Dobson. The French men were in touch up till the break trailing by a couple but fell off the pace to go down to their seventh loss (12-30). Wigan, for the 3rd match-up, were at Brutus again the following week before yet another 9,000 plus crowd and the match was closer even than the earlier edition with both defences having their say; Hansen's last minute try claimed a merited (16-16) draw for the visitors.

There was a sense of a wobble again; maybe questioning a self-belief in accepting what had already transpired. The two points needed though beckoned and were obtained at struggling Huddersfield a week later (22-20) to maintain their present standing on the back of a brace of tries from Mogg. The play-off spot more or less assured with two rounds to play for after finishing 10th on the ladder just a year before. The last two games were lost without any consequence. Harlequins motivated by the feisty loss in the rain at Brutus earlier took the spoils (24-34) at the Stoop and Catalans lost their final league game to Wakefield at home (32-38) already knowing that Warrington where coming in the first round of the play-offs. It was all quite surreal; A Wembley visit in only their second season followed immediately by a 3rd place in the league the year after. Who across the Channel would have believed it?

Warrington who would come to Perpignan for the French clubs first ever play-off game on the second weekend of September were one of only six Super League clubs who had played every year since the competitions inception in 1996, with however little success. Their visit to Brutus would represent only their fourth post season game and thus far a single victory back in 2006 at Headingley. They had lost twice in the regular season to the Dragons in 2008 and this third clash would offer nothing new. Catalans had it in the bag by half-time racing away to a twenty points lead with the flying Murphy already half way to his eventual haul of four tries playing a big part in the relative newcomers stunning

(46-8) win at their first attempt. The following morning's headline on the front page of *L'Indépendant* said it all: *"Les Dragaons crachent le feu"* (fire-eaters).

The success enveloped the ville. The municipal authorities for the following weeks visit of Wigan erected hanging posters promoting the tie from lamp posts and around the centre of the town and the local buses ran rolling ticker tape messages of support, *"Allez les Dragons!"*. For the first time the national press represented by the hugely poular national sports daily *L'Équipe* showed some real interest at last. A full page piece in particular caught the eye with a feature profiling the merits of stand-off Thomas Bosc of the Dragons and USAP's mega signing, the All Blacks Daniel Carter. Wigan though were in no mood to let the party roll on. The Cup loss in 2007 still festered.

Without a win in the present campaign after three attempts, the Lancastrians were desperate to turn the tables on the French side. The draw in August at Brutus had laid the platform. The ground record crowd was broken yet again (9,985) for this eliminating semi final tussle which saw both sides in the wrestle up till the break before the locals collapsed (26-50) conceding half a dozen second half tries with wing Richards in his element with a 22 points haul.

The dream was over but what a ride 2008 had been. Mogg became the 2nd Catalans player after fellow Australian Murphy to gain recognition in the annual Dream Team selection too. As they soared to heights far above their expectations for a new club in a different setting and culture, it was also a time for passing on. Coach Potter had got himself fixed up at high flying St Helens who had been impressed in what he had achieved across the Channel in just three years with the newcomers. Three players from the antipodes were also moving on as well as the assistant coach McFadden. Wing Murphy had been with the club since their UTC days and played in the French competition. Although slight of build, he had real pace and was an intelligent footballer; his strike rate was impressive with 53 tries in sixty-six appearances. He would stay on for an additional term helping out with their reserve set up and youngsters and returned to Australia in 2010.

His inside centre partner Wilson formerly of the West Tigers was a popular, hard working player who gave the sang-et-or that loyal and dependable service in their infancy years; he returned to Sydney and continued his involvement in

Clint Greenshields was the most celebrated of all the overseas players to wear the sang-et-or with 146 appearances. Along with Ian Henderson, the only ones to put in a 5 year stint at Brutus, and the clubs record try scorer to date with 85 tries. Consistency was his draw card. Leading try scorer in 2008 with 18 tries and the same number too in his final year 2012. Became the 3rd player in 2008 after Murphy and Mogg to be nominated for the Dream Team. Would represent France in the inaugural Four Nations in 2009 and after a last hurrah at North Queensland Cowboys in 2013 would return again to France to carry the Tricolours one last time in the World Cup that autumn and play his last ever competitive game, appropriately at Stade Gilbert Brutus against Samoa. A Dragons legend.

the game as a Development Officer with the NSWRL. A bit surprisingly too Khattabi returned home to Provence after his three year stint in Perpignan with a dozen tries to his name; never will he forget though the try he scored on a certain May day in 2007 when he rewrote a bit of history as the first Frenchman to cross the white wash in a Challenge Cup Final at Wembley.

The third player retiring was the Kiwi prop Chan. He was one of those players specially recommended to the club by fellow international great, Stacey Jones for their debut season. Chan was of Chinese origin born in Auckland. He was a late bloomer not making the NRL till his mid twenties after starting out at the Taupo Hawks and Bay of Plenty, turning out at full-back. His wanderings across the Tasman took him to the Northern Eagles and then on to Parramatta where he played off the bench in the Eels Grand Final loss to the Newcastle Knights in 2001. He was good enough then to be picked up by Melbourne Storm before finally arriving in Perpignan in 2006 at the age of 31 years. Possibily Chan wasn't the most spectacular of players or even Catalans most valuable but his presence in the group was exceptional. In many ways he helped them to be bigger and better than their parts.

It was against Leeds at Aime-Giral in only their fifth ever game and they were taking a right tonking. The Leeds heavies were throwing their weight about and some pushing their luck. The locals were annoyed and Chan landed some punches and was the first ever Dragon to be dismissed. He had set out his stall. From then on he was going to be their enforcer. He would be the one the French lads would look up to when things warmed up; he would always be there for them; "Le Padre" tendering his flock. His trade mark at Brutus was his resolute march back behind his own posts after the Dragons had scored. None of this exaggerated celebration stuff for him; but gritty resolve to go again and again. It was something ingrained into him from his time at Parramatta and both Ferriol and Casty continued in the same vane. Chan returned to Sydney and driving trucks as well as coaching in the local comp at Wentworthville Magpies.

( ) Denotes Play-off games

2008 FIXTURES	RND	DATE	VENUE	RESULT	ATT
CASTLEFORD	1	09/02	WHELDON RD	W 21-14	
HULL KR	2	16/02	GILBERT BRUTUS	L 20-24	8,350
LEEDS	3	22/02	HEADINGLEY	L 6-34	
WARRINGTON	4	02/03	HJ STADIUM	L 18-38	
BRADFORD	5	08/03	GILBERT BRUTUS	L 18-20	7,450
ST.HELENS	6	15/03	GILBERT BRUTUS	W 24-10	7,828
HARLEQUINS	7	21/03	THE STOOP	W 24-22	
WAKEFIELD	8	24/03	GILBERT BRUTUS	W 28-20	8,120
HULL FC	9	29/03	GILBERT BRUTUS	D 28-28	8,450
HUDDERSFIELD	10	04/04	GALPHARM	W 20-16	
WIGAN	11	11/04	JJB STADIUM	W 26-24	
FEATHERSTONE	CCR4	20/04	POST OFFICE RD	W 22-12	
CASTLEFORD	12	26/04	GILBERT BRUTUS	W 38-30	8,745
HARLEQUINS	13	04/05	CARDIFF	W 18-16	
BRADFORD	CCR5	11/05	ODSAL	L 16-46	
ST.HELENS	14	17/05	KNOWSLEY RD	L 10-28	
HUDDERSFIELD	15	24/05	GILBERT BRUTUS	W 48-0	7,785
BRADFORD	16	08/06	ODSAL	W 24-16	
WIGAN	17	14/06	GILBERT BRUTUS	W 45-38	9,125
WARRINGTON	18	21/06	GILBERT BRUTUS	W 52-14	9,040
WAKEFIELD	19	01/07	BELLE VUE	W 30-14	
HULL FC	20	06/07	KC STADIUM	W 30-18	
HARLEQUINS	21	12/07	GILBERT BRUTUS	W 32-26	6,225
LEEDS	22	19/07	GILBERT BRUTUS	L 24-37	9,880
HULL KR	23	01/08	CRAVEN PARK	L 16-30	8,471
WIGAN	24	09/08	GILBERT BRUTUS	D 16-16	9,535
HUDDERSFIELD	25	16/08	GALPHARM	W 22-20	
WAKEFIELD	26	23/09	GILBERT BRUTUS	L 32-38	8,320
HARLEQUINS	27	07/09	THE STOOP	L 24-34	
WARRINGTON	PO	13/09	GILBERT BRUTUS	W 46-8	(8,442)
WIGAN	PO	20/09	GILBERT BRUTUS	L 26-50	(9,985)
				Total	135,751

Regular season median: 8,350

SUPER LEAGUE: P27 W16 D2 L9 PTS 34 PF 694 PA 625 POS. 3RD
CHALLENGE CUP: P2 W1 L1 PLAY-OFFS: P2 W1 L1.

2008	GAMES	TRIES	GOALS	POINTS
GREENSHIELDS	30	18		72
MURPHY	18	16		64
WILSON	24	7		28
MOGG	27	7		28
PELO	25	13		52
BOSC	30	7	122(1dg)	273
MCGUIRE	20	7		28
FERRIOL	16	1		4
GORRELL	21	7	4	36
GUISSET	26	2		8
RAGUIN	31	8		32
CROKER	23	2		8
MOUNIS	29	7		28
CARLAW	28	3		12
GOSSARD	4			
ELIMA	17	8		32
GRIFFI	3			
DUPORT	15	4		16
CHAN	28	4		16
BENTLEY A	4			
BENTLEY K	1			
FAKIR	20	3		12
STACUL	14	2		8
CASTY	28	2		8
KHATTABI	14	5		20
BAILE	6	1		4
TOUXAGAS	19	3		12
QUINTILLA	5			

(28)

Chapter 5

– BARCELONA –

The ground was moving everywhere in 2009. The RFL for the first time in a decade added two extra teams to the Super League competition as they introduced a new three year licensing system and ceased promotion and relegation for the first time since the competition's launch in 1996. Salford and the Celtic Crusaders based in Bridgend made up a 14 team entry and the play-offs would involve eight sides rather than 6 previously. For the first time since it's inception the competition at last started to look like what was originally intended with representation from London, Wales and France. An add-on was the introduction of a second French club in Toulouse Olympique into the part-time Championship. A national and European dimension to the game was at last becoming a reality.

After Potter's successful three year tenure in Perpignan, it was time to turn a page as the Australian coach crossed the Channel to take over at St Helens from Daniel Anderson. The former St George Illawarra full-back had truly laid the foundations in the South of France with a Wembley Cup Final appearance and a 3rd place league spot in just three short years. Kevin Walters another Australian would take his place beside the Mediterranean. Walters, a Queensland legend along with his two brothers Kerrod and Steve, had established a dynasty in the land of the Maroons with Kangaroo and State of Origin representation.

Chan, Wilson and Murphy had been Potter's most able lieutenants in those bedding-in campaigns but they too had moved on to be replaced by a noted Kangaroo prop in Jason Ryles, Manly threequarter Steven Bell and Brisbane scrum half Shane Perry. Everything seemed in place for Walters to build on solid foundations and keep the still relatively new boys moving forward. Landing the Nike swoosh brand to their armoury was another feather in their cap as they swanned up and down the Champs-Élysées in Paris in their new playing apparel with the Government's Cultural Minister in tow.

The first sign of turbulence was the postponement of the warm up game at Toulouse Olympique with a near hurricane strength winds roaring across the Midi. They did get a run out the following weekend against a French Select from the local competition in Perpignan. They won as expected (36-18) but suffered the loss of the experienced Raguin with a serious cruciate ligament injury which would side line him for most of the year.

Huddersfield would be the opener in 2009 at Brutus. The Giants had been indifferent the year before but would show real signs of progress in Super League XIV starting with this one. The prop Ryles was the big catch for the Dragons in this their 4th campaign but the towering former Kangaroo got a rude awakening on his debut. A mighty collision floored the big fella early on and the towering former St George Illawarra star was assisted from the field and took no further part in the game. This loss appeared to rock the locals who looked under-cooked already. They couldn't get their combinations working while the Yorkshire men inspired by full-back Hodgson and half-back Robinson had just too much guile as they established a ten point lead at the break. It got no better as the visitors stormed away to a convincing (30-6) success with the sang-et-or reeling to their heaviest opening day defeat so far before a crowd of 7,533. Fortunately they got back on their *vélos* rather smartly with a commanding victory at Warrington (40-20) a week later which had club boss Guasch purring, "It's the victory of courage and talent to the end of a real match of Super League. What happiness in this hell!" he concurred. Yet another former Kangaroo Carlaw had been dumped and carried away in no time leaving Catalans with just five Antipodeans at their disposal to turn it around. Behind at the interval the French lads stood tall and strong with a heroic second forty led brilliantly by Carcassonne's Baile, who was everywhere.

The opening fortnight was to set the template for their season. Which side would turn up? Remarkably, the home fans wouldn't see them win a league game until Easter Monday in 2009, with a Round 9 game against Wigan. After the success at the Halliwell Jones it was down-hill all the way with five losses on the bounce all to Yorkshire opposition. At Hull FC, the Dragons had always found the going hard and this time was no different (12-28). With Ryles still unavailable after his knock out in Round 1, coach Walters decided to pull in Australian Greg Bird from Cronulla. The talented utility player had suddenly become available after being ditched by the NRL for domestic reasons and the Dragons pounced when Bradford couldn't secure a visa for him.

The Kangaroo and State of Origin player made his debut from the bench against Castleford at Brutus on the opening weekend of March but brought nothing new initially to the party as they where edged out (22-24). Wakefield who had started promisingly spanked the French next up at Belle Vue (10-30) with Catalans still missing the weight and presence of Ryles and Carlaw. Only the presence of the two promoted sides sitting below them on the competition ladder prevented embarrassment. Ryles was back in harness the week after at home to Bradford with Bird starting for the first time in the back row. This game represented the club's 100th since their entrée but unfortunately wasn't celebrated. They got mighty close to the Bulls but a last minute try for the visitors did for them (24-30) despite a man of the match performance from Bird and four tries scratched out by the video official scant recompense.

Even with Carlaw returning, Headingley and the Rhinos as usual would provide next to nothing. But any glimpse of improvement the week before at Brutus had dissipated in the wink of an eye as Leeds tore them apart with five first half tries. A couple of late tries massaged the reality of it all though (14-42). The Bulls were back in Perpignan again quick time but it was the Challenge Cup calling. Walters was already in a predicament with a one win out of 7 tally, representing their poorest ever start. It had been nip and tuck a fortnight earlier but would the Cup be the incentive required to lift the Dragons out of their stupor?

This turned out to be an incredible game. One of the greatest comeback ties of all times to decorate the famous 'Auld Girl.' On the first Sunday in April, in front of the BBC cameras, the Dragons just weren't at the races in a lamentable opening half, taking four unanswered tries and a deficit of twenty points to turn around. Within a couple of minutes of the restart a further converted score took it out to 0-26. Bradford where already looking in the velvet bag for the 5th round draw it appeared. Then suddenly and dramatically it all turned upside-down as the Catalans inspired by Bosc grabbed four tries in a ten minute burst just before the hour mark to bring the Dragons back into the frame at 22-26 with Brutus rocking. It all seemed too much to take in when Tadulala stretched the visitors lead further though with a converted try on 60 minutes but this proved just a hiatus as the locals roared on yet again and would not be denied as three Frenchmen Baile, Gossard and Bosc claimed converted tries in the final quarter to take the spoils (40-38). Bosc, magnificent, finished with eighteen second half points in probably his best ever 40 minutes spell.

Inspired by the Cup result, Walter's team had a productive Easter with maximum points achieved in the three league games played. In the capital to take on their nearest neighbours Harlequins as ever would be feisty foes on the Maundy Thursday. For the first time too a French man in the middle in the form of the Tarnais whistler Thierry Alibert in charge of a Dragons encounter. The Catalans got a handle on this one early doors with three tries in the opening half hour and just did enough to keep the Londoners at bay for the duration with the former Kangaroo Carlaw leading the way (28-24). The coach had switched the talented Bird to stand off at The Stoop alongside Bosc and that combination blossomed alongside the sunshine on Easter Monday against Wigan before the largest crowd of the season so far of 9,490. It was tit for tat in the opening half of a free flowing encounter with the sang-et-or just edging it. Bobby Goulding the newly appointed French team coach in attendance was enamoured with Catalans half-back pairing saying that they were the key to unlocking the visitors defence. "We made the difference grace to our excellent defensive effort in the second half," confirmed coach Walters (40-24).

Salford would close the hectic three match festive programme five days later, again at home. The Reds buoyed by their stunning win at Leeds earlier couldn't repeat their performance. Although the Lancastrians opened the scoring a converted try that was all they where going to get. The locals responded with three tries of their own by the break before running away with it (38-6) and a victory which would put them on the edge of play-off respectability in 9th place. Their season at last re-launched maybe?

Well, the roller-coaster provides as many down turns as upward ones and for 2009 anyway Catalans were always about finding the ascents at precisely the right moment. Hull KR on Humberside would bring them down back to earth with a sudden bump after the Dragons prosperous Easter ride. Indeed the Spring time would prove calamitous for the French outfit with that defence, lauded by Walters earlier, truly went missing big time leaking nearly 150 points in that month. The influential Mogg was still absent after picking up a knock in the Cup match but more important was the loss of their dynamic Easter half-back pairing of Bird and Bosc at Craven Park. The Robins ran riot on the last weekend of April running in eight tries as the Dragons floundered (10-44).

The Super League was bristling in their launch in 2009, rightly proud of its expanded geographical reach that year. Games would be played in England, France, Scotland, Spain and Wales. The Dragons would cross Hadrian's Wall for the first time that May time as the Magic Weekend wound its way up to Edinburgh where the French side would tussle with the champions Leeds. 30,122 attended the opening day and while the sang-et-or admired Murrayfield and its splendid city landscape views the Rhinos helped themselves to a thirty-zero half-time lead with a trio of touchdowns in a five minute spell, killing them. They did get some self-respect back with a spirited second half response but still no nearer the Leeds machine that term (16-36). Bird still entangled with personal problems and court appearances, had to fly back to Sydney more than once during his eventful year in Roussillon. He only just made the Edinburgh kick off in time and in June disappeared completely, missing four games.

He picked up an injury in Scotland's capital and missed the Cup tie at St Helens a week later too. His performances as one would expect with his travails were up and down but at the fag end of the year he would prove to be the real deal.

It was heart-breaking after seeing off the Bulls in such dramatic circumstances at Brutus a month or so earlier to be awarded with a Cup 5th round draw against the holders St Helens at their Knowsley Road den. The French side made a fist of it in the opening half conceding a converted try in the last minute to push the hosts into a ten point advantage at the turn around before pulling away impressively later on (8-42). It was to be Catalans third Cup exit to Saints in four years. A week later the Dragons at least would have a chance to redeem themselves in the league game back in Perpignan. With Bird back on board and Mogg pairing up with Bosc at half-back Catalans showed their better face in a breathtaking encounter. The locals captivating early on raced into a two score advantage by the break and in doing so registered their 500th point in Super League. The lead changed hands three times in a palpitating last forty before Saints stole it with the decisive try 2 minutes from the final bell (28-32). A fine performance but a ninth defeat never the less, pushing them back down to 12th spot at the half way stage and all to do to reach a play-off spot for the second consecutive year.

At least the struggling Welsh team would offer easier pickings next up even down in Bridgend with Guisset playing his 100th game for the club. The French side had to avoid a banana skin and did so even after conceding an early score. Cyrille Gossard to the fore made his presence felt, instigating openings which saw Walter's team comfortably ahead at the turn around, with four tries recorded. The Crusaders made a game of it later but the visitors had enough to gain the vital competition points (30-18). With a week off for the Cup quarter-finals the Dragons could really prepare and set out their stall for the arrival of Leeds at Brutus, always eagerly awaited. It was another cliff-hanger as per the Saints clash in the last home game but this time the French side had the last word with Stacul's last minute try securing the win. It was close all the way as the two protagonists shared the ten tries equally with two penalty goals from Bosc proving crucial (32-30).

With another 2 competition points in the pocket the Dragons were on the coat-tails of four teams all on 14 points with all still to play for as the home straight appeared on the horizon.

The Dragons perform their callisthenics in Barcelona's Olympique Stadium on the eve of their momentous match with Warrington.

STAR GAME 2009 SUPER LEAGUE XIV ROUND 17 WARRINGTON WOLVES
at Stade Olympique Montjuic Barcelona on Saturday 20th June

This just had to be Dragons crossing the border to play a match in Spain and to the Catalans spiritual home of Barcelona. It would be a big test of the still comparatively new club to mobilise its support in such numbers as to be able to garnish the Olympic bowl that was Montjuic. They came from everywhere for this special and unique event; from Perpignan, Ceret, Ornaisons and Lézignan a round trip of over 400 kilometres. They poured into Place d'Espagne from early morning and in conga formation up through *las Ramblas* to the heart of the city in their gold coloured T-shirts and white sombrero hats. Out on the mesmeric hillside that is Montjuic, coaches were parked in lines as far as the eye could see, nearly a hundred in number who had ferried a good number of the estimated 15,000 who had made the celebratory trip.

The actual game seemed to get lost in the surroundings of the venue and occasion. As one peered across the home stretch of the running track images of Christie's lunge for Olympic gold back in 1992 came into view while the two formations continued their pre-match warm ups. The Old Wire's fortunes had definitely taken an upward turn since Tony Smith had arrived as coach in the spring. With Bird still back in Sydney the Dragons had to plug the centres with the ageless Croker, leaving Mogg to partner Bosc in the halves.

Warrington were first to impose when Bridge crossed for the opening converted try early on with their quick passing exposing some lack of mobility in the home ranks. The forward battle between Morley and Carvell against Ryles and Ferriol was immense. Catalans didn't help themselves as in turn McGuire kicked out on the full and Mogg had a clearing kick charged down. With the home support urging them on the French side got level when Croker burrowed over from close in after wing Bell had set up the position with a determined run from deep.

The Dragons slowly asserted themselves with Mogg very much orchestrating things and Ferriol making inroads down the middle. The former was causing the primrose and blue all sorts of problems and it was his lovely long cut-out pass on 20 minutes that put Stacul over in the corner to put the Dragons in front for the first time. The rest of the half was scoreless though Mogg's super covering tackle on Riley saved their bacon.

Bosc subsequently added a penalty goal to extend their lead to six as the second period unfolded. Mogg then undid his earlier efforts losing the ball from Ryles off-load inside his own 20 metres. From there the Lancastrians hit hard transferring the ball rapidly left for the increasingly influential Matt King to pick a great line going between Mogg and Crocker from fifteen metres out for the equalising score 12-12 on 48 minutes. In reality from then on Warrington had all the aces and the Catalans just couldn't find the inspiration they had shown against Leeds even after Greenshield's had intercepted and broke clear only to be reeled back in by a chasing Riley.

Jérôme Guisset and Adrian Morley lead out their sides for the first ever Super League game played in Spain in front of a crowd of over 18,000. A cavalcade of nearly a 100 charabancs brought thousands down from Perpignan for the occasion. What a day!

Just before the hour mark the visitors hit the lead for the second time when Riley picked up a clever little kick dabbed into the corner getting his nose in front of Stacul to collect and plunge over. The Catalans still had their moments though especially when Greenshields slid a neat kick behind the Warrington defence only for the supporting Bosc to fail to get enough downward pressure on the ball as it trickled over the white wash. The clincher came ten minutes from the end, when with the Dragons tiring, John Clarke went from dummy half centre field from 40 metres out to score in the right hand corner exposing some poor defence. Hicks added a penalty just minutes from the final bell to rap things up for the Lancastrians.

Catalans coach Walters disagreed with the decision to kick that 46th-minute penalty but also hoped a Barcelona game could become a regular fixture. "We took those two points and I think that was a critical play because I thought we could have kept the pressure on", he said.

"It was disappointing to lose but it was a tough game and we'll take something out of it. I knew that a good game would be on the cards and it was a good crowd in a good stadium. They seemed to enjoy it and we like coming down here so we could possibly make it an annual event."

The visitors coach Smith added, "We were frustrated with ourselves in the first half. If you're not playing smart and you make a couple of errors on top if it; you get hurt. That put us behind the eight ball, particularly against a big team like that. They're as big as anything in Super League so to come over here and get the money is a tough ask. You've got to be smart to do that and we proved that in the second half. We were better and we needed to be. There was a lot of commitment to one another and we saw that with how we recovered from a couple of their breaks."

Catalans 12-24 Warrington. HT: 10-6. Weather: Humid & overcast. Attendance: 18,150 Referee: Thierry Alibert. For Catalans: 2 tries from Croker (16) & Stacul (20) & 2 goals from Bosc. For Warrington 4 tries from Bridge (7), King (50), Riley (60) & Clarke (70) & 4 goals from Hicks
Catalans: Greenshields, Stacul, Croker, Baile, Bell, Mogg, Bosc, Carlaw, McGuire © Guisset, Elima, Gossard, Fakir Substitutes: Ryles, Ferriol, Perry, Touxagas
Warrington: Mathers, Hicks, Bridge, King, Riley, Grix, Monaghan, Morley © Clarke, Carvell, L Anderson, Westwood, Harrison Substitutes: Johnson, Rauhihi V Anderson, Woods

Although the Dragons fluffed their lines on the pitch in Barcelona it was still a monumental day in the club's evolution. It was the biggest crowd to watch a Super League game across the Channel passing the 17,873 for PSG's opener against Sheffield on the very opening day of the new professional era. The timing for the Dragons couldn't have been better too because in 2009 their fearsome neighbours down Avenue du Maréchal Joffre USAP where on the prowl. The town's union team had been wary of the competition developing up the road. When it was little village Pia or suburb St Estève rustling up a few hundred for the French competition no concern but the Dragons had quickly made their mark after Wembley and a 3rd finishing place in 2008. That year the *L'Équipe* sports daily did a piece on the two rival clubs with the article highlighting the respective stand offs Thomas Bosc and the All Black super star Daniel Carter who had signed a short-term contract for the unionists for the following year. Just sharing a page in the illustrious journal and framing these two respective players side by side was a statement in itself.

In 2009 USAP would go on and win the Top 14 competition for the first time since 1955 and they would also reach the Paris Final twelve months later. Some saw Carter's signing partly as a response to the new fledgling arriving on the scene. But their success didn't roll over the new rugby league set up who when considering the vastly different media profile between the two punched well above their weight. Bernard Goutta the USAP coach had played league as a junior at Pia but was content with the situation commenting, "Last season, on the same day and time, we pulled 12,000 to Aimé-Giral and them 8,000 to Brutus. Getting twenty thousand Catalans watching the rugby; not bad eh!" Some supporters would follow closely the two especially with a wrap around season and Super League in the summer. USAP players were often seen at Brutus over the years. Paul Goze the union club President though was openly hostile and fought bitterly against the development of Stade Gilbert Brutus. He had wanted an enlarged Amie Giral to host both clubs but he was never slow in coming forward to announce who would be the junior partner.

Well after the Barcelona weekend it was back to business and the quest for points towards qualification in the new 8 team play-offs. Castleford had benefitted from the new licensing structure after finishing bottom in 2008 and had regrouped well and on the last weekend of June sat in the final eighth qualifying spot with the Dragons in town and serious about closing the four point gap. Catalans, highly motivated to gain revenge from the earlier loss at home to the Tigers, couldn't have had a worse start conceding two tries in the opening ten minutes.

Fortunately they got their act together in time bringing the sides level by the break. Greenshields was their lynch key man in this one, offering something of substance both sides of the ball and enabling Walter's side to get the two vital and timely points (22-20); their fourth away success in 2009 and one place won on the ladder too. Hull KR had followed Catalans into Super League a year later and like the French side had adapted quickly. Back on home terra firma the week after Castleford, the Robins of Justin Morgan high flying in 3rd slot, would be a formidable challenge. Fortunately for the sang-et-or it would be one they would rise too with gusto. Baile had the game of his life scoring a hat-trick of tries in the centres; two in the opening quarter would prove decisive giving his side a solid two score advantage at the break. A cameo appearance put in for this one from the unfathomable Martins who, unfortunately drifted in and out of Brutus over the years without ever realising his true potential. A late Bosc drop goal pushed them into safe territory before Baile got his third on the bell (23-12) keeping his team still in the hunt with just a couple of points separating five sides vying for the last two qualifying places, just as the RFL would have hoped for.

A week later at the JJB Stadium Catalan born Mounis also celebrated his 100th game for the club following on behind Guisset. Bird was back after an extended stay back in Sydney and showed Wigan his best face. The Cronulla strong man landed back in the early hours jet lagged and was only expected to fill in on the bench but as Mogg pulled-up in the warm up he started at stand off. He showed his pedigree early on putting Greenshields clear and got a vital score to keep his side ahead later on. Bizarrely when the latter was in the bin leading into the break Catalan grabbed two quick fire tries to hold a narrow advantage at the turn round. Losing Guisset early on and Croker hobbling on one leg, they didn't quite have enough as the cherry & whites edged it (24-22). With another side in direct competition for a top 8 place Harlequins to arrive a week later. It was hot and sultry beside the Mediterranean as the Tour de France arrived in Switzerland with a certain Bradley Wiggins handily placed in 3rd place and everyone else packing their buckets and spades ready for their vacations.

The Londoners as determined and feisty as usual in these encounters gave nothing away in a tight opening forty. The high temperatures favoured the locals who accelerated away though after the citrons. With defences tiring in the heat the gaps opened up and ten tries accrued with the hosts adding an extra five to the two earlier (38-16). The game will be remembered though by an exquisite individual try from Bosc from 40 metres out. He kicked ahead twice over the opposition and gathered to score between the uprights in the blink of an eye but what made it unique and eye catching was he alternated feet in the process!

The home straight was now well in view. The Giants had shown in round 1 at Brutus that they where becoming the real thing in 2009 under Nathan Brown and further confirmed it in round 22 with a second convincing win over the French outfit (36-12) at the Galpharm. Cudjoe, a rising force in the centres for the claret & gold, claimed a hat-trick of tries. The Dragons were thereabouts up to the break but faded badly after. Celtic Crusaders and the rearranged game at Salford followed, offering something more manageable, against the bottom two sides. The Welsh side with just three wins to their account were dispatched comfortably (34-0) at Brutus on the opening day of August before the lowest crowd of the season 7,420 and Salford fell too after a tight affair at the Willows (18-16). A stumbling show against the Reds with McGuire's last minute intervention saving their bacon.

The four points picked up well consolidated their 10th placing but with just four games left the room for manoeuvre was now becoming constrained. Catalan really pushed the boat out in 2009 with not one but two fixtures relocated. After the epic effort to stage their Warrington fixture in Spain their penultimate home game against Hull FC went up the road rather than south to Beziers and their impressive sea-shell shaped Stade de la Méditerranée. The town just inland from the coast is a real rugby union stronghold with eleven Championship titles to their name but where rugby league had much earlier had had its place, when S.O.Beziers contested the inaugural weekend of the code in October 1934. And it would be where sixty years later the game would bid farewell too to the Kangaroo legend Mal Meninga playing his last Test in the illustrious green & gold.

The struggling Airlie Birds arrived in the *Hérault department* having never lost to the Catalans in France. This would be Hull FC's last throw of the dice to stake their own claim for qualification. It was stern and tough with just one converted score to the visitors at the interval. Just as Baile had undercut the Robins earlier with a hat-trick of tries this time it was Elima who would replicate the feat against the other Humberside challenge in a determinant second period which would bring home the goods with bravado (18-6). They were back in the 'Eight' for the first time since February. Unfortunately the victory in Bezier had left traces with half a dozen picking up knocks and compromising their preparation at Odsal eight days later against the frustrated Bulls facing their first ever none play-off qualification. Steve McNamara's side would make hay sauntering to an easy win (42-18) raking up eight tries in the process as the Frenchmen still lodged in 7th spot turned their thoughts to Wakefield two weeks later at Brutus.

Trinity under John Kear where flying high in 2009 on target for their best ever finish. On the penultimate weekend they had the 7th spot already in the pouch but could still go further. Catalan had been well beaten in the earlier fixture at Bell Vue in March but here needed the points more maybe than the visitors knowing that St Helens a week later at Knowsley Road, where they'd never won, awaited them. It was a tense opening in Perpignan for their last home game of the year with the 37 year old NRL great "Toots" Croker bidding farewell to Brutus for the last time after yeomen service to the Dragons since 2007. Wakefield drew first blood opening a ten point lead before the hosts responded with a couple of tries; what did for the Dragons though was their indiscipline which saw the Yorkshire outfit land three crucial penalty goals before the break and would be their undoing. McGuire though did get his team in front with a quick brace of tries on the resumption but it didn't last as Trinity finished impressively with a flourish and three further tries (20-34). Bernard Guasch was disconsolate and made his sentiments known; lambasting his players after the encounter, "It's lamentable. For the first time in four years I'm ashamed. I've announced to them this evening in the changing rooms that they're all free to leave. Better some leave themselves rather than me firing them!" The President had spoken; over the years his hands on involvement, was and would be, always close and intimate.

So on to St Helens where they had never before won. The Saints of Potter running neck and neck all year long with the champions Leeds for the Hub Cap (League Leaders Shield) of top dog, were beckoning. Cunningham, Gidley, Pryce, Long et al in their pomp couldn't be taken in their lair could they? Well the response had to be immediate from a French side who's heart jumped to life by resuscitation cardiac from their comatose state of a week earlier as Pelo plonked the ball over in the corner on just 3 minutes. On quarter time McGuire got a second try and after that the visitors would just not let go as they went to record a famous victory against all the odds and expectations (24-12) and in so doing saved their whole season in just 80 minutes of action thwarting a late run by Bradford on the rails for the defining 8th placing. Phew!

How different to twelve months earlier when they sauntered into the play-offs. Of course this finishing position wouldn't have been good enough in 2008 and would leave Walters the unenviable task of performing on the road from then on. For their second successive play-off campaign it would be the surprise package Wakefield at Belle Vue awaiting the French on a damp Saturday night in late September. The same Trinity who'd delivered misery to the Dragons during the regular season with home and away defeats. For this pair of qualifiers it was knockout football no less. No second chances and it showed. Both sides tense and not giving anything away with only a penalty goal to the good for the hosts in the opening half hour. Then dramatically the game sprung to life and in the space of five minutes the 'sang-et-or' struck with venom sealing the Yorkshire men's fate with three tries and two conversions with Mogg omnipresent. After the break Catalan put the shutters up rolling with the punches. Wakefield would hit back

Greg Bird presence grew throughout 2009 hindered by his frequent trips back to Sydney. When the Dragons reached the Semi-Finals of Super League for the first time he was the man to look out for. At Headingley on his swan-song he was the one asking questions of the Rhinos defence, time and time again.

late on but not enough as a Bosc drop goal and penalty steered the visitors into week two (25-16). It would be the clubs first play off success across the Channel.

Huddersfield who completed their best ever campaign finishing 3rd lay in wait at the Galpharm the following Friday after their loss at St Helens. The Giants, like Trinity, had beaten the French side twice in 2009 in the league but there was something stirring in the air in Roussillon that autumn and it was palatable. Somehow they turned the emotion of that last home defeat to their advantage. A historic first win at Saints followed and now success at Wakefield. In a highly charged opening beneath the rolling Pennine hills with the visitors conceding three penalties in next to no time the tone was set. The resolve was there and Catalan would not submit to the giant charges of Mason and Crabtree. Greenshields and Robinson would break the dead lock exchanging first half tries and there was but a sliver between the foes. Huddersfield would only crack after the hour mark when Pelo and Elima plundered tries and it was done and dusted (16-6). The thirty or so French fans who travelled were overjoyed but thousands back home watching on television in bars and clubs in Albi, Carcassonne, Limoux and Perpignan were standing tall too. Unbelievably Old Trafford was just eighty minutes away!

Headingley had never conceded to the French challenge and that was putting it mildly. The Dragons in earlier visits had never really contested and received lots of grief. But this was a major semi-final leading to the Grand Final. McGuire and Duport exchanged tries early on but Catalans took water seriously in those vital minutes going into the break taking three tries and on the return a fifth from Donald. A three score gap and an ignominious ending stirred the visitors straight in the face. But Bird, Mogg and crew demanded no such retreat as the Dragons dug deep. In the last half hour they truly won their spurs with a come back of gigantic proportions. Duport ran round Senior and claimed a marvellous hat-trick of tries and Mogg would land their fourth as they closed in on the champions. It was serious enough for Sinfield to land a drop goal to quieten their nerves at (27-20). It was a heroic defeat and as the *L'Indépendant* reporter Arnaud Hingray commented: *"Les Catalans ont été* (have been) *grands!"*

A season which had started badly for Kevin Walters finished in near glory. It was topsy-turvy all along and never boring as epitomised by Greg Bird's transit involvement while Mogg still showed his class and stature in the games he featured in; he missed more games than in his previous two seasons. The significant progress though for many was the French players, at last maturing into decent Super League quality players. Olivier Elima with 19 tries became the first French player to be the leading try scorer at Catalans and in tandem with Baile and Pelo registered forty touchdowns between them. The mould at the Dragons of local player's contribution seen as peripheral had been broken. Bird returned to Australia as did Ryles, who never really settled. Perry struggled to make an impact at scrum half and also returned Down Under along with the popular Croker who had played at Wembley in 2007 and had been a super signing.

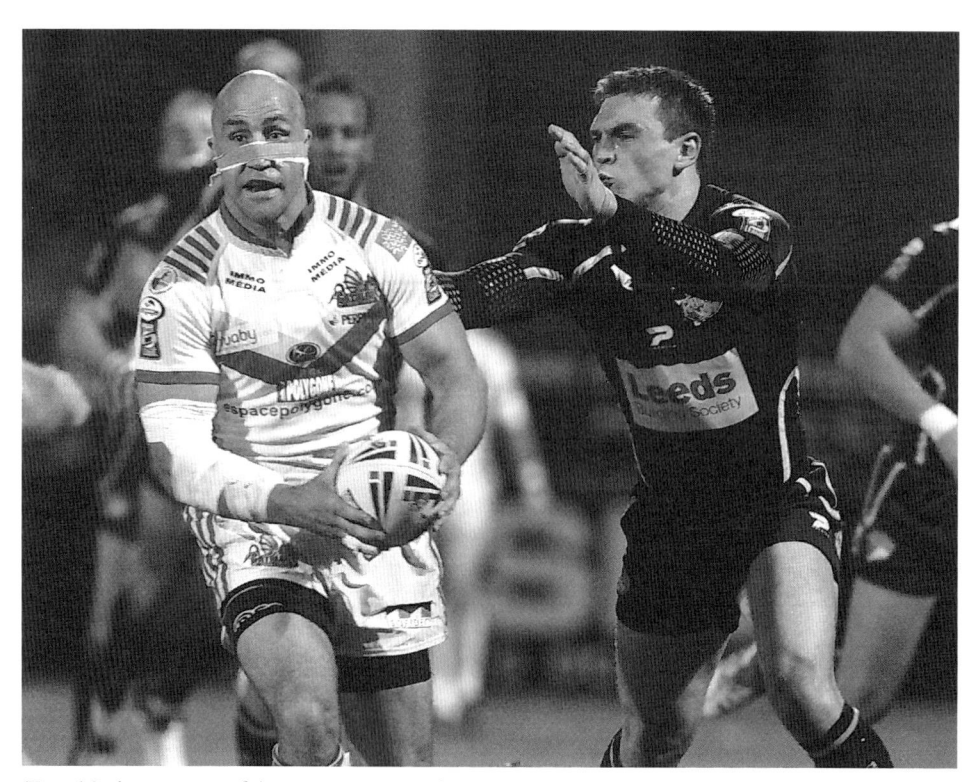

'Toots' Croker was one of that super quartet of Greenshields, McGuire and Mogg. Jason here very much in the wars against Leeds in their first ever win over the Rhinos but always turned for up Catalans despite arriving as a 34 year old NRL veteran of more than 300 games. Decisively he got on to the end of Stacey Jones's dink into the in-goal at the HJ Stadium in that famous Challenge Cup Semi-Final victory over Wigan in 2007. He would play 62 games at the Dragons – an age-less warrior. Last heard running a cafe in down-town Canberra.

( ) Denotes Challenge Cup game

2009 FIXTURES	RND	DATE	VENUE	RESULT	ATT
HUDDERSFIELD	1	14/02	GILBERT BRUTUS	L 8-30	7,533
WARRINGTON	2	21/02	HJ STADIUM	W 40-20	
HULL FC	3	27/02	KC STADIUM	L 12-28	
CASTLEFORD	4	07/03	GILBERT BRUTUS	L 22-24	8,150
WAKEFIELD	5	15/03	BELLE VUE	L 10-30	
BRADFORD	6	21/03	GILBERT BRUTUS	L 24-30	7,620
LEEDS	7	27/03	HEADINGLEY	L 14-42	
BRADFORD	CCR4	05/04	GILBERT BRUTUS	W 40-38	(6,450)
HARLEQUINS	8	09/04	THE STOOP	W 28-24	
WIGAN	9	13/04	GILBERT BRUTUS	W 40-24	9,490
SALFORD	10	18/04	GILBERT BRUTUS	W 38-6	8,327
HULL KR	11	26/04	CRAVEN PARK	L 10-44	
LEEDS	12	03/05	EDINBURGH	L 16-36	
ST.HELENS	CCR5	10/05	KNOWSLEY RD	L 8-42	
ST.HELENS	13	16/05	GILBERT BRUTUS	L 28-32	9,065
CRUSADERS	14	23/05	BRIDGEND	W 30-18	
LEEDS	15	06/06	GILBERT BRUTUS	W 32-30	7,913
WARRINGTON	17	20/06	BARCELONA	L 12-24	18,150
CASTLEFORD	18	27/06	WHELDON RD	W 22-20	
HULL KR	19	04/07	GILBERT BRUTUS	W 23-12	9,073
WIGAN	20	10/07	JJB STADIUM	L 22-24	
HARLEQUINS	21	19/07	GILBERT BRUTUS	W 38-16	8,324
HUDDERSFIELD	22	26/07	GALPHARM	L 12-36	
CRUSADERS	23	01/08	GILBERT BRUTUS	W 34-0	7,420
SALFORD	16	07/08	WILLOWS	W 24-16	
HULL FC	24	15/08	BEZIERS	W 18-6	9,803
BRADFORD	25	23/08	ODSAL	L 18-42	
WAKEFIELD	26	05/09	GILBERT BRUTUS	L 32-38	8,755
ST.HELENS	27	11/09	KNOWSLEY RD	W 24-12	
WAKEFIELD	PO	19/09	BELLE VUE	W 25-16	
HUDDERSFIELD	PO	25/09	GALPHARM	W 16-6	
LEEDS	PO	02/10	HEADINGLEY	L 27-20	
				Total	126,073

Regular season median: 8,327

SUPER LEAGUE: P27 W13 L14 PTS 26 PF 613 PA 660 POS. 8TH
CHALLENGE CUP: P2 W1 L1
PLAY-OFFS: P3 W2 L1

2009	GAMES	TRIES	GOALS	POINTS
GREENSHIELDS	29	13		52
STACUL	13	6		24
BELL	23	9		36
MOGG	21	5		20
PELO	29	17		68
BOSC	28	6	84(2dg)	194
PERRY	16	1		4
FERRIOL	30			
MCGUIRE	30	8		32
GUISSET	31	2		8
RAGUIN	7	3		12
CROKER	16	3		12
MOUNIS	26	2	9	26
CARLAW	23	3		12
BAILE	29	12		48
ELIMA	30	19		76
GOSSARD	27	3		12
DUPORT	16	6		24
QUINTILLA	1			
BENTLEY K	13	3		12
TOUXAGAS	12			
FAKIR	16	1		4
RYLES	22	2		8
CASTY	29	1		4
MARTINS	4	1		4
BIRD	23	5	3	26

(26)

Chapter 6
– BOAR LANE–

A fracas around a late night birthday celebration in Leeds on the very opening weekend of Super League XV wasn't the best way to launch Catalans fifth year in the competition – a year which would see them drop to bottom place after being 3rd in 2008 and only eighty minutes from Old Trafford the year before. The Dragons fell at the first hurdle at Wakefield that February afternoon. After the team retired to their Leeds hotel, a small group of them decided to celebrate Rémi Casty's 25th birthday by nipping out to a nearby fast-food restaurant adjacent to a public house in Boar Lane. Remi was joined by Jean-Philippe Baile, Olivier Elima, newcomer Setaimata Sa and Dimitri Pelo. During their visit an altercation took place between the players and some local lads which ended with the police involved.

Two of the players Pelo and Sa ended up being detained in the local police station pending further inquiries and didn't travel back with the rest of the group the following day. Subsequently it was reported that the two players involved were given ten and nine months suspended prison sentences and fined £1,000. It was felt by some that it possibly set the tone for a turbulent campaign on and off the field in 2010 something so far they'd never really come up against. 'Le Padre' Alex Chan wouldn't have approved for sure! But after that it all just kind of rolled down hill for Kevin Walter's crew with no one or group arresting the malaise. They had finished so well in 2009 and only a few people had moved on. True the admirable Crocker and the influential Bird had gone, as well as bizarrely Duport (to Toulouse Olympique) who scored a hat-trick of tries in that Semi-Final at Headingley on the penultimate weekend of 2009. Queenslander Dallas Johnson was considered a stellar capture from Melbourne Storm for sure and that solid triumvirate of Greenshields, McGuire and Mogg were still at the heart of things.

Walters was in buoyant mood more so with the performances of the French team in the 2009 Four Nations, "Playing against Australia, New Zealand and England is a great way to get experience and the team has definitely made progress since the World Cup. It was only in the last 15 or 20 minutes of games that they fell away and that is a big step forward". His only concern was the shortened inter-season for the internationals adding to that of 2008 in Australia. Two warm up games in January were programmed with Castleford travelling to Perpignan (lost 12-14) and the Dragons popping up the road to play Championship outfit Toulouse Olympique (won 46-22).

Unfortunately the catastrophic start of the previous year was about to play out yet again. The Wakefield loss on the opening weekend of February was just the start (20-28). In rainy cold conditions the Dragons were level at the break and a Sébastien Martins try soon after saw them ahead but then three unanswered tries secured the points for the hosts. With the goings-on off the field still in their nostrils they were a bit tender going to London the following week. Fortunately they had Greenshields and Carlaw fit for that trip to the capital but to no avail. As standard, Harlequins true to form raised their game against the French. It was a tight one again but with Ferriol getting his marching orders late on, the hosts prevailed (4-16).

The opener at Brutus was to be St Helens the losing finalists of Super League 2009, a real challenge and a level up on the two precedent fixtures. Catalans started like a house on fire with a brace of unconverted tries inside 10 minutes raising the home support. But that early promise crumbled dramatically with Elima's sudden dismissal by Steve Ganson for a high challenge on the Saints influential running half-back Lomax with still nearly an hour to play. The air of hope and expectation from the Dragon's balloon there and then just went pop. They never recovered conceding eight unanswered tries in the heavy and troubling loss (12-42). They were certainly attracting the ire of the English game officials with 2 red cards and one yellow – Dallas Johnson at Belle Vue – with the season only three matches old.

The sombre mood in the camp was going to take some lifting with the discipline on and off the field raising its head. Of course Wigan at the DW Stadium and top of the table would be a formidable challenge under any circumstances but on the last Friday of the month it would turn the mood even blacker for the French. They had shipped half a dozen tries by the break with a quartet from wing Richards alone; Mogg as captain in place of the suspended Elima seeing his ship well torpedoed and listing badly. The damage was severe at the conclusion (0-58) the heaviest loss in the club's short history.

Adam – left by the side door without a fond Adieu unfortunately during the calamitous 2010 campaign. But Mogg was great for the Dragons. Arrived in their second year from Canberra Raiders. A real leader on the pitch scoring 26 tries as well as a Dream Team nomination in 2007. A big ticker too – in the 800 metre training runs he was always the one to catch. A real thorough-bred.

Adam Mogg would be the main victim of this humiliation as it transpired to be the iconic Queenslanders final game in a sang-et-or jumper. He didn't deserve this send off at all. He also appeared to leave by the side door without any real formalities and a fond 'au revoir' to the fans for his services rendered. A mysterious deep rooted injury issue was mooted as reason of his sudden departure. He had been after all, one of the pillars of the club in its infancy setting a real example as a prodigious trainer to the aspiring French contingent; he had played State of Origin as a winger before departing for Roussillon but was a more than solid midfield general at Brutus in his 83 appearances. He left them after just four games and rock bottom and far from that Wembley appearance in his debut year and a 3rd place in the league the campaign after.

Salford at least on the opening weekend of March would prove a respite. A post Mogg Dragons had to reshuffle with Sa moving inside. The City Reds as then had found promotion the year before a challenge and their second term was no different. They went into this fixture at the Willows pointless like their opponents. The visitors had just that bit more direction up front from a returning Elima in the forwards but they had to battle back from a half-time deficit to claim their first points (24-12) of their fifth campaign to get them off the floor and up into 12th spot with late tries from Raguin and Sa the key.

The week following, Castleford made their second crossing of the year to Perpignan and as in the friendly earlier would prove too much for the French side yet again (16-20). On a freezing night and a howling gale blowing off Canigou the Dragons not for the last time couldn't handle a lively Chase in mid field even if the locals had had the best of the early exchanges. After suffering on the road at the start of 2010 with four displacements to one at home they just couldn't make home advantage tell and let the Tigers take control in the later stages. From bad to worse though for Catalans as their best here Greenshields was carried off the field in the closing stages with a serious leg injury. The talismanic Australian, who thus far had only missed a handful of games since he landed beside the Mediterranean more than three years earlier, would not be seen again till late June. A big hole had to be to filled and even more so after Mogg's shock disappearance too. With these two totem poles absent the question was whether there was enough quality, direction and leadership in the group to compensate for their loss.

Debutant David Guasch the nephew of the club's President drew the short straw as the replacement for the irreplaceable Greenshields in the last line of defence a week later in Wales at Celtic Crusaders. Since the year before when they played in the south of the Principality at Bridgend, they had upped sticks and headed north to Wrexham. Under Brian Noble and giving a first run out too to the rugby union legend Gareth Thomas, the new Crusaders had thus far proved sterner stuff than their promotion year. On a wet night at the Racecourse Ground even with a Frenchman in charge in Thierry Alibert the Dragons couldn't find a way to win. It was tight as a drum with just three tries registered.

Ferriol clattered Thomas in the opening minutes to welcome him to the fold but the visitors, lacking inspiration, fell to their 6th defeat (8-14) in seven. On the last weekend of March the improving Hull KR under Justin Morgan came calling. The Robins had entered the competition a year after the Catalans and in

2009 finished an impressive 4th on the ladder. This game saw the first appearance of the campaign for skipper Thomas Bosc after his persistent ankle problems and he celebrated it in style with a first home victory (16-10) in a tough game which the hosts held most of the aces with the Robins points assembled only in the dying embers. With Easter round the corner it was a convenient time to claim the valuable two points and more so at Brutus where the fans hadn't seen their favourites victorious in nearly eight months.

The big off field news in 2010 at the club was centred on the construction of the new stand behind the posts at the western end of Stade Gilbert Brutus. The first diggers and workmen arrived in March and the Easter matches against Yorkshire giants Leeds and Bradford had to be swopped over to Aimé-Giral down the road. The municipally owned ground in the Moyen-Vernet quarter had had a major face lift before the Dragons had moved in three years earlier with the conversion of the main Bonzoms stand to a cantilever, reseating both the stand opposite and that behind the posts. The semi circular nature of the latter structure was a carry over of the old athletics track and had the extra disadvantage of not being covered.

The economic success the Catalans had achieved for the town and its immediate surrounding area in bringing Super League and its travelling away support had been a bit of a revelation and why the different public authorities had dipped into their pockets to develop and extend the Dragons facilities. The costs of the new stand which would seat 2,500 would be over £5M. As well as the covered seating the structure would provide administrative office space, a new boutique, several bars and a top deck sponsor's lounge with panoramic view. Into their fifth year the club had ticked all the boxes thus far and this was the recognition and recompense.

On the field the busy holiday programme promised further challenges. It's always considered a time for evaluation as the competition completes a third of its journey. Teams still in the hunt by then had to be moving in the right direction. The normal Good Friday away trip to the Stoop this time round was replaced by high flying Huddersfield at the then Galpharm Stadium. With the Rhinos and the Bulls at home the following week Walters compromised his chances in the West Riding going with a young guard and only four overseas players. With back-rower Touxagas and Avignon teenager Tony Gigot selected in the centres you kind of knew what the mind set was. It proved cover your eyes time as the avalanche duly arrived with 26 unanswered points by the break. With Brough pulling the strings the damage was severe again and the misery complete at the end (6-48). Pelo got their solitary try in the same week he and Sa had been summoned by the local police force for their part in the incident in Leeds back in February.

Back on old ground three days later at USAP's home territory for Leeds even if the Rhinos form thus far had been far from convincing. The dependable Carlaw had to be pulled out of the pack to link up with another back-rower Touxagas in the centre positions as the Dragons fumbled around trying to get those fingers inserted in the dyke wall. At least it would be a bonus getting Ferriol back to shore up things in the engine room. Nice pre-match touch too with two eminent characters of the game Leeds President Harry Jepson and former XIII Catalans king pin Robert Llobet both well into their 90's and still going strong giving the proverbial celebrity kick off. Although Guisset gave the home side an early lead with a converted try it was the visitors who asserted themselves with a quick fire response of four tries all in the opening quarter and 26 points by the turn round. The Dragons at last found some desire and application in the second act to at least still hold their heads up and some credibility in the (24-34) loss with McGuire's second effort for the Rhinos in the last 5 minutes steadying the visitor's edginess.

Bradford had been going well and buoyed by their draw at Headingley the week before found themselves in the top half of the table after missing out to the French side the year before and qualification for the play-offs for the first time in the Super League era. The Bulls had always found rich pickings this side of the Channel and rested undefeated in the league match-ups. Catalans had men back for this Round 11 clash with Chris Walker and Baile boosting the distressed back division. Not that it made much difference as the Bulls replicated what Leeds had done days earlier making the difference in the opening salvos. The hosts didn't appear capable of connecting up with their second half effort against the Rhinos and fell behind as Sheriffe's try on the half-time siren took the visitors more than two scores in front. Little inspiration and tackles missed with the Bulls racing away at the death (14-36) with Sheriffe completing his hat-trick. Abiding memory was Menzies picking Baile's pocket with an audacious intercept and going 50 metres for the visitors fourth incursion. The Dragons management made note of that in their diaries.

Only now the Londoners keeping Catalans off bottom spot as the qualification possibilities already drifted increasingly northwards. Although Walter's debut year had gone horribly wrong too they had won all three of the corresponding Easter games to keep them in the hunt. The only positives here were that the re-located games at Aimé-Giral against the two Yorkshire heavy weights had garnered over 17,000 spectators and that the upcoming Challenge Cup could take their minds off the perilous league position.

2010 would be a year of many surprises but the news of an erupting volcano in the far north Atlantic wouldn't have been one of them. The Icelandic mountain of Eyjafjallajokull exploded high into the sky that April and the volcanic ash drifted far to the south and east right into the flight paths of planes leaving UK airspace. A calamitous situation unfolded with a lock down and for Salford in particular as they were expected in Perpignan for a 4th Round Challenge Cup tie on the third weekend of April. With flights grounded Shaun McRae had to get his side mobilised for a trip which, instead of taking a few hours, would now be several days on the move overland and navigating a Channel crossing too.

The inconvenience wasn't just for the Salford team as Leigh travelling to play at Limoux where also involved and Toulouse Olympique travelling the other way to St.Helens. For the Dragons though they were more preoccupied with their own form and seeing the Cup as their only realistic chance of saving their season. As the City Reds had provided the French side with one of their only two successes thus far in 2010 they would be fancied at least to make the draw for the next round. It was a tentative opening at Brutus between two sides down on confidence. With Walker injury prone, Pelo was back in at full-back and the hosts down further with Sa and Johnson missing too. On a bright warm afternoon the Dragons hit the lead early on only to show their fragility taking a brace of tries from the Salford flyer Broughton as the opening half concluded leaving the home side just a couple of points to the good. The heat and fatigue caught up with the Lancastrians though and as the second period unfolded so did the visitors resolve. With twenty unanswered points it would be a comfortable home success (30-8) and a safe passage into the next round of the Cup were they would face the Celtic Crusaders in Wrexham in three weeks time.

Sometimes the Cup can be an elixir and lift for teams but that didn't translate for the French as they continued to flounder in Super League. A week after their third win of 2010 they collapsed at Warrington (6-40) and not only that found themselves rock bottom of the comp after Harlequins shock win up at Wigan. The tender, young Gigot filling in at hooker suffered the charges of Morley while skipper Bosc still not 100% carrying his ankle niggles. Only McGuire held the line of resistance as the old Wire took complete charge early on with 6 tries by the break. It wasn't pretty and the local daily *L'Indépendant* didn't spare them with a front page story screaming, *"Derniers! (Last!)"* and what added salt to the wound was the news that arch rivals down the road USAP had just finished top of the Top 14 at the conclusion of their regular season. On Scottish soil again a week later to Murrayfield and Magic Weekend as May came into view; a new opponent too in Castleford following on from Leeds the year before. In front of a crowd 25,401 on the second day the Dragons showed some improvement but not enough against a bottom half placed side who's kicking game taunted the French side all afternoon; four tries resulted plus an interception and they where done for (18-34).

From one Celtic country to another for the Catalans a week later and Wrexham again to be precise for a Challenge Cup 5th Round tie against the improving Crusaders. A bright early summer's afternoon in rural North Wales suited the visitors more than the murky March night earlier and at last they made a bit of hay. In a real nail-biter, the French side nearly let it slip after roaring out of the blocks with 30 points on the board by the break. Sa with his best effort of the campaign to date grabbed a hat-trick of tries.But a near collapse around the hour mark nearly cooked it for the visitors conceding three tries in a dramatic 5 minute spell which brought the two protagonists level. There was still a good quarter of an hour to go to find a winner but nothing accrued until captain marvel Bosc, on cue, secured it (35-34) with the last kick of the game with a one pointer and a quarter final place in his pocket. Phew!

The Cup was proving a godsend and the last eight draw had smiled on the Roussillon club with an away tie at Championship club Batley to be played at the end of the month. The question being asked now, was with two home league games lined up before the trip to the West Riding, could the cup run eventually stimulate a revival and see an upturn in their Super League fortunes. Hull FC first-up would be as tough as ever in Perpignan with a near unblemished record there. The Airlie Birds going well in a top-end position proved again too strong dominating early on with a couple of converted scores. The visitors pack, a right handful, out-muscled the locals with the Dragons getting only late consolation scores to massage the difference (14-28). Salford after turning over St Helens at home would come buoyed up the following week and with Harlequins also picking up points, a chasm was lurking in view down at the bottom. To save face and give them any chance of escaping the last spot on the ladder the City Reds had to be taken. After exhausting all the options at half-back the club decided to bring in a new face in the Australian Brent Sherwin released by Castleford. Unfortunately another tepid performance as the side couldn't lift itself after conceding two tries early yet again this time inside 6 minutes. Salford scrapped for everything determined not to make it three losses to the French in 2010. As at Hull the week before the hosts response was too late and too little even if Bosc claimed all his sides points on his 100th game in the sang-et-or. The mass was already said for his team (14-22) if not for the captain.

Only the Cup could from now on bring some relief to the distressed Dragons. The question was being asked if a Karl Harrison motivated Batley from the Championship could be the one to bring further humiliation to the French on the famous Mount Pleasant slope. Although there was some rain about on the last weekend of May in Yorkshire this was not a ploughed mud heap in January when the part-timers could have had a say. It turned into a near massacre with the Gallant Youths of old leaking 13 tries as the visitors clacked up their biggest ever winning margin to date (74-12) with even strong-man Ferriol, who in five years in Perpignan only managed a career total of 8 tries, claiming a brace. The Catalans took out all their frustrations on the minnows. But any hope that the latest success with a Cup Semi-Final place against Warrington already safely in the pocket, would signify that a Super League revival of sorts was around the corner, like the others would prove groundless.

Back-to-back weeks in Yorkshire first on Humberside and Hull KR and then at Wheldon Road against the Tigers saw further losses but they were on a real hiding to nothing here as sandwiched in between would be the international against England with nine Dragons players involved. The Robins gained revenge for the loss at Brutus with a comfortable win (6-24) grabbing early scores with the visitors not able to take the chances created. The preparation for the re-arranged clash with Castleford the following Tuesday compromised their chances as those on international duty stayed over after the game at New Craven Park. Their 15th defeat was anticipated (20-24) but they gave it a-go failing not by much with a returning McGuire to the fore. The Tigers who where a bottom-end side in 2010 claimed their fourth victory of the year against the French including the pre-season run out revealing just how far they were off the pace from the season before when one game from Old Trafford.

With two thirds of the Super League virtually completed and the Dragons six points adrift at the bottom Kevin Walters tenancy in Roussillon was more or less done for. One of the early runners to take over was John Kear at Wakefield who would be the Catalans next opponents in Perpignan. The experienced Yorkshire man had coached the French national team and appeared to be interested in the proposition. He was though still under contract at Belle Vue and the Dragons not keen to pay compensation, didn't pursue it.

A year later with Trinity in near financial melt down one thought that Kear may have had regrets he hadn't pushed harder. The Yorkshire side had won the year before in Perpignan on the last home game of the season nearly scuppering the French side's qualification hopes but this time there was a glimpse of light in a success (30-23) coming back strongly after being led at the interval. Greenshields back on the bridge after three months out injured was a moral-booster, scored a crucial try that got them back into it. The crowd of 5,055 here was the lowest turn out for a home game in Perpignan since St Helens visit to Canet Village in their debut season.

It was probably a bonus that the gap between the Quarter and Semi Final of the Challenge Cup in 2010 was one of the longest – 10 weeks – meaning that there was something for the Catalans fans to hold on to as especially high summer looked particularly foreboding for the Dragons with all the top four sides to be met in the coming weeks. Hull FC had invariably been difficult to manoeuvre at the KC Stadium so the French sides effort on the last weekend of June was one of their better losing efforts (8-10) showing real determination especially in defence. Just three tries in total and all in the opening quarter saw the offence take a back seat.

Some of that starch in defence though would certainly be needed when competition leaders Wigan arrived on a hot July afternoon a week later. Rather than the Englishmen bending in the Mediterranean sun though it was the locals who felt the heat. It was tit-for-tat early doors but the Dragons inability to hold on to the ball played into the visitors hands enabling them to get a grip on the proceedings first half with a couple of converted scores and a penalty without any response from the hosts. The Lancastrians had it done and dusted with an electric three try burst in just 8 minutes soon after the restart and a 26-0 score line said it all. Even with Coley dismissed just after the hour mark Catalans found it difficult to respond with any conviction even if a brace from Greenshields indicated just how much he had been missed. Skipper Bosc was disappointed, "This which annoys you the most is the taking of 30 points here at home (16-32). With the Cup Semi Final around the corner we've got to try and get that sorted."

If it doesn't rain it pours and high flying Saints at their bastion Knowsley Road a week after was the worst case scenario possible. But against all expectations the Dragons pulled off what would turn out to be the best success on the road of 2010 and repeating the triumph of the year before. Even if Wellens had the hosts first on the score board it was the Dragons who dominated the opening half with a quartet of converted tries and an unlikely score line of 24-10 in their favour. Carlaw the former Kangaroos forward yet again showing his versatility and presence in the backline was much in view with half-back Sherwin in charge mid-field. The sang-et-or had to summon up all their defensive capabilities late on to withstand the glowering Graham stamping about. But they held out (30-20) for a famous victory on what would be their last ever visit to the old, exhausted place.

The only downer on the Lancashire trip and result was that Harlequins would continue to confound them by turning over Bradford on the same weekend and kept the Dragons still four points adrift of both of them and Salford. With the Londoners still to come to Perpignan, followed by the Crusaders, getting off the bottom was still doable. There was however, throughout Walters second term, a deep malaise below the surface, intractable, that was in process now of playing itself out. After the real tonic of Knowsley Road you'd have thought the Welsh side there for the taking at Brutus but not so, as they fell in the facility of it all just a week later (22-26). Greenshields celebrating his 100th appearance in the sang-et-or and the first overseas player to do so didn't finish the game and it would be touch and go if he would be available for the all important Cup Semi Final in three weeks time at Widnes. Sebastien Munoz the Director Sportive of Catalans announced it as, *"À l'image de la saison"* and the daily paper the morning after headlined it, *"La confiance, ça va, ça vient"*.

While Wigan had always been the Catalans first choice, bridesmaid Warrington were not far behind. The cherry and whites were always the ones to choose for the grand opening night back in 2006 and subsequently invited to the regions capital, Montpellier not once, but twice. However when it came to the Catalans capital of Barcelona in 2009 it was the Wire who got the nod. From the start Warrington fans travelled across the Channel in such numbers that few clubs bettered. The first few years maybe as many as 2,000 journeyed over, occupying hotels and filling local restaurants and bars. The early years saw Perpignan in Super League as the most exotic thing to happen to the game and competition since Paris St-Germain in the opening years but this time with the sunshine, beaches and vineyards. It was like a huge lung full of fresh air for the North of England code.

By the time the Dragons had got the go ahead to join the competition back in 2006 the Australian David Foti then living in Carcassonne had quickly seen the potential and opportunity opening up for a go-between the new club and locality and visiting supporters. The sociable Aussie a 'treiziste' through and through set up his Catalans Sports Tours operation facilitating this development. From the very start Dave was liaising with supporters groups across the Channel organising their stays including often at his own expense picking up small groups of people from airports as far away as Gerona and Nimes. The other thing he loved being involved in too was co-ordinating with junior league clubs such as Newton-le-Willows and Saddleworth from Oldham who would bring their youngsters to play against local French teams and then concluding on the Saturday perched on the terraces at Brutus watching a Super League game in the evening sunshine to cap it all off.

Simultaneously as these developments and initiatives were unfolding the French Super League club where busily setting up an expansive supporters operation of their own. *'Les penyas'* as the supporters groups were called where officially recognised by the club with their own membership structures and Presidents. It was very hands-on approach too by Guasch and his team with regular meetings throughout the year focusing on real issues. The club management worked hand in glove with them. There are touching eighteen *'penyas'* varying in size from around 50 members to as many as a couple of hundred and located through out the Roussillon region as far south as Céret and Albères on the Spanish border and there are even two up in the Aude area near Carcassonne and Lézignan an hours drive from Perpignan. The former is based in a village near to Carcassonne just a few kilometres on the train up the Aude Valley at Verzeille. Several Dragons players attend their AGM and share an aperitif with the members. For each home game *Les Dragons du Lauquet* organise a coach taking sixty or so of its members to Perpignan.

By 2010 though, the financial crisis everywhere was affecting the numbers of British fans making the annual trip over as the pound devalued appreciably

100,000[th] British Supporters Tribute Day with the arrival of Warrington on a steaming hot July. Held in the town centre at the side of the Castillet. Guasch in his element even if the team weren't – pressing hands of the regions movers and shakers-he had already the €7M envelope in his pocket for the new stand so enjoyed this day.

against the euro. There was no doubt that in the early years of the Dragons the away support, in both numbers and character, was crucial to the clubs initial development in building up the crowds. Fortunately the club realised long term it would have to develop there own support and that is where the penya phenomena fitted in. Guasch wanted to reward Warrington and its fans for making the staging of the Barcelona game so successful and why they chose the Wolves to celebrate the mythical '100,000th British Supporter on Tour' idea.

The case for the Dragons and their home base at Stade Gilbert Brutus to develop was fortunately built on their early successes at Wembley in year two and a 3rd Super League placing the following year. 2009 with the hiring of those 100 packed local charabancs heading south across the border into Spain and Barcelona with the Mayor of Perpignan and other local heavyweights in tow the case for further capital investment was being made. The unfolding events in the 2010 campaign were mere hiccups along the journey to something substantial and long lasting. With the Dragons bottom of the league that summer the decisions had been already made and the €7M budget approved with the bulldozers and cranes already on site. It was something for the supporters to hold onto that year as the team failed big-time to deliver.

It's completion would hold the key to the clubs future as a major component of the competition and would enable them to join the 'big boys' at the head of the table if not yet in silverware but in their ability to expand commercially through revving up its income streams to fund player recruitment and junior development.

STAR GAME 2010 SUPER LEAGUE XV ROUND 23 WARRINGTON WOLVES at Stade Aimé-Giral Saturday 24th July

The Dragons had partly planned their season around this fixture. Unlike the season before when Warrington travelled to Barcelona this particular game was organised around the theme of '100,000th British supporter' who had crossed the Channel since the advent of the Catalans entry into Super League since 2006. The club awarded the honour to the Wolves as one of the best supported English sides. A sumptuous banquet including a huge paella was prepared in the open air in the centre of Perpignan for more than a thousand supporters of both clubs plus management, local dignitaries and press. It had been difficult for the Dragons to the raise the bar in their present circumstances but Guasch and his team rose to the challenge impressively and not for the first or last time.

Maybe because of the clubs back-room staff's efforts in arranging the pre-match function there was spill over in how the team prepared and presented themselves that particular afternoon. A year before a stronger Catalans outfit fluffed its lines at the Olympique Stadium, so would it be possible for the bedraggled 2010 version to do any better?

The Wire arrived bouncing after dispatching the leaders Wigan away a week before while the hosts lost at home to the 11th placed Welsh outfit the Crusaders. But on this high summers day the Dragons would be reborn and play the game of their lives. Inspired by the Sherwin and McGuire leadership and a Carlaw in his pomp behind, they took the game to the visitors in an absolute cracker. Nip and tuck from the off and stayed that way to the very end. Catalans in the ascendancy early on but the visitors roared back to level it at the break. The Dragons laid the victory within minutes of the re-start as first full-back Stacul crossed and then a couple of minutes later a charge of outrageous proportions from a Casty breathing fire gave them the cushion which would see them take the spoils but only just.

Vinnie Anderson scored from a sublime Solomona intervention for the visitors before Sherwin swept over a crucial drop goal still with a quarter of an hour to go to give the locals a seven point advantage. Heroic defence was the order of the day as Tony Smith's lads threw everything at the French rearguard and only once found wanting as Briers crossed for a converted try with 3 minutes left. However it was the Dragons leading by just the single point who had the momentum with a Fakir try ruled out by the video official on the very last play. What an aperitif before the Cup Semi Final show down!

Catalans 29-28 Warrington. HT: 16-16. Weather: Hot and sunny.

Attendance: 7,852. Referee: Ian Smith. For Catalans 5 tries from Vaccari (7) Carlaw (30), Bell (35), Stacul (42), Casty (46) & 4 goals from Bosc and 1 drop goal from Sherwin

For Warrington 5 tries from Hicks (12,38), Clarke (40), V Anderson (56), Briers (77) & 4 goals from Westwood

Catalans: Stacul, Bell, Raguin, Carlaw, Vaccari, Bosc©, Sherwin, Casty, McGuire Fakir, Mounis, Elima, Johnson Substitutes: Guisset, Sa,Touxagas, Simon

Warrington : Mathers, Hicks, Grix, Atkins, Riley, Briers©, Myler, Morley Monaghan, Harrison, V Anderson , Westwood, Solomona Substitutes: Carvell Clarke, Cooper, McCarthy.

The win against Warrington in the dress rehearsal for the Cup game two weeks later was a much needed tonic. Bradford the week after with a certain Menzies in the pivot role were taken (24-22) for the French sides sixth victory of the campaign and the first time in 2010 that they'd had

Around a thousand supporters of both clubs regaled themselves in the summery weather before the Wire match feasting on the Giant paella provided with lots of good Roussillon wine to aid the digestion. Great time was had by all!

two successes consecutively and for that opening weekend of August off the bottom at last passing Harlequins on points difference. The points won built on a dominant opening period and a ten point cushion at the break. It was a tense last quarter before Bosc's late penalty goal clinched it and a super way for prop Casty to celebrate his 100th appearance in the sang-et-or favours – the 5th to do so in Catalans fifth year. Having Walker back too boosted the backline and a bonus following the former Brisbane man's long three month injury lay off.

The Cup Semi-Final was to be staged at Widnes's Halton Stadium a mere 7 miles from their opponent's stamping ground at the Halliwell Jones Stadium. Could the powers that be not have found something more palatable than this especially after 2006 when the Dragons had fronted up against Wigan at the same stage of the competition at the same said HJ Stadium. A decent turn out of Catalan colours massed together on the Sinclair Avenue side of the ground to give their favourites a shout or two. This though would be by some distance far from the team's winning performance against the cherry & whites. Sherwin was no Stacey Jones and when Harrison plundered over inside 10 minutes the Wire procession was about to roll out relentlessly.

The Cup holders, quickly into their ascendancy, were just too big, too fast and too good; and had the thirst already for another Wembley visit already on their lips. Primrose & blues colours everywhere were flying amongst the 12,265 crowd with a dominant Louis Anderson to the fore with an impressive hat-trick of tries. Twenty four points in the opening half and another 30 after it told the tale of total dominance by Tony Smith's crew. A try in each half from Greenshields was the sum total plus the conversions from Bosc. For the Australian full-back though some consolation in that his opening effort took him past Justin Murphy's club record haul of 53 tries racked up in seasons 2006-8.

Catalans tenuous lead over Harlequins on the league ladder proved exactly that a week later for the wooden spoon honour. Their heads still in their hands after their no show on the biggest day of the season the week before at Widnes with a Wembley trip unbelievably at stake. Against the Londoners they just didn't seem to have the desire or ability to lift themselves from their stupor. The visitors took their chances and then closed ranks to defend what they'd got. A fat zero at the break sang-et-or and London ten to the good. Even after getting themselves back into it with two early quick fire tries after the break they still didn't possess the self belief to make it tell as Brian McDermott's charges bounced back to grab the victory in the closing stages (12-16). QED.

Going to Headingley the week after must have felt an afterthought. The last place in the world to be where they'd never won before even with much better formations than the Dragons where presenting in 2010. If in Super League your bellwether is often found some place near to Wigan and Leeds what one does the other follows. Even with early optimism Catalans took a 58-0 walloping at the then JJB Stadium back in Round 4; here at the entrails not just of a season but of a changing of the guard and turning of a page. Four unanswered tries before quarter time and they were already done for. They suffered here like never before (6-52) because nearly 12 months earlier with Bird flying they'd nearly created Super League history.

They were now just going through the motions; even the possibility of getting off the bottom didn't appear to interest them as by now the points difference had moved in the Londoners favour. Huddersfield would bring the curtain down at what had been their poorest campaign by far in this their 5th year. As two weeks before they couldn't register any points in the opening half as the aspiring Giants claimed the competition points to press their qualification credentials with some ease (12-26) leaving the hosts to leave by the side door. It was the end of their poorest campaign to date and unexpected. Their total nine wins, worse than their debut year in 2006.

There were a lot of goodbyes with some more felt than others. McGuire in particular deserved a better send off at the end of his fourth year in Roussillon with his 99 appearances in the sang-et-or. Ten players would depart including the forlorn Queenslander Johnson who had arrived as the marquee signing of 2010 but never made the impact expected. Maybe for him it was a case of being in the wrong place at the wrong time. The left flank trio of Frenchmen Elima, Baile and Pelo, so much in view the year before, didn't turn up. Elima struggled to raise a gallop that year, Baile injured for the most of the year with half a dozen or so appearances only while Pelo completely lost focus maybe affected by the palaver in Leeds on the opening weekend. It was particularly tough on youngsters such as Gigot and William Barthau making their debuts in a group short of direction and confidence.

In hindsight though the unpicking of the original senior players group starting with Chan leaving in 2008 and followed by Croker the year after, was where it all started to unravel. It was covered up somewhat with the flying visits of Bird and Ryles in 2009 but the team Potter managed was breaking up. Mogg disappearing suddenly after just a handful of games early opened the floodgates and Greenshield's three months out injured completed the shipwreck. It was tough on the amiable Walters on the bridge. A really likeable bloke who would return to Australia and coach at Melbourne Storm would still have the satisfaction regardless of taking Catalans to 80 minutes from both Old Trafford and Wembley during his tenure.

( ) Denotes Challenge Cup game

2010 FIXTURES	RND	DATE	VENUE	RESULT	ATT
WAKEFIELD	1	07/02	BELLE VUE	L 20-28	
HARLEQUINS	2	14/02	THE STOOP	L 4-16	
ST.HELENS	3	20/02	GILBERT BRUTUS	L 12-42	7,825
WIGAN	4	26/03	DW STADIUM	L 0-58	
SALFORD	5	05/03	WILLOWS	W 24-12	
CASTLEFORD	6	13/03	GILBERT BRUTUS	L 16-20	6,810
CRUSADERS	7	19/03	RACE COURSE GD	L 6-14	
HULL KR	8	27/03	GILBERT BRUTUS	W 16-10	6,620
HUDDERSFIELD	9	02/04	GALPHARM	L 6-48	
LEEDS	10	05/04	AIME-GIRAL	L 24-34	8,230
BRADFORD	11	10/04	AIME-GIRAL	L 14-34	8,884
SALFORD	CCR4	18/04	GILBERT BRUTUS	W 30-8	(5,235)
WARRINGTON	12	25/04	HJ STADIUM	L 6-40	
CASTLEFORD	13	02/05	EDINBURGH	L 18-34	
CRUSADERS	CCR5	09/05	RACE COURSE GD	W 35-34	
HULL FC	14	15/05	GILBERT BRUTUS	L 14-28	6,512
SALFORD	15	22/05	GILBERT BRUTUS	L 14-22	5,115
BATLEY	CCQF	29/05	MOUNT PLEASANT	W 74-12	
HULL KR	16	06/06	CRAVEN PARK	L 6-24	
CASTLEFORD	17	15/06	WHELDON RD	L 20-24	
WAKEFIELD	18	19/06	GILBERT BRUTUS	W 30-23	5,055
HULL FC	19	25/06	KC STADIUM	L 8-10	
WIGAN	20	04/07	GILBERT BRUTUS	L 16-34	7,612
ST.HELENS	21	09/07	KNOWSLEY RD	W 30-20	
CRUSADERS	22	17/07	GILBERT BRUTUS	L 22-26	6,208
WARRINGTON	23	24/07	AIME-GIRAL	W 29-28	7,852
BRADFORD	24	01/08	ODSAL	W 24-22	
WARRINGTON	CCSF	08/08	WIDNES	L 12-54	
HARLEQUINS	25	14/08	GILBERT BRUTUS	L 12-16	6,152
LEEDS	26	20/08	HEADINGLEY	L 6-52	
HUDDERSFIELD	27	04/09	GILBERT BRUTUS	L 12-26	5,708
				Total	93,818

Regular season median: 6,620

SUPER LEAGUE: P27 W6 L21 PTS12 PF409 PA747 POS. 14TH
CHALLENGE CUP: P4 W3 L1

2010	GAMES	TRIES	GOALS	POINTS
GREENSHIELDS	13	11		44
BELL	26	8		32
RAGUIN	27	8		32
SA	25	9		36
PELO	20	3		12
MOGG	4			
BOSC	22	3	61(1dg)	135
FERRIOL	23	1		4
MCGUIRE	25	6		24
GUISSET	26	3		12
ELIMA	26	7		28
MOUNIS	27	2	7	22
JOHNSON	28	1		4
GUASCH D	1			
BAILE	7	1		4
BARTHAU	7		3	6
GOSSARD	21	1		4
CARLAW	30	7		28
TOUXAGAS	5	1		4
BENTLEY K	16	1		4
MARTINS	8	1		4
FAKIR	22	3		12
WALKER	12	6	2	28
CASTY	26	4		16
GIGOT	17	1	2	8
STACUL	12	2		8
VACCARI	18	9		36
SIMON	10			
BENTLEY A	9	1		4
SHERWIN	14	1		4

(30)

Chapter 7
– ACT 2 –

The departure of Kevin Walters at the end of 2010 culminated in the biggest turn over of staff since their debut. After five campaigns it was time to turn over the page. The new season would resemble a completely fresh start and at last lay the platform for a team and a club respecting its French origins. There had been much speculation about who would land the Head coaching position. Initially John Kear's name was banded about as the front runner. He had been involved before with the French game both at Paris Saint Germain and the national team. But he was still under contract at Wakefield Trinity and they indicated compensation would be required to permit him to leave. At the time the West Yorkshire club's long term future in the competition was under threat. It was understandable that Trinity would want to ease their financial position but did John Kear really push hard for a release knowing the uncertainties in the air at the time?

Trent Robinson a young Australian from Sydney was cutting his coaching teeth in France the year the Catalans joined Super League. Robinson a former Parramatta back-row forward had been forced by injuries to finish his playing career at Toulouse Olympique, then being coached by Justin Morgan, in 2005. After Morgan had left for fresh pastures at Hull KR the Toulouse club gave the rookie coach Robinson the reins for the new season. In 2006 he took TO to the Championship Final where they lost to the Catalans of Pia 21-18. He seemed to leave the French game after a four-year stay by the side-door. However back home in Australia after the disappointment of the Final loss in Toulouse only re-motivated the former St Gregory's student to seek a coaching career full-time. His initial appointment over there was up the coast at the Newcastle Knights as one of the assistants to the legendary Brian Smith.

After several years there gaining experience the young Robinson impressed Smith sufficiently enough to take his assistant with him to the Sydney Roosters where in 2010 they shared a NRL Grand Final loss to St George Illawarra. Robinson may have been a back field applicant to take over the Dragons job but his French credentials would in time prove his making. At the time a string of untried Australian assistants were heading to Europe and Trent Robinson would be just one of them. The year before Robinson arrived in Perpignan, Michael McGuire at Wigan, had won a Grand Final at the first attempt so he was already in good company. What though Robinson had was not simply an experience of France but a genuine desire to be part of a real renaissance built around a Catalans Super League club at the heart of the French game. His French girl-friend from his Toulouse days had travelled with him back to Sydney and they had already a young family in tow by the time they set up home in Thuir on the outskirts of Perpignan, in the autumn of 2010. On the first day of training for the new squad Robinson for the first time since the clubs inception designated French as the first language, with the overseas players expected to assimilate. For the first time too both assistant coaches were French with the retired Jérôme Guisset taking his place alongside Laurent Frayssinous.

The ability of the club as it grew to attract quality overseas players from day one was beneficial for them. The day Stacey Jones walked through the doors the template was laid. Jason Crocker and Adam Mogg followed the latter, fresh from a State of Origin debut, a year later. In their roller-coaster year of 2009 the Kangaroos Greg Bird and Jason Ryles both continued this trend. As well as the experience brought to the team the effect it had on the French players especially the younger blokes was uplifting. Just sharing the same training pitch and rubbing shoulders with this calibre of player was inspirational. They set levels of professionalism and expertise not seen in these parts since Puig Aubert's days. For his debut season, Robinson well and truly pulled the bunny from the magician's hat, in landing the veteran Steve Menzies from Manly via Bradford. It was synonymous of Robinson's intelligent approach that he could entice a player of Menzie's calibre to the Catalan cause.

The other new faces for his baptism season included a couple of experienced robust forwards in Lopini Paea fresh from a Sydney Roosters Grand Final appearance and hooker Ian Henderson returning to the competition again after being a Super League winner with Bradford back in 2005. Two young untried Australians scrum half Scott Dureau from Newcastle Knights and utility back Ben Farrar from Manly arrived as the club continued her quest to resolve the eternal troublesome pivot spot once again. Wakefield's Fijian centre Daryl Millard was a late arrival following the Yorkshire clubs administrative problems while wing Damien Blanch another Trinity player joined a growing band of players already with Super League experience. Seven of their 2010 overseas players would depart with only Greenshields and Sa retained.

2011 was an important year for the club with the competitions licensing process up for renewal. After their disappointing last place finish the year before it was vital that a dignified response ensued. The club needed to build consistency in its performances both on and off the field. The big news of the year would be the completion of the new stand behind the goal posts which would seat under cover nearly 3000 spectators as well as accommodating club offices, club shop, restaurant and bars plus sponsorship facilities. It was a huge statement by the club and a real vote of confidence by particularly the vital public bodies who invest hugely in sports facilities. Bernard Guasch was an astute tactician in playing the political game knowing which levers to press. The season before he had made a big thing of the Warrington game which commemorated the *100,000th* visit by British supporters since Super League arrived in the town and celebrated with that giant paella out in the open air next to the Castillet and enjoyed by nearly a thousand supporters and local dignitaries.

The club's President knew how important the new structure would be in the next phase of the Dragons story. Phase one, the original refurbishment of Stade Gilbert Brutus in 2007, was just the opener but this new €7 million development reflected the clubs growing status and aspirations. Guasch had to withstand some fierce opposition from the USAP union club who had opposed the development favouring instead the enlargement of their own Aime-Giral.

The whole saga generated much public debate and it was interesting how much support the Dragons received from the wider sporting community within the city. Knowing what the status-quo was in their debut season Guasch's resolve held firm. It would be a landmark victory.

Trent Robinson's familiarity with the French scene would see him around the barriers often watching the French league games in places such as Carcassonne and Toulouse as well as Perpignan early in 2011. His Sydney baggage additionally included another Australian from the Roosters in Keegan Smith, son of Brian and nephew of Tony the Warrington coach, who would succeed Rodney Howe as the fitness conditioner. The story on the bloc was that the training would put emphasis on speed sessions rather than endurance and his game plan was to produce an open expansive style and talk of a return to the French *flair*. Yes, everything in the shop window looked promising in the early January window but at that moment in time Robinson's credentials were only assumptions and nothing more. Only the demanding months ahead would reveal the real story and whether the rookie had the wherewithal to deliver on these promises.

The troubled Crusaders now under the guidance of Iestyn Harris would be the first challenge of two pre-season warm up games for Robinson's new look squad. At what would be a two-sided stadium for the imminent future, the Catalans looked ring rusty and where undone (22-34) by a Welsh performance well marked by the exploits of lively half-back Sammut who bagged three tries. A week later in Toulouse against the Championship side on a damp and dismal afternoon the Dragons won comfortably (24-0) with Menzies once again absent with Robinson wanting to the keep the maestro for the more serious tasks ahead. Prior to the opening weekend of fixtures in Cardiff for the Millenium Magic weekend with the Dragons going up against the usual foe Harlequins he wanted to take any pressure off the players. He stated that he hadn't set any long term targets for the new season and that after three months together, "We've still a lot to do. The group has blended well on and off the field. My main concerns are the combinations between the players occupying the 9, the 7 and the 6, between the half-back and the second-rowers and half-back and the centres. That will take time."

Greg Mounis accompanied Robinson to the Super League launch at Old Trafford on the eve of the competition, having decided to give the local lad from nearby Baixas, the skipper's arm band giving further evidence of how much the Australian coach wanted to stamp the French flavour on the team and club in this their sixth year but added, "I want first of all to see everybody express themselves. For me each player must know how to be his own captain."

The Londoners in Cardiff weren't very accommodating though a few days later giving Robinson his first taste of defeat (4-11) in a tense battle on a slippery, heavy field causing lots of handling errors from both teams. Menzies made his debut from the bench marked XXL alongside Casty, Fakir and Henderson but to no avail. Baile, who started at hooker announced, *"C'est une nouvelle ère".* Two of the three tries scored came in the opening ten minutes to the Quins from Gale with Greenshields all at sea. The French side, even with lots of possession and territory, couldn't conclude anything, well not until the 78th minute when Farrar got over in the corner with their only expansive play of the game.

Wakefield were next up for Robinson's home debut and he would be well aware how the coach John Kear would be approaching this particular fixture with his club crumbling but defiant. And so it proved as once again Kear used adversity as a motivating tool. It was a poor opener for Trent Robinson's side who were never in it after Marciano scored an interception try and wing Penny had danced around several Catalans players as immobile as the Maginot Line. It didn't get any better as Trinity raced away with it winning convincingly seven tries to two. It couldn't be disguised as anything other than a desperate start against a side and club expecting to finish at the bottom of the pile. After five efforts at Brutus the new coach couldn't change the opening days 'blues', maintaining the tradition thus far of never starting with a win there (14-38). The only bright note for the locals was a debut for a young hooker from St-Paul-de-Fenouillet up in the Agly valley, Eloi Pelissier. Fortunately for him better times lay ahead.

It could only be upwards after that performance and the struggle at Cardiff. Hull KR though would be a mightier challenge on Humberside a week later as unlike the earlier opposition they had qualified for the play-offs the campaign before. As against Trinity in France the weekend before the Dragons started badly conceding two early scores before getting their act together to level it up at the break 12-12. Wing Blanch got them into the lead for the first time just minutes after the turn round and from there inspired by the impressive Dureau and Henderson centre field, recorded only their second ever victory at New Craven Park (31-18). Off the mark at last and no better way to celebrate for *'Fefe'*, alias rugged prop Ferriol bringing up his 100th appearance in the sang-et-or *'maillot'* or jumper.

To confirm against Saints the week after though would be another story. This time though the Catalans showed much more resolve than the last time at Brutus. Greenshields was still out after picking up an injury in Cardiff and centre Daryl Millard made his home debut after his transfer from Wakefield. Still another poor start with the Lancastrians scoring two unanswered tries by quarter time and Graham a killer third just before the oranges. But the locals kept battling away with Dureau and Menzies getting across the white to ensure a tight finish. It was insufficient though with the visitors edging it (16-22). It was a performance that gave Robinson something to build on and successive away trips coming up at Castleford and in Wales would be an indicator.

It was the first sight of Robinson's team on Sky TV at Wheldon Road. The French side had experienced a very frosty reception there earlier but this ground had given them some successes since their debut and they travelled with some hope especially with co-captain Greenshields returning to the fray. For once the Dragons got out of their starting blocks early with Dureau and Blanch registering tries but the Tigers responded to peg them back before Dureau the former Newcastle Knight grabbed a second as the interval hooter sounded. But the French outfit couldn't build on their one score lead as the elusive stand off Chase weaved his magic putting the Tigers into the lead for the first time approaching the hour mark. A long range interception try from wing Youngquest minutes later decided it (24-34) and Stacul's late effort just massaged the deficit.

In West Yorkshire Robinson had decided to use utility man Sa at stand-off to counter Chase and with Greenshields fit again the experiment was continued a week later in Wales against the Crusaders. The half-back positions at the Dragons had for five years never been fully resolved. Jones was at scrum half for the first two years and had his injury problems. By the time Bosc had immerged as a genuine stand-off possibility in 2008 Jones had departed with Mogg, more a natural centre or wing filling the void, not it must be said without some success. Walters had brought in Perry from Brisbane in 2009 but this didn't really gel and the following year Bosc struggled with injuries and fitness. The arrival of a genuine no.7 in Dureau was hopefully going to be the key but as 2011 got into full swing Bosc was still months away from returning after major knee surgery during the close season. Gigot, the former Avignon junior, who had featured regularly in his debut season the year before in difficult circumstances, was being given the opportunity to develop under Robinson's guidance. But he lacked experience and early on in 2011 he was struggling to come up to scratch and soon the new coach started to look at Sa and Farrar as fill-ins.

The Crusaders coach Harris was, like Kear, under pressure already with a similar four competition points reduction following administration but with that earlier lift of that pre-season win in France still in mind may have courted a similar outcome in Wrexham. Sa would have the same role as the week previously to use his physical presence to put another lively half-back off his game, this time the charismatic Sammut, who had toyed with the Catalans in the friendly earlier. But this time with points at stake the French entity had the conviction. A hat-trick of tries from Greenshields and a brace from Farrar did the trick giving the visitors their second away triumph of the year (32-22).

March had indicated some progress and Salford at Brutus should have consolidated that. Except that the Reds flying wing Broughton hadn't read the script. On a crisp evening by the Mediterranean Sea before a watching Federation President Nicolas Larrat the local combination minus their organiser in chief, Dureau, produced a limpid performance satisfying no one. Broughton scored all four of his teams tries – two in each half – to win it (12-22) more or less single-handedly with his pace and opportunism just too much for the out of sorts sang-et-or. Only Remy Casty playing his 100th game came anywhere near what was needed or expected. Robinson was not impressed, "You can't blame Gigot and Sa. It's not their fault we lost. We lacked a bit of intelligence when completing our sets. It is the role of the No.7 to manage these moments but also the 9 and 1. Tonight Salford where stronger in defence than we were in attack", he lamented. A characteristic 7,000 gate being the norm for early season games in these parts departed a wee bit anxious especially with what lay ahead.

STAR GAME 2011 SUPER LEAGUE XVI ROUND 8 WARRINGTON WOLVES at the Halliwell Jones Stadium on Sunday 3rd April

Following a stuttering start and especially those two opening defeats at home to Wakefield and Salford the Catalans decided to set up base for the week in Lancashire ahead of two mammoth challenges against reigning Cup holders Warrington and Super League Champions Wigan five days later. For the clash with the famous primrose and blue the Catalans had to do without several first choice picks such as Bosc, Paea, Fakir, Sa and Blanch. They were on a hiding to nothing. It all started badly for them too when in the opening minutes they lost Greenshields with a dislocated elbow. The Wolves smelt blood and within ten minutes wing Monaghan was over in the corner for the opening try. With Stacul to full-back, Millard on the wing and Raguin pushed out into the centres the French visitors had it all to do. They closed ranks and held firm. Just after quarter of an hour Catalans found their inspiration when Millard scored a converted try set up by Raguin with aplomb to put them ahead. A fabulous cat and mouse race was on. The old Wire retook the lead through Monaghan again with a converted score just before the half hour before Vaccari responded with the try of the match.

It was Bevanesque in style when the spindly flyer collected a ball near the side line and hemmed in on his own 20 metre line. He dodged past a couple of defenders as he traversed the terrain before straightening up slipping another couple of tacklers before hitting the open field. Then it was a straight foot race between the

Bevanesque! Vaccari was a quick winger with spindly legs who couldn't play anywhere else. He wasn't a star but an honest lad, who against Warrington in April 2011 would score probably his finest ever try and certainly the most valuable he would ever record in the sang-et-or colours. Trent Robinson's early career at Catalans had been decidedly wobbly and in need of a real lift. The Dragons would spend a week in Lancashire playing Wire on the Sunday and visiting Wigan the following Friday. It would change their season and their destiny sending the young Aussie coach on his way to success and later, much fame at Sydney Roosters. Fred's try that day at the Halliwell Jones Stadium was a launch pad. Brian Bevan's statue just metres away would have definitely nodded in approval.

Villeneuve lad from the valley of the Lot and Bridge from half way. A try worthy of winning any game and one Vaccari will always cherish. Dureau's conversion brought the two protagonists level at 10-10 as the siren sounded for half-time.

The Challenge Cup holders wanted to defend their home unbeaten record were recharged after the break when wing Riley got them back in front squeezing in at the corner. It was turning into a battle royal. Ferriol the rough and ready vineyard owner from Brugairolles was in his element like a toddler in a sand pit clattering into Carvell and Morley. He doesn't score many tries but when he does they tend to count. His trundle to the posts just before the hour mark was his 7th in five campaigns in the sang-et-or and with Dureau's conversion the lead changed yet again. With quarter of an hour to go half-back Myler found a chink in the Catalan defensive line to grab his side's fourth try.

This was the deciding phase in the whole match. The visitors battered and reduced already from Greenshield's exit so early were on the ropes. However fortune favours the brave and with less than ten minutes remaining Dureau got the decider against all expectations pinching Briers kick centre field to race 40 metres to the posts as the lead changed for the seventh and what would be last time. Everyone was on the edge of their seats. The Catalans led magnificently by Dureau and Henderson held the line, all hands on deck as the penalties rained down from Phil Bentham -15 in total conceded. In the dying embers of the contest Dureau was carried off on a stretcher and Henderson sin-binned with a couple of minutes remaining, yet somehow they had the wherewithal to hold on in adversity, typified by Stacul's crunching tackle on Hodgson millimetres from the white wash. It was more than a win though as it transformed their season. Club President Bernard Guasch was regaled, "A grand player was born today. Eloi Pelissier played a special match and he wasn't alone. I made my feelings known to the players last week and they've responded in the way I hoped. We had a half-back pairing impeccable today in Farrar and Dureau. They organised everything and the players behind have benefited from their organisation".

Warrington 20-22 Catalans.HT: 10-10 Weather: Fine & dry. Attendance: 10,056
Referee: Phil Bentham. For Warrington 4 tries from J Monaghan (7,26), Riley (46) Myler (65) & 2 goals from Hodgson. For Catalans 4 tries Millard (16), Vaccari (34) Ferriol (56), Dureau (72) & 3 goals from Dureau
Warrington: Hodgson, J Monaghan, Bridge, Evans, Riley, Briers ©, Myler, Morley M Monaghan, Carvell, Grix, Blythe, Clarke Substitutes: Wood, Higham, Solomona Cooper
Catalans: Greenshields, Stacul, Baile, Millard, Vaccari, Farrar, Dureau, Ferriol Henderson, Casty ©, Raguin, Menzies, Mounis Substitutes: Baitieri, Pelissier Simon, Martins

The Catalans dressed and massaged their battered torsos in the short interlude before their second monumental challenge at the Champions Wigan the following Friday at the DW Stadium. Greenshields and Baile wouldn't reach the starting gate. But their predicament was eased somewhat with the return of Sa and Blanch while Dureau passed a late medical after his knockout blow at

Warrington. What transpired that mild, damp Friday evening will go down in the Dragons folklore. The dancing feet of Sam Tomkins launched by Leuluai put the Warriors four up in one turn of the stop watch and most in the ground sat back for more of the same thinking that the French visitors would have had enough of the heroics for one week and drained of energy to lift again. How wrong the Wigan faithful would be as Robinson's band used their success at Warrington to not only claim a famous Lancashire double but as a springboard to resurrect their whole 2011 campaign. By quarter time they had rattled off four unanswered tries with Dureau orchestrating things majestically. It didn't stop there as Menzies and Vaccari added two more before the break giving an unbelievable score line of 30-10. So unbelievable that the BBC Radio Merseyside team of Ray French and Alan Rooney covering the Saints game at Wrexham the same evening asked the sports desk back in Liverpool to confirm not once but twice the validity of the score update!

Rémi Casty elated! He didn't score many tries as a prop but the one at Wigan was probably his best. This effort put them ahead 18-4 with hardly quarter of an hour gone and heading for their best ever success at the DW Stadium. The Lancashire revolt well and truly launched and from then on in an upwards trajectory.

Wigan were shell shocked. After the pause the Dragons just ratcheted up the winding cog to maximum with three further scores by the hour mark with a score line then reading 10-46 for the French men. The cherry and white got consolation tries in the last fifteen minutes to make the final score (47-28) look more acceptable but it couldn't hide one the biggest upsets of 2011. Assistant coach Jérôme Guisset was overjoyed, "It's the rewards of all the effort put in during the close season. The systems of play introduced by Trent are starting to show through. The concept of the group is hyper important. Today everybody worked for the bloke next to him; we really play to *'treize'*.

The Catalan club had ticked the box with the public bodies that were going to deliver them in 2011 a brand new grandstand behind the posts. As their sixth campaign unfolded the on-field fortunes appeared to mirror that of the new structure as it was rising week by week into the Perpignan skyline. The new facility and its potential income generating were fundamental to the continued growth of the franchise. After the calamities of 2010 it was crucial with what was happening off the field that the playing side was redressed. The magic week in Lancashire was the launch pad in re-establishing themselves as a potential major force.

Rather than expecting them to tumble down the competition ladder before the Lancashire escapade the four points won saw the Catalans climb into the top half of the table for the first time really since Potter's last year in 2008. It put them in fine fettle ahead of the crucial Easter period where markers are put down to determine end of season achievements. Hull FC at home the weekend before the holiday period would be a tough one as the Airlie Birds had never previously lost in Perpignan. Any side with the likes of Fitzgibbon and O'Meeley in the forwards were going to be a handful as was the case the year before. There were just two points in it up till the break and two tries apiece. But that defensive toughness honed at Warrington, again brought them home, rendering the East Yorkshire visitors scoreless after the pause. It was mighty tough all the way until the evergreen magician Menzies charged down a kick and ran nearly the length of the field pursued by England wing Briscoe to score in the corner for a memorable try just five minutes from the end.

With their first ever win at Brutus to Hull FC (28-10) in the pocket the two Easter games promised more rich pickings. A faltering Harlequins team at the Stoop on Good Friday saw the French side race out of the blocks to establish a comfortable half-time lead with four well taken tries being the key. They wobbled a bit second half and needed a Dureau one-pointer to steady the nerves to bring them home (37-30). Bradford Easter Monday saw a near full house at Brutus before the SKY cameras for the first time in France in 2011. It was tight as a drum this one highlighted by a monumental thunder storm during the proceedings limiting the amount of open play as the pitch was awash. Just two tries shared in the opening half and the two kickers sharing a penalty each after. Still a draw (8-8) kept their unbeaten run intact even if the Bull's curse endured. Ian Henderson against his former club came up with anther top performance confirming the value of his recruitment while Mathias Pala originally from Provence debuted in the centres.

Huddersfield's visit the following Saturday would represent the Dragons biggest test since the two big "W's". The Giants second on the ladder would provide a formidable challenge with their pack capable of matching the Catalan six physically. With Menzies and Sa joining Greenshields on the injured list the Dragons had to draw from outside their original roster and pull in Touxagas from St Estève to bolster their pack. Although Ferriol had got the Catalans off to a flyer with a try in the opening minute by quarter time Huddersfield where in the box seat courtesy of two converted tries from Gilmour and Grix. This was their third hard fought battle in as many games against Yorkshire opposition and it was bringing the best out of the locals. With thirteen French players on view it was just the tonic. The confidence of winning and the harmony of the group was developing a mental toughness. Stacul filling in for Greenshields was exemplary at full-back. Baiteri, French born but reared in Sydney, grabbed a vital equalising score on the hour. Dureau won it for his comrades (13-12) with his second decisive drop goal of the holiday programme. Coach Robinson was elated, "The victory's fine but I'm proud of doing it with thirteen French blokes. When I arrived here it was to construct something around local French players and create a real identity. I think this evening we have made a big step in that direction".

The month of April had been colossal for the Dragons undefeated in six games. Their longest undefeated run since 2008 with wins against all the top three sides. From a stage looking like going down hill they were already now cemented in the top half of the table. All the anguish and disappointments of Kevin Walter's last year was now well and truly behind them as they awaited Championship club Leigh away in the Challenge Cup.

It was the first ever meeting between the two on a damp Friday evening in May at the Sports village venue. As at Featherstone in 2008 the Championship side rose to the occasion playing out of their skins inspired by an opening which saw them register two tries with little more than ten minutes gone. Tries before the break from Blanch and Baile got them back into the fray but the loss of Farrar early and later Casty both with serious knee injuries unsettled them. But when needs be, the stronger react. Stacul got over in the corner early after the return to put the Dragons in front for the first time which they would not relinquish as their defence consolidated with Henderson as ever setting the example.

Jamel Fakir had a second celebration commemorating his 100th game for the Dragons and only the sixth French player to cross this bar. Injuries were mounting as mid-season approached and Leeds the week after was not the best place to go as the Catalans had never won there. With thirteen French born players on the team sheet and front liners Menzies, Greenshields and Dureau sitting it out the task would be a challenge to stay competitive. But they achieved that with merit with a battling performance defending for their very lives. The deficit at the break was just a converted try and only a three try burst in the last ten minutes from the Rhinos eventually undid the French side's resistance blowing out the score to (6-30).

Successive weekends in the West Riding saw the Catalans Wembley hopes vanquished as Huddersfield proved too strong at the Galpharm for the visitors lamenting their poor handling and lapses in concentration in defence. As at Headingley they very much made a game of it. Conceding tries just before and after the break did for them, even though a Stacul try kept every one on the edge of their seats before the Giants sealed it with two tries in the last ten minutes. Having Dureau back from injury was a plus but the pairing with Bosc was still malfunctioning. The lad from St Estève was still struggling for form and fitness. He had played on one leg it seemed for much of 2010 with a persistent foot injury and a tendon injury later complicated things. A remedial operation was deferred and his close season rehabilitation severely compromised. After the Cup exit Bosc wouldn't be seen until the last game of the regular season in September. Following the youngster Gigot at stand off in the early part of the campaign Farrar had adapted well to the no.6 shirt but his involvement was terminated with his busted knee at Leigh. Sa the following weekend at their May adopted home of Yorkshire would be Dureau's fourth half-back partner so far.

Skipper Mounis had become the first Catalans player to celebrate his 150th game at Huddersfield and a week later it was the turn of Raguin to reach his 100th in the game at Wakefield. The accumulation of this number of games at this level although nothing out of the ordinary for established English sides, it was for the French entity a significant development and achievement. They had now half a dozen players with sufficient experience to contribute significantly to the teams overall level of performance. Belle Vue and Trinity in early summer were more accommodating than a cold Perpignan in February even for the Dragons as the competition passed its half-way stage. The visitors were highly motivated for this tie after their crushing loss at home earlier. With Greenshields back in harness they were always comfortable here registering four tries in each half in a free flowing game in the sunshine with the former St George Illawarra player claiming one of them in the (42-22) win.

Flaming June kicked off with the 'on-the road' game against Wigan up at Montpellier, the capital of the Languedoc Roussillon region. The public authority there is a big player in the world of sport and the Dragons big beneficiaries of their generosity. As major funders of the new grandstand at Gilbert Brutus the Catalans wanted to show their face in the regions capital and what better place than the new state of the art Stade Yyes du Manoir Stadium to welcome the Super League Champions Wigan. The Dragons sent a posse of players up in the days ahead to drum up support in this most modern and sensuous of Mediterranean cities pictured with members of the local all conquering handball team. There was one problem though. The day of the match clashed with the Final of the Top 14 union match in Paris in which the local Montpellier club had qualified for the very first time. Wigan fans were rather lost in the delightful *Place de la Comédie* where a giant television screen relayed live for the locals the images of the action from the French capital.

Catalans fans travelled in numbers up to the regional capital Montpellier and the Stade Yves du Manoir in 2011. From day one the Dragons wanted to spread the word with games played around Le Midi at Carcassonne and Narbonne – as well as Beziers 2009 and Toulouse 2013.

After their ravishing at home by the French side back in April there was a certain sense of trepidation of how an injured champion would respond. The Catalans though had nothing to fear as they once again showed they well and truly had turned a corner. In a herculean tussle the locals would win the defensive battle, just. Sam Tomkins magic feet were the danger for Catalans early on with a couple of tries countered by replies from Baile and Millard. Just a couple of points in it at the break. In the second half the Dragons kept Wigan pointless with a blanket defence exemplified by Sa's cover tackle on wing Richards millimetres from the whitewash. Millard steadied the good ship Catalan with a try late on to give Robinson's lads the side's first ever double against the Lancashire juggernauts (20-12) and in the process taking them up to 5th on the ladder. The club President Guasch was pretty content even if the targeted five figure gate hadn't quite been reached (9,372). The competition in the city for sports fans attention had been fierce with not only the rugby union but the highly popular handball and water polo teams also playing at home. Guasch believed that this was just an opener in this part of the world and he intended to repeat it.

Iestyn Harris brought his Welsh Crusaders side over the week after. So different than a year earlier under Brian Noble but now a club in decline and bottom of the table suffering administrative problems and points reduction. Harris got his lad's up for it with a combative performance but the locals won with a bit to spare (31-18). It was 1-1 with their next opponents Huddersfield after the Cup loss earlier at the Galpharm. This round 18 tie was switched to Halifax's Shay ground as remedial turf work was programmed at their home base.

The Sky TV coverage was a fair call as a tough, exciting contest unfolded between two sides wanting to consolidate their respective positions towards the top of the league table. The home side just had the better of things in the opening period with a 2 to 1 try advantage. It was to stay tit-for-tat all the way in a game memorable for two long distance scores by Hodgson for the home side and Dureau for Catalans as well as a mercurial touchdown on the corner post for wing Blanch. Sa's yellow card compromised the Dragons position late on in the feisty affair. The Giants just had enough to cross the line ahead (20-28) and in doing so went top of the Super League.

Castleford had well and truly been the French side's bête noire in 2010 turning them over four times including a pre-season run out. On the last weekend of June Terry Matterson's lads crossed the Channel one place behind the Dragons and already the win at home in round 5 in the pocket. The coming of the Tigers heralded the opening of the new stand and it was well garnished with 8,695 turning up on a hot summers evening. From the off the Dragons were breathing fire in turbo mould. Although the Yorkshire side countered an early Menzies try it was more or less over by the break with the Catalans rattling off a further four tries and a 16 points cushion. After the citrons it was more of the same in an expansive free flowing performance replicating their effort at Wigan notching up their first fifty point competition haul since Warrington five years earlier.

Although Bradford had never lost a Super League game in France the Catalans had a fair record going the other way with wins at Odsal in 2007, 2008 and 2010. The first Saturday in July here saw them grab their fourth success (34-28) courtesy of an imperial performance from the very evergreen Menzies returning to his old stamping ground. Ball in hand playing at stand-off he was sublime in the afternoon sunshine but for most the memory of his vital try saving covering tackle will be the one that will endure. The next weekend Leeds crossed over for their always popular visit to Perpignan bringing with them a good following as usual.

It was unusual for them though, sitting behind the French club on the ladder. Leeds surly and combative as ever where overwhelmed by yet another exemplary showing from Robinson's confident charges registering seven tries in their biggest victory over (38-16) Yorkshire's best in front of the Catalan's first ever five figure audience at Gilbert Brutus.

St Helens though put a spoke in the Dragons wheels in round 22 at the Stobart Stadium in Widnes, their temporary home. The French were thereabout up till the break but the Saints back line destroyed them late on scoring all six of their tries in a comfortable win (18-40). The Dragons missed the direction of king pin Dureau at scrum half giving a debut to the local boy Remi Marginet as well as rough-house prop Ferriol suspensed after his red card at Odsal. A faltering Harlequins a fortnight later would give the locals their fourteenth success (48-22), led impeccably at stand off by the Kiwi Sa well aided by Marginet again filling in for the injured Dureau. The two points achieved consolidated their 5th place in the league table and guaranteed their play-off qualification with still a month to go.

It's difficult to say how the two blank weekends either side of the Harlequins game affected Robinson's side on the home run-in. But it appeared that somewhere there they lost some focus. They took another forty points in the loss (8-40) to Hull FC at the KC Stadium in early August the biggest of the season. Warrington the following week promised a big match up against competition leaders thirsty for revenge. The Lancastrians had never won at Gilbert Brutus and the French would be propelled into 4th spot in the case of victory. It turned into a real battle royal. There wasn't a great deal between the protagonists. Briers playing out of his skin inspired the Wire to a laudable success won (12-25) courtesy of two break-out counter attack scores from Bridge and Atkins.

After the Cup Final weekend the fast improving Hull KR would be visitors to Perpignan in the penultimate round. The Robins had the Tigers and 8th place very much in their sights while the Dragons loss of momentum put their present standing under pressure from a resurgent Rhinos. The locals mind set didn't seem to be quite right from the moment Newton clattered Casty in the opening minutes. The Humberside team super motivated were always ahead and the Catalans playing catch-up. It was close though at the end with the ten tries shared equally and only Dobson's early struck penalty goal being the difference (28-30).

The French club had set it sights on a home draw when qualification had been realised but now back in 6th place behind Leeds even that aspiration was threatened by both Hull clubs going into the last week of the regular season.

Skipper Greg Mounis had hoped that the issue of a home tie would have been sorted before the trip to the Willows and Salford on the last weekend knowing full well the sentiments that would surround this particular game. The Reds would be saying farewell to their old Weaste location after more than one hundred years and would want to leave the 'Old Dame' on a high. A 10,000 crowd the best in years assembled to say their goodbyes. It was an emotional day for all but in the cold light of day the visitors needed the points more than the Lancastrians. The Dragons were able to put all their energy just on the actual 80 minutes of play leaving all the paraphernalia to others. And it worked a treat for them. Their forwards gained the ascendency early on leaving Dureau and the returning Bosc in the halves to orchestrate the proceedings with style. It was competitive up to the break but one-sided after with the French running away with it (18-44) with Menzies the iconic Australian having the privilege of registering the very last try at the Willows in the last minute of play. Before the game we had had both national anthems and recognition of the historic ties between the *'Les Diables Rouges'* and the Catalans from when the legendary Gus Risman had taken his champion side across *La Manche* back in 1934 to launch the code in that part of continental Europe.

To reach the play-offs for 3rd time for Catalans in six campaigns especially after their complete *'deroutement'* the year before was a monumental achievement. It was more than satisfying that it would be Hull KR returning to Perpignan just two weeks after their victory there on the season's penultimate weekend. The Robins had battled hard to make the play-offs like the Dragons had done in 2009 beating Castleford at New Craven Park in the decider. It was bizarre in some ways that a side who had given everything to get there couldn't make anything of the prize. The famous momentum that teams aspire to at the business end of the campaign was certainly with Justin Morgan's lads but it appeared that this was just a game too far for them. There was no juice or inspiration in the tank. They had left all that on Brutus two weeks before. The Dragons roared out of the blocks and were three tries to the good before 20 minutes had passed led majestically by Menzies. It was 22-0 by the break and the Catalans already thinking of extending their season for at least another week. It was all too easy at the end with ten tries racked up and half a century of points accumulated (56-6).

Wigan would be next up at the DW Stadium. The title holders would be thirsty for revenge after losing both regular season games to the French outfit. Eight days after they had squashed the spluttering Robins the Dragons themselves received the same medicine. It didn't quite feel like the same indigestion as the Catalans battled early doors and it was point less up till quarter time. The third try conceded to Farrell on the half-time bell was the game breaker. They just couldn't regroup and the tie ran away heavily from them (0-44). Robinson was philosophical about it, *"C'est une leçon"*, but concluded, "We will go and improve on these failings to return stronger."

The Catalans had finished their seventh campaign identical to their start with just 2 wins out of the seven last games played. But in between something of real substance had been achieved. Act 2 had seen the re-birth of a new team under a new young coach who brought to the scene for the first time a real French connection. A bloke who knew something about French culture and life and wanted to make that tell. He would soon bind himself to the task at hand having for the first time two assistant coaches in Frayssinous and Guisset who where both French. His presence was everywhere around the game watching the internationals and behind the barriers too at Toulouse, Carcassonne and Lézignan following the local game. His foot print had been deeper and wider than any previous incumbent. It's what the French game wanted and needed.

The RFL were delighted with the Perpignan based club and duly awarded them a B Grade licence. They had got themselves off the canvass impressively and back with the front runners. Their on-field form mirrored their stadium development at Gilbert Brutus perfectly. The club won the 'Club of the Year' accolade and Robinson 'Coach of the Year'. Well recompensed.

The arrival of some fresh, young French faces was welcome too. Eloi Pelissier a hooker from up the nearby Agly valley made his debut and by seasons end became the first Catalan player nominated for the 'Young Player of the Year Award'. Steve Menzies, Scott Dureau and Ian Henderson proved outstanding successes with the first two selected for the phantom Super League Dream Team. It was the first time two players from the club had featured simultaneously and brought the overall total to five following on from Justin Murphy in 2006, Clint Greenshields in 2007 and Adam Mogg in 2008. Indeed the renewal couldn't have been bettered and the timing near perfect. 2012 must surely see both the team and club kick on further.

A contemporary great Stevie Menzies would sprinkle gold dust around Brutus at the end of an illustrious career covering two decades and over 500 senior games in Australia, England and France. 'Beaver' would play 71 games for the Catalans scoring an impressive 29 tries for a forward. His anticipation legendary with interception tries his speciality. At 39 years old he would become the oldest player ever to feature in Super League.

( ) Denotes Play-off game

2011 FIXTURES	RND	DATE	VENUE	RESULT	ATT
HARLEQUINS	1	12/02	CARDIFF	L 4-11	
WAKEFIELD	2	19/02	GILBERT BRUTUS	L 14-38	7,113
HULL KR	3	27/02	CRAVEN PARK	W 31-18	
ST.HELENS	4	5/03	GILBERT BRUTUS	L 16-22	7,095
CASTLEFORD	5	12/03	WHELDON RD	L 24-34	
CRUSADERS	6	18/03	RACECOURSE GRD	W 32-22	
SALFORD	7	26/03	GILBERT BRUTUS	L 10-22	7,156
WARRINGTON	8	03/04	HJ STADIUM	W 22-20	
WIGAN	9	08/04	DW STADIUM	W 47-28	
HULL FC	10	16/04	GILBERT BRUTUS	W 28-10	8,025
HARLEQUINS	11	22/04	THE STOOP	W 37-30	
BRADFORD	12	25/04	GILBERT BRUTUS	D 8-8	8,946
HUDDERSFIELD	13	30/04	GILBERT BRUTUS	W 13-12	7,825
LEIGH	CCR4	06/05	SPORTS VILLAGE	W 22-16	
LEEDS	14	13/05	HEADINGLEY	L 6-30	
HUDDERSFIELD	CCR5	22/05	GALPHARM	L 16-30	
WAKEFIELD	15	29/05	BELLE VUE	W 42-22	
WIGAN	16	04/06	MONTPELLIER	W 20-12	9,372
CRUSADERS	17	12/06	GILBERT BRUTUS	W 31-18	6,742
HUDDERSFIELD	18	18/06	HALIFAX	L 20-28	
CASTLEFORD	19	25/06	GILBERT BRUTUS	W 54-20	8,695
BRADFORD	20	02/07	ODSAL	W 34-28	
LEEDS	21	09/07	GILBERT BRUTUS	W 38-18	10,688
ST.HELENS	22	15/07	WIDNES	L 18-40	
HARLEQUINS	23	30/07	GILBERT BRUTUS	W 48-22	8,471
HULL FC	24	12/08	KC STADIUM	L 8-40	
WARRINGTON	25	20/08	GILBERT BRUTUS	L 12-25	9,495
HULL KR	26	03/09	GILBERT BRUTUS	L 28-30	8,252
SALFORD	27	11/09	WILLOWS	W 44-18	
HULL KR	PO	17/09	GILBERT BRUTUS	W 56-6	(8,413)
WIGAN	PO	25/09	DW STADIUM	L 0-44	
				Total	116,288

Regular season median: 8,252

SUPER LEAGUE: P27 W15 D1 L11 PTS 31 PF 689 PA 626 POS. 6TH
CHALLENGE CUP: P2 W1 L1
PLAY-OFFS: P2 W1 L1

2011	GAMES	TRIES	GOALS	POINTS
GREENSHIELDS	20	12		48
BLANCH	30	21		84
FARRAR	14	3		12
SA	24	7		28
STACUL	18	8		32
BOSC	8	1	5	14
DUREAU	27	11	95 (5dg)	239
FERRIOL	25	2		8
HENDERSON	31	6		24
CASTY	25	1		4
RAGUIN	30	9		36
MENZIES	23	12		48
MOUNIS	31	4	1	18
GIGOT	8		1	2
BAILE	24	9		36
GOSSARD	7			
MILLARD	23	8		32
VACCARI	19	11		44
SIMON	21	1		4
MARTINS	8			
FAKIR	24			
PAEA	21	3		12
BAITIERI	29	5		20
DUPORT	3	2		8
PELISSIER	25	2		8
TOUXAGAS	3			
PALA	2			
MARGINET	2		9	18
ANCELY	2			

(29)

Chapter 8

– FORTRESS BRUTUS –

Early doors at the Dragons, a type of myth grew that the French team would be more than likely be dominant at home with the Mediterranean sun on their backs. But even when finishing incredibly in 3rd spot on the competition ladder in only their third campaign in 2008 under Mick Potter they had a less than 50% regular season success rate in Perpignan. It had always been a challenge for them from day one especially with the local competition just down the road in USAP. The union club had a formidable home record which helped to consolidate their support at Aime-Giral. The Dragons on the other hand had fluctuated and this didn't assist developing their attendance levels at home. Unlike their British counterparts Catalan fans find it difficult to follow their team home and away making it more relevant for home success to be achieved.

2012 would see the first full season with the new grandstand behind the posts at the western end of Brutus operational from the off. The panoramic viewing lounge at the top soon accommodated several hundred invited guests on match days and by seasons-end a spanking new state of the art boutique had opened at ground floor level. This towering new structure obliterated the last remnants of the old cinder running track which once circulated the terrain.

The more enclosed nature of new look Brutus just added to the atmosphere. With three covered seating areas now in situ the club felt that at last it could start to catch the shirt-tails of the big boys across the Channel, especially after Trent Robinson's stellar first year at the helm.

The Franco-Australian coach continued his recruitment policy of bringing in Super League players from other clubs rather than from Australia. Blanch and Millard had arrived the year before but what raised peoples eye brows was the landing of internationals Leon Pryce and Louis Anderson from St Helens and Warrington respectively. The former the most decorated player of the Super League era at the time and the latter a recent double Challenge Cup winner. It was statement of intent. With club and coach of the year accolades in their pockets they were not going to rest on their laurels.

For the first time the Catalans arranged two home pre-season games against Super League opposition in Wakefield and London Broncos who arrived in Roussillon in January. The Yorkshire men spent a full week in France sharing the Brutus facilities with the Dragons ahead of the first run-out. Pryce's debut attracted much interest being the first Englishmen to carry the sang-et-or colours. A much changed Trinity under new coach Richard Agar were beaten (46-10) whereas London a week later where tougher up front and only six points a drift at the turn round before going down (44-22), with the only set back being a serious season ending knee injury for lively wing Fred Vaccari during the Broncos clash.

The vagaries of winter would take a hold of the Super League XVII opening on both sides of the Channel in 2012. Odsal would have a deep coat of the white stuff on the first weekend of February when Catalan came calling. Only the herculean efforts of the Bulls supporters got the game played with snow stacked around the touch lines. Pryce missed his debut with a muscle strain against his old team while young Eloi Pelissier, one of the finds of the previous year, received a bad head injury at Lézignan for St Estève leaving them so exposed in the hooking position that Robinson turned to the experienced former Hull KR player Ben Fisher playing then at Batley to hop over to fill the breach.

The Odsal bowl had been a receptive hunting ground for the Dragons in contrast to Perpignan where Bradford had never lost but on that cold uninviting February afternoon Catalan got their new campaign off to a flyer with a convincing (34-12) win inspired by their Australian scrum half Dureau on the back of a strong pack performance well aided by three substitutes of note in Menzies, Fakir and Ferriol. The French side additionally brought some of that inclement weather back with them and more. A cold snap encroaching from the Alps engulfed the Mediterranean region like never before sending temperatures plunging to − 20°C and rendering Gilbert Brutus unplayable on the day in question frustrating everybody more especially the Hull FC team and supporters who had made the trip over.

Things had warmed up a bit a week later with the arrival of Castleford, permitting Pryce to make his home debut. However it was his opponent the ubiquitous Kiwi Chase who stole the show creating a hat-trick of tries for the Tigers winger Griffin. The Dragons had to come back from a ten point half-time deficit to claim the points (28-20) with Menzie's contribution being the deciding factor. This opening success at home represented their first ever at Gilbert Brutus.

STAR GAME 2012 SUPER LEAGUE XVII ROUND 4 ST HELENS at Langtree Park on Friday 24th February.

Setaimata Sa was a bit of a conundrum at Catalans from the day he arrived under Walters tutelage. He got involved in some off the field stuff at the time and he appeared to be going down as one of the *étrangers* not well remembered. He did have later under Robinson who knew him from the Sydney Roosters connection, some better moments but none better than this particular Friday in the heart of Lancashire.

The Dragons certainly played better games in 2012 than they did on their debut at Langtree Park but their last 20 minutes at Saints new home will go into the pantheon of the Catalans Dragons story. After some right drubbings in the early days Catalan had picked up some wins at Knowsley Road but this Round 3 tie just didn't seem to be heading for another even after skipper Casty's early try had cancelled out Foster's opening effort. They looked well out of it at the break down 20-8. When Makinson got over again for another converted score just after the break it really looked all over for the visitors.

The Dragons tornado though unknowing to us all was just winding up. Blanch's score on 58 minutes seemed just to offer some solace to the score line but when he added his second after Duport had exposed the home sides left-side defence again with their fourth try there was a discernable stirring in the wind. But surely Wheeler's try 10 minutes from the end would bring St Helens home at 32-22. Cometh the hour; cometh the man and that would be in the form of the big Samoan Sa. He stole over for an opportunist try converted by Dureau making it a six point ball game and it was now all-on as one of the competition's greatest ever escapes was unfolding in front of our very eyes.

With one last throw of the dice the French visitors stormed down the field for one mighty last effort with seconds left on the clock. Into the left hand corner the sang-et-or went but Saints defence numbered-up just in time. With the time keeper's finger on the buzzer one last play was permitted as Catalans had one desperate fling. Dureau kicked high to the posts as the final hooter sounded as Menzies leapt highest to tap the ball back to a supporting Baitieri on the inside, heading for the posts. Frenzy was the key word here as the Franco-Australian somehow still kept the ball alive into the hands of Bosc who then found Henderson who in turn moved it leftwards to Dureau once again moving to where the move originally started.

The former Newcastle man didn't catch the ball but just flicked it on basketball style to Sa. With the stadium now in complete uproar the Samoan could hardly

Super League's finest try! Or at least one of them unfurled at Langtree Park on a crisp February night in 2012. Daryl Millard scored the Dragons best ever try and surely the Fijian's most memorable. Siren already sounded but somehow the French side kept the ball alive!
Millard wasn't one of the greatest under the high ball but he will be remembered for the try of the decade for Catalans anyway at St Helens. He would score another memorable try that season too against the Wire on the Easter Monday when he sailed up the popular side touchline from deep inside his own half giving the jubilant fans a little wave as he passed by.

believe what was being played out. He got his pass out to the Fijian Daryl Millard who feinted to go for the corner post, cut back inside the one trailing home defender to stretch out one very, very long arm to plant the ball just over the whitewash. Incredible.

That tied the score of course still leaving Dureau to convert for victory. Cool as cucumber the Australian sent the ball right between the uprights and was immediately engulfed by his euphoric team mates to cap a sensational finale. Within minutes the images of this breathtaking score were all over the internet worldwide with one clip even having its own particular musical sound track!

The win full of audacity sent Catalans on that particular Friday night top of the ladder as the only undefeated side with three straight wins; their best ever start. A beaming coach Trent Robinson summed it up, "I said at half-time they could still do it. I have the confidence that this team has the capacity to score tries. Confidence is the key in these types of situation. They have the instinct of playing expansively and are not afraid of making mistakes."

St Helens 32-34 Catalans. HT: 20-8. Weather: Cool & dry. Attendance: 13,108

Referee: James Childs. For St Helens 5 tries from Foster (4), Laffranchi (16), Wheeler (36,69), Makinson (46) & 6 goals from Foster. For Catalans 6 tries from Casty (9), Blanch (58,67), Duport (65), Sa (72), Millard (80) & 5 goals from Dureau.

St Helens: Wellens, Makinson, Shenton, Wheeler, Foster, Gaskell, Lomax, Laffranchi Roby ©, McCarthy-Scarsbrook, Soliola, Wilkin, Puletua Substitutes: Hohaia Flannery, Flanagan, Clough.

Catalans: Greenshields, Blanch, Duport, Millard, Bosc, Pryce, Dureau, Casty © Henderson, Paea, Menzies, Sa, Baitieri Substitutes: Ferriol, Fakir, Mounis, Raguin

The team management would have identified the red rose visits to St Helens and Wigan on subsequent weekends as fundamental to how the team would go in 2012. The previous season the Lancashire fortnight designed and made their campaign with those tremendous wins away at Warrington and Wigan. Everything fell into place after that leaving Robinson's star soaring. The cherry and whites never quite forgot that forty plus points thumping even more so after going down at Montpellier in the return fixture too. They were sore as hell pride wise and really took it out of Catalans in that end of season play-off massacre at the DW Stadium with that painful (0-44) score line.

The Dragons arrived in good fettle obviously after the emotional high of Langtree Park but equally wanted to lift that dirty stain inflicted on them back last September. Anderson for Menzies was the only major change from the previous week. Catalans carried on where they left off eight days previous leading at the break 12-10 courtesy of a sumptuous try from Dureau. But disappointingly they collapsed in the second period taking twenty six unanswered points. The early loss of Henderson didn't help matters but they simply couldn't handle the physicality of the Wigan forwards led by O'Loughlin and Hock and ended a well beaten side. Their attacking prowess had been asphyxiated by the swarming home side's defence reducing their output to 6 'off loads' as against 22 the week before against the Saints. Robinson alluded to the team's short comings, "A lot of tackles missed and it was too easy for Wigan to progress around the play the ball area. We lacked energy and couldn't get our offensive moving".

After two weeks on the road it was a bonus to have successive games at Brutus in the form of Salford and Hull KR. The City Reds had started the season well and took the lead in Perpignan early on through a Howarth try before the Catalans got into their stride. They had lost this corresponding tie the year before so it was satisfying seeing them dominate this particular fixture with a big contribution from the right wing pairing of Blanch and Duport who both came up with a brace of tries. The French international centre had been a bit of an enigma since breaking through as a teenager under Potter and playing at Wembley back in 2007. He wandered off to Toulouse for a year and then broke knee ligaments playing for France forcing him to miss most of 2011. He had played impressively too against England in the Test on his home ground in Avignon back in October.

With a twenty point lead at the break the French side had this one in the pocket early on and won well (40-18) registering 8 tries in the process and securing their 5th place on the competition ladder. Ben Fisher made his debut after transferring over from Batley to fill in for the absent Pelissier injured playing for St Estève at Lézignan. Hull KR also arrived having won at Brutus the year before and have experienced success there in the past. Under new coach Craig Sandercock they were as awkward and difficult to manoeuvre as usual with former local favourite Dobson causing his usual head aches. The Robins led at break with the Dragons just edging it around the hour mark with tries from Blanch and Bosc. They were more than willing to take a two point penalty to get them across the line at (20-12).

Wakefield had looked disorganised with a completely new set up under new coach Agar in the pre-season run out in January and by the end of March still had only one win to show for their efforts. Trinity though had a decent home record against the French and they were to build on it here. They ran the Dragons ragged in the first half opening up an eighteen point lead with four converted tries. The French side continued to alternate Greenshields and Bosc between wing and full-back but at Belle Vue the defence was absent, with key players Menzies and Anderson missing. They rallied later on but it was not enough going down (22-32) and their second consecutive away loss.

The busy Easter league programme is considered one of the pivotal moments of the season and the first ever visit to Perpignan of the promoted Widnes struggling at the bottom was good as any to get the festivities under way. Although

Scott Dureau at the top of his game – hands aloft not once but twice – to embrace Millard and then with his match winning conversion from wide out. The popular former Newcastle Knights half-back would rack-up 96 appearance for the Perpignan based club in his five year stay scoring an impressive 792 points. He became the only Dragons player to be selected twice for the Super League Dream Team (2011and 2012).

the Vikings had taken some drubbings already they were competitive for the first half hour or so at Brutus on a lovely Spring like afternoon with Kite's try countering two early Dragons efforts giving a hopeful score line 12-6. But it fell apart horribly and quickly for Denis Betts' forlorn troops, taking four converted tries in eight minutes, two by debutant wing Damien Cardace. One of which displayed wing play at its best, swerving outside the flaying arms of full-back Briscoe centimetres from the touchline after a run of 60 metres.

The teenage wing from Lézignan would claim two more touchdowns in a man of the match performance and with promise of more to come. Injuries didn't help the Lancastrian's cause especially to the emblematic skipper Briscoe. Catalans ran up 13 tries in an all-time record victory of (76-6) setting them up comfortably before London and Warrington over the coming holiday weekend. For the trip to the capital the Catalans could align the tandem Anderson-Menzies again and both scored tries in a feisty affair with only four points in it at the break before the basement battlers relented (36-18) leaving the visitors in 3rd place on the ladder.

Everything was set for an Easter block-buster with table toppers Warrington on the following Monday. This traditional holiday game was becoming popular over here but even more so this particular year with a record crowd of 11,526 assembled and covered as seems the custom now by Sky Sports. This game was everything the sang-et-or had hoped for. A blistering start with Paea and Bosc over in the opening ten minutes and already the Wolves chasing their tail.

Warrington responded well with Higham and Riley reducing the deficit but unable to keep out the irresistible pairing of Anderson and Menzies who carried on where they left off at the Stoop, registering tries before the break, leaving the visitors with all to do, down 22-12.

Henderson, at the top of his game, led the way as the Catalans expansive game ran the 2011 League Leaders winners ragged in the end (44-16) exemplified by the cerise sur le gateau moment and Millard's parting final touch from 80 metres out down the tribune Bonzoms touchline, rounding full-back Hodgson in style and racing away to cross, simultaneously giving a wave and wink to the delirious fans. *"Quel try! Quel match!"*

For some that match was the summit of their season and not repeated. It was one of the most dazzling performances under Robinson's tutelage, full of verve and audacity. The Dragons were slowly but surely consolidating their top four credentials and for the first time ever rested undefeated in Perpignan at Easter. From pre-season and the recruitment of Pryce and Anderson both winners at Warrington and Saints respectively, talk was about this generation of Catalans players taking out a title. The idea of a Wembley return raised its head and the club even issued a Challenge Cup shirt.

The next four weeks would have a distinctive Yorkshire feel including two Challenge Cup ties. Hull KR at New Craven Park in the Cup would be the first hurdle to climb. Pryce a former Lance Todd trophy winner was a key figure in this premier success guiding his new team mates first over the finishing line with a brace of tries in the opening period. With a strong wind coming off the North Sea and behind the French visitors it was imperative to have some points on the score before the change round. At 20-0 the Catalans would have felt content with their first half efforts. The battling Robins made a real game of it second period to bring it back to a two point difference but the Dragons defence had just enough resolve to hold out (20-18) with Paea's man and ball tackle denying younger brother Mickey a match winning score on the bell.

The following weekend the French side were back but this time in the West Riding to take on their ultimate *bête noire* Leeds Rhinos at Headingley in what would be the club's 200th game. It was a real milestone for the French knowing what little impact the earlier PSG had shown and a testament to their resolve and enterprise against some of the heartland sceptics. Still, the Rhinos skipper Kevin Sinfield celebrating his own 450th appearance in the blue & amber put things into perspective about durability. On this special night Headingley would retain its mystique for the Frenchmen being the last citadel still to fall to them.

Leeds were out of the blocks like a champion sprinter with both wings Jones-Bishop and Hall over for scores within the opening ten minutes with the former getting his second before the half hour mark as the Dragons back line struggled to cope. The pace and precision of the Rhinos back line would become a recurring nightmare for not only the Catalans in 2012. Anderson and Menzies once again showed their worth with tries apiece to keep the visitors just in touch but it was not to be enough as the champions showed their spurs surging away (34-18) with a capital try full of bravado from a fired-up Bailey. It was a feisty affair with Delaney-Baitieri fronting up and with the promise of more to come later in the campaign.

Sheffield would meet Catalans for the first time in a 5th round Challenge Cup tie at Brutus the following week. The Eagles under the astute guidance of Mark Aston had become a force in the Championship and would go on to take the title in 2012. Here they were left floundering in a one-sided contest, illustrating the chasm between full and part-time professionalism. On a dry and full-size track the South Yorkshire men couldn't cope. The promising teenage winger Cardace grabbed a hat-trick of tries to add to the quartet he picked up against Widnes as the locals cruised to a comfortable 26-0 lead at the break. A further seven tries accrued after the change round giving a final score line of (68-6) with wing Finigan getting a consolation try for the spirited but out-classed Eagles.

The Giants of Huddersfield, joint leaders with Wigan promised an epic battle at Brutus on the opening weekend of May as the competition reached its half-way stage. Another five-figure crowd gathered in great expectation to witness this top 4 joust and they were not to be disappointed. It was nip and tuck all the way with just a couple of points in it at the turn round as Crabtree and O'Donnell locked horns with Paea and Casty up front. The exciting young winger Cardace confirmed his promise registering his 8th try in just his fifth run-out while showing pace and poise to create the opening for Pryce's score, the best of the match. The protagonists exchanged tries in the second period and it looked like Bosc's late drop goal would be the sole difference before Duport crashed over just before the end to give a (27-20) score line.

The BBC cameras were in Perpignan for the first time in two years for the outstanding tie of the 6th round of the Cup the following week for the match against the Challenge Cup holders Warrington. The Wolves without stars Morley, Myler and Michael Monaghan were considered vulnerable possibly. The Dragons buoyant after their convincing Easter Monday success over the primrose & blue were already thinking about a return to Wembley.

However the mindset of Tony Smith's charges was evident from the outset with long striding wing Monaghan putting the visitors in front inside ten minutes of play with a converted try. Although Lopini Paea replied for the home side and brought them level, Warrington took a real hold on the tie around the half hour mark. Hodgson had put them ahead with a penalty goal before the wily Australian chimed in with an opportunist score, soon followed by wing Riley grabbing a third touchdown and suddenly the score line had blown out to 20-6. The Cup holders had well and truly thrown down the gauntlet.

Disappointingly, a full strength Dragons line-up just couldn't respond. Out muscled up front by the old warhorse Wood and shouldered impressively by new gun Hill, the home side's effort lacked both resolve and punch. Although Simon and Fisher brought them back into it early in the second period it never quite felt convincing. Wood extended their lead and when Bridge intercepted Baitieri's pass and galloped away it was over at (22-32) with Duport claiming a consolation score as the game ran down. The loss was palpable and cutting. However they tried, from that day on, a big part of their season had ebbed away. The Lancastrians would prove to be both their pinnacle and nemesis in 2012.

The ramifications of the heartfelt Cup loss was to become evident over the subsequent weeks. A stuttering performance on the synthetic pitch at Widnes a week later was the first signs that it would take some time. They raced away from the side they had racked up a record score at Brutus before Easter with three tries in the first quarter of an hour through Greenshields, Pryce and Duport and then allowed the Vikings back into the contest by the break at 20-18. Widnes took the lead within minutes of the re-start before Louis Anderson and Lopini Paea brought some order to the proceedings with a couple of scores around the hour mark helped by the sin-binning of a Widnes lad. A lack of resolution in defence and some enterprise from the locals made it a hair raising last few minutes before Thomas Bosc and Scott Dureau secured a nervy victory with a couple of tries (42-34).

After Edinburgh and Cardiff it was time to bring the Magic Weekend closer to home and the superb new Etihad Stadium of Manchester City. As was the norm now that the French would play their notional derby of sorts against their nearest neighbours the London Broncos. There had been rumours doing the rounds, in the end unfounded, that this was the only match not to be televised by Sky as it was programmed for the dead end slot of midday on the Sunday. With some of their critics salivating over the prospect of three men and a dog or two making it to kick off-time for the 'Outsiders Derby' Alan Rooney and Ray French announced across the listening world of BBC Radio Merseyside that maybe not far off ten thousand had dragged themselves away from their bacon butties to be present.

On the hottest day of the year across the Channel the Catalans again repeated their start at the Stobart Stadium a week earlier racing away to a dominant lead with four unanswered converted tries from Paea, Casty and a brace from Pryce by the break. As at Widnes it was *déjà-vu* as the Londoners fought gamely to get back into the contest bringing it back to a six point ball game by the hour mark before three further converted tries from Casty, Menzies and Fakir sealed it at (42-18). Two unconvincing performances then against the two basement sides in early May at least consolidated the French side's top 4 standings. Maybe a certain lassitude had enveloped the Catalan camp. Wembley was always going to be a more realistic target one thought for a premier title than Old Trafford and maybe this sentiment was still lodged in the minds of more than one or two in the Dragons camp.

Although the club had continued to progress with the refurbishment at Gilbert Brutus and getting themselves off the canvas, playing wise after 2010 the absence of television coverage for the first time was a set back. Orange Sports had become defunct after taking over from Canal Plus's initial involvement. With the Perpignan club and the French game in general always battling uphill for media recognition television was considered an absolute necessity for the flag-ship club and competition.

Charles Bietry had been involved with Canal + Television as well as the Paris St Germain Omni-sports organisation which launched the PSG Super League club earlier. He had always had a soft spot for the treize and spoken highly of its merits. By 2012 Qatari money had started to flow into Paris and more particular into the failing PSG football club. It didn't stop there as Paris Handball was taken over by the cashed-up Gulf State and its petro-dollars. Qatari's Al Jazeera Television who had spread its tentacles across both the Middle East and Europe in recent years then got involved with the launch of a new pay-per-view Sports Channel marketed locally as Bein Sports.

The glittering opening big night gala took place at a swish Parisian venue with all Europe's sporting galactic stars on view including Lionel Messi and Cristiano Ronaldo on the 1st June when Catalan was lining up at Salford's spanking new stadium at Barton. How bizarrely then between sporting worlds so different that the Dragon's skipper Casty should by video link be invited to the ball from the changing rooms minutes before taking the field to announce that Super League and more particularly the French participation would be a small part of Bein Sports content from day one.

Maybe the images of stardom transmitted from across the Channel inspired Casty's lads as they tore the Reds to pieces in the first quarter of the game with already four tries racked up by Millard, Dureau, Stacul and Paea without response. Then just as if the theatre lights went down abruptly the stark reality and their flickering doubts returned with a vengeance.

It just wasn't the best preparation before taking on the competitions leaders Wigan a week later up at Montpellier. Unlike the year before the Lancastrians were invited this time to the venue of the newly crowned French Ligue 1 soccer champions MHSC at their cavernous Stade Mosson home. The Catalan club pulled out all the stops to rally support working with the French Federation and organised a specially chartered train from Perpignan taking nearly a thousand fans north to the regional capital along with forty bus loads and 4 making it on their bikes! Bein Sports were to commence their first live transmission with former Dragons prop forward Adel Fellous given a roving pitch side mandate with the microphone while the exuberant and highly popular Rodolphe Pires sharing the commentary with Louis Bonnery up in the grandstand. Pires from Albi in the Tarn was lost to rugby union when Canal Plus pulled out. His return was received more than enthusiastically by the games followers across the Channel. His vibrant personality and passion for the game is a shining light. Bietry was there just as he had been at Stade Charlety in Paris on Super Leagues very first opening night against Sheffield.

Unfortunately the French side flunked their lines on yet another special occasion out manoeuvred and out muscled by a vibrant Wigan performance as they had done at the DW back in Round 5 and of course the annihilation in last seasons play-offs. That spectacular spanking given by the French in 2011 now well digested and paid back with interest. Even with a man in the bin the cherry and whites dominated up front in the first half and only a contested score awarded to Blanch kept them remotely in touch. The loss of Anderson in the last play before the turn round with a serious arm injury spelt more bad news. It was one way after that as Wigan's speedy backs took over with panache and as conclusive victory as you could wish for at (14-36). Off the field it had been a successful venture with the biggest ever crowd (13,858) to watch the Dragons play in France and the debut of a new and potentially best ever television partner in Bein Sports.

A week later at a very windy and wet New Craven Park in Hull skipper Casty celebrated his 150th game for the club and only the second player to reach that

Josh Charnley gets a killer try in Wigan's win at Stade Mosson home of Montpellier Ligue 1 soccer team. The Lancastrians had a special relationship with Catalans from the off and that opener at Aime-Giral. This was Wigan's second trip to the regional's capital.
Later Wigan will play the Dragons in London and maybe Guasch would reciprocate and invite the cherry and whites to Paris further down the line.

milestone behind Mounis. This was a real arm-wrestle if there ever was one in front of the Sky camera's. A ball like a piece of soap and a gale blowing meant scoring would be a lottery. The Catalans hadn't been doing much digging of late but here they rediscovered some real resolve to get the two points with Dureau being the lynch pin. His 35 metre drop goal and penalty goal in the last few minutes making the difference (13-10) as the French club recorded their first ever league double over the Robins on top of the earlier Challenge Cup success. Trinity came calling to Brutus on the last weekend of June. They had started to show their better face, moving away from the basement teams, and had well-beaten the Dragons at home. This would be an encouraging and straight forward success though for Robinson's side ahead of their crunch matches against sides challenging for the top spots. Blanch got a hat-trick of tries and Menzies a brace in a comfortable success (34-10).

Catalans played a Sky match on a Monday night for the first time at Warrington a week later, less than a week before the Wolves Cup Semi-Final. This one had the connoisseurs salivating. What got them going was the sheer intensity of the confrontations. As some said the real season had just began and for Catalan to be involved was a huge statement. Robinson had got them voted as club of the year in 2011 but taking them from there was going to be the difficult one.

The 2nd place on the competition ladder was at stake with the protagonists tied at 1-1 so far after the Wolves Cup success in Perpignan. There was just one converted try to the home side registered in the first period and that contested after some questioned whether one of Warrington's forward had been grounded before releasing the ball centimetres from the visitors line and also whether it was forward by the time Westwood gobbled it up to cross. Atkins scored a fine opportunist try in the second period to put daylight between the sides. But Catalan roared back at them as action-man Baitieri got them just a score behind around the hour mark following Menzies sublime intervention. Maybe that little bit of composure and pace out wide was still not quite there. Still the Lancastrians were more than content to run the clock down with two late penalties and a drop goal to secure the points at (6-15).

The Monday night away game for the Dragons though would mean a short-turn around for the re-scheduled Round 2 tie with Hull FC to be played on

Bastille Day the following Saturday. There was some ill feeling around this one. The East Yorkshire club thought the Catalans hadn't done enough to get the game on back in February but it was difficult to see what the hosts could have done differently against the severest cold snap in half a century.

You would have thought the national holiday would have drawn out the punters for this feisty one but surprisingly people had better things to do and less than 8,000 turned up; the lowest turn out since neighbours Hull KR's visit back in March. Whatever it was the Dragons would be up for this one. Prop forward Julian Bousquet a young promising mountain of a lad from Lézignan made his debut too. They felt they didn't get the rub of the green at the HJ Stadium earlier in the week plus the rumblings between the sides from the earlier episode saw them pumped up. In warm conditions Dureau gave a master class alongside Pryce. The half-backs got three first-half tries between them, leaving the locals comfortably ahead at the break by two scores with only the visitor's enterprising wings causing them any heartache. Dureau finished with a 20 point haul at the end as Catalans sauntered home (44-12); by far the biggest ever winning margin against the Airlie Birds and the win represented the clubs 100th in all competitions with another milestone reached.

The French side had gone to Warrington vying for 2nd spot on the competition ladder. Two weeks later it was St Helens with this time the 3rd spot up for grabs. These were heady times for the French club as they had led both the Lancastrians and Leeds for most of the year; a first in their young history against two of the real juggernauts. Of course after the events of February at Langtree Park there was great anticipation building around the re-match with again Sky television in attendance. With a 9pm kick off on what had been a sweltering day beside the Mediterranean a palpating encounter awaited us. It was certainly that, with as much action and controversy to last a season.

Since day-one most of the Catalans home games had been televised live, with Bein Sports now on board following on after Canal + and Orange Sports. Of course from the RFL's point of view the arrangement was handy as it meant fewer match-day officials were required. Sky had possibly found the cost too much to dispatch their giant screen on a regular basis for these encounters so it meant the home supporters having to twiddle their thumbs awaiting the video official's pronouncements. Over time this had started to become an issue, none more so than in 2012. Controversial refereeing by British officials in France is part of the game's folklore. Who can remember Billy Thompson at Narbonne in 1980 being smuggled out of the Stadium in a Gendarme's uniform after a disputed England-France Test Match!

Maybe at the start the Dragons were considered a bit of a party gate-crasher. Not to comment too much but know their place and be thankful for the invite. After seven years the French felt they had well earned their place and where indeed now looking for a place at the top table so to speak, demanding recognition as a full paid up member. This sentiment bubbled over in 2012 no more so with this St Helens clash. It was felt here that previous coaches had bit their lips so as not to the cause offence regarding any perceived bias against the French. This was to change especially from this game and later on, as the mild mannered Trent Robinson went on to the attack. Late challenges on Dureau and forward passes not picked up by linesmen also drew the Australian coach's ire but what really blew up on that steamy late night at Brutus against the Saints was the hotly disputed try of young wing Cardace not given by the video official in the closing stages with the game finely balanced.

The locals had the visitors back peddling, putting their fingers in the dyke wall down to twelve men after Puletua's yellow card for a high challenge that laid Mounis low. The French side threw everything at the Lancastrians as Dureau's angled kick to the corner soared skywards. Millard and opponent Makinson both leapt high to challenge for a contested ball with the Fijian's height and size winning the day leaving Cardace an easy pick and grounding centimetres from the corner post. Referee Thaler would as customary here refer it upstairs. After what appeared an eternity the video ruled out a possible match changing score for hardly discernable contact on Makinson. Without video evidence what would the officials have concluded? This raised several issues. One being were the Dragons playing under different rules to everyone else having all their home games televised. A side and relevant issue was that the fans in the stadium having to endure all this paraphernalia without any recourse to the images being viewed by the official stuck in a van outside the gates of the ground.

Accepting all of the shenanigans above there was still the question of whether the French side were actually good enough on the night to claim, what would have been their first ever league double over St Helens. They started well enough with an early try from Duport and concluded the half with a Raguin try making it 15-10 with Dureau claiming two conversions; a penalty and a drop goal put the hosts in the box seat. However they couldn't build on that. The visitors retook the lead after a fine try from Flannery and added to it when the Catalan rear guard went absent gifting Makinson a walk in score. However hard they tried Catalans just couldn't find the key to unlock a ferocious St Helens defence and finished pointless after the break. The Saints had denied the French club a place on the podium and became the first side to win at Brutus (12-25) in 2012 in the league. The Dragons were learning the hard way that just being in the top four was still not quite enough.

The emotion draining mini epics and the controversy around the games against both Warrington and St Helens for some was a turning point from then on in. Three poor performances followed with an indifferent winning effort against London struggling home (19-12) and heavy away losses in Yorkshire against Huddersfield (36-18) and Hull FC (30-10). The week before their Wembley Challenge Cup Final showdown with Warrington, the Rhinos Leeds arrived at Brutus with a full strength side, eager to do the business and a 4th place in the standings up for grabs. It was a wonderfully palpitating encounter with Leeds chasing the Dragons all the way to the finishing line with Watkins in the centre revealing a burgeoning talent. Catalan lost Pryce with a leg injury early on and Sa shuffled inside but looked to be struggling on one leg to make any difference. The pace and class of the Leeds backs nearly got them the spoils with four tries in the last quarter of an hour as it finished (38-34). The French side had turned up for this one and maintained their standing but the visitors revealed possibly more. In similar circumstances could Catalan have gone to Headingley a week from Wembley and got any where near such a performance?

With a welcome break for the Wembley weekend the Catalans were refreshed going to a floundering Castleford the first weekend of September. Their top 4 aspirations still intact and now in their own hands they could see the finishing line more clearly now. They tore into the Tigers from the off rattling off five tries by the break and adding another three later with the departing Greenshields excelling with a hat-trick in a runaway (46-26) victory.

It just left recoiling Bradford six days later to navigate. Before that though a thunderbolt hit the club with the news that Robinson had accepted an offer from his former NRL bosses Sydney Roosters to take over the reins from the departing Brian Smith. It all happened very quickly. Robinson with his French connections had proved such a near perfect fit for the Dragons. The hope had been from the off that the bi-lingual Aussie could break the mould of the previous antipodean incumbents and build something more substantial and lasting. But like the others just a staging post for other things. The club needed somebody to do a Wayne Bennett and a build a dynasty over a decade or more; not just a few years and off. To be fair to Robinson the allure of the NRL and the club where he grew up was just too much.

The coach though would conclude his second and final regular campaign on a high. Bradford though had never lost a league game across the Channel but this version had experienced calamitous goings on through out 2012 with players and officials going unpaid and even the prospect of them not even finishing the season. Coach Potter had soldiered on unpaid to get them across the finishing line – just. They had though shown great resolve to get back on the proverbial horse and were pushing Wakefield for the last play-off spot. But it was all in vain as Trinity won at Salford and the Dragons still needed the points to keep Leeds at bay and finishing ahead of the title holders for the first time ever. It was a nervy Brutus especially when the locals conceded a couple of tries in the opening few minutes but by the break had edged into the lead. They finished in a flourish with nine tries and a score line of (50-26) even if their bête noir Sammut in the opposite corner grabbed an incredible quartet of tries in the losing process.

Robinson was off then but not before becoming the Catalans most successful coach over a season with a haul of 36 competition points just a couple ahead of what Potter achieved taking the Dragons to 3rd spot in 2008. Within weeks too Potter landed a plumb job also as head honcho at Sydney Tigers in the NRL. Bernard Guasch didn't hide his disappointment in losing the young Australian coach but could take some solace in that the French outfit had groomed two aspiring head coaches for the games marquee competition.

The Dragons had qualified for the play-offs for the 4th time in seven campaigns but how would Robinson's recent decision to jump ship effect their preparations?

First-up would be Wigan, the winners of the League Leaders Shield, who had two convincing successes already under their belt against the French side in 2012. More poignantly too the embarrassing memory of a 44-0 thrashing against the Lancastrians at the DW Stadium in the second round of the play-offs the year before. In the days leading up to the clash Bernard Guasch, CEO Christophe Jouffret, Robinson and Dureau were at Langtree Park in St Helens for the presentation of the Albert Goldthorpe Medal to the former Newcastle Knights scrum half. The award given annually by the League Express publication for best player was another first for the French club. The following evening John Kear visited the Thistle Hotel at Haydock to address the Dragons players prior to the show down with Wigan.

Any motivation gleaned there though didn't transpire into anything remotely like a victory as they failed to make any impression at all. They succumbed as brusquely as twelve months before with a near replica score line (6-46). Carmont gave Duport a night to forget running over, through or around the Provence lad claiming a hat-trick of tries two inside the opening ten minutes. They just never recovered from the Wigan blitzkrieg with Leuluai fending off Mounis too easily for try number three with little more than a quarter of the game gone. Where was the intensity and commitment shown at Warrington back in July on that damp murky Monday evening. Charnley's long distance score running past the whole French team rather summed it all up.

After such an impressive regular season to come up so short at the vital stage of the year was such a shock that it wasn't really viable to imagine progress from that point on. For some, the manner of that loss, just couldn't be recouped. Somewhere along the line, possibly around the losses at Warrington and at home to St Helens, an element of disbelief appeared to set in. Leeds would return the following weekend and although Catalans made a game of it sharing the eight tries it always looked that the visitor's class and composure would tell ultimately (20-27). The Rhinos looked undaunted about the prospect of a trip to Wigan whereas the Dragons had lost its appetite for such a challenge.

The campaign had just got too long for them maybe. They had always looked their best in 2012 when both Menzies and Anderson where in tandem together either in possession or defending especially the latter.

Féfé the vineyard owner from Brugairolles near Limoux – alias David Ferriol – was a real throw back to an earlier era when France produced rough-house packmen like Marcel Bescos and Aldo Quaglio who could tough it out with the best props around. Ferriol, a man of the soil, so attached to the sun bleached terrain of the Aude found it difficult to contemplate pastures further afield whether it be Northern England and Sheffield or the beaches of Sydney. Many believed he could have scaled such heights.
But it would be to Limoux where he would grow up and play with his mates and think, if only maybe. It could have all started and just finished there but for Catalans Dragons. This would be his last chance to gain some real recognition of his talent beyond a local competition meandering along. The prop was already 27 years old before he got his chance in 2007 There was never any messing around with Ferriol and his opponents knew it too The stare was enough. In tandem with Chan they were formidable in those vital, early years. In his first year he would play at Wembley and he would go on to wear the coveted sang-et-or number 8 jumper 144 times, the last time against Leeds at Brutus in the play-offs of 2012. The Rhinos won that game and later Jamie Peacock wandered down to the home sides changing room and presented Ferriol with his jersey, signed 'RESPECT'. "Tout est dit".

Between them though this pairing missed over twenty matches through injury and played together just a dozen times. Pryce and Dureau too had their moments but too fleetingly together especially in the crucial matches. The scrum-half though continued to be the darling of Brutus racking up the points again as in his debut year seeing him pass the 500 points registered in total. He made the Dream Team again in 2012 the first Catalans player to be nominated twice. Alongside him though more revelatory the first ever selection of a French player in skipper Casty. In its totality, a season of progress again as Robinson built on their 6th place the year before when they were awarded club of the year by the RFL. The new stand behind the posts was opened and made the ground more complete in every way. For the first time the club attracted five crowds of more than 10,000 at home where they lost only once in the regular season. They were already a million miles of where they were back in 2006.

( ) Denotes Challenge Cup games & Play-off game

2012 FIXTURES	RND	DATE	VENUE	RESULT	ATT
BRADFORD	1	05/02	ODSAL	W 34-12	
CASTLEFORD	3	18/02	GILBERT BRUTUS	W 28-20	7,455
ST.HELENS	4	24/02	LANGTREE PARK	W 34-32	
WIGAN	5	04/03	DW STADIUM	L 12-36	
SALFORD	6	10/03	GILBERT BRUTUS	W 40-18	8,158
HULL KR	7	17/03	GILBERT BRUTUS	W 20-12	7,337
WAKEFIELD	8	25/03	BELLE VUE	L 22-32	
WIDNES	9	31/03	GILBERT BRUTUS	W 76-6	9,156
LONDON	10	05/04	THE STOOP	W 36-18	
WARRINGTON	11	09/04	GILBERT BRUTUS	W 44-16	11,526
HULL KR	CCR4	14/04	CRAVEN PARK	W 20-18	
LEEDS	12	20/04	HEADINGLEY	L 14-38	
SHEFFIELD	CCR5	28/04	GILBERT BRUTUS	W 68-6	(3,102)
HUDDERSFIELD	13	05/05	GILBERT BRUTUS	W 27-20	10,684
WARRINGTON	CCQF	13/05	GILBERT BRUTUS	L 22-32	(7,000)
WIDNES	14	20/05	STOBART STADIUM	W 42-34	
LONDON	15	27/05	MANCHESTER	W 42-18	
SALFORD	16	01/06	SCC STADIUM	L 30-34	
WIGAN	17	09/06	MONTPELLIER	L 14-36	13,858
HULL KR	18	22/06	CRAVEN PARK	W 13-10	
WAKEFIELD	19	30/06	GILBERT BRUTUS	W 34-10	8,842
WARRINGTON	20	09/07	HJ STADIUM	L 6-15	
HULL FC	2	14/07	GILBERT BRUTUS	W 44-14	7,388
ST.HELENS	21	20/07	GILBERT BRUTUS	L 12-25	10,387
LONDON	22	28/07	GILBERT BRUTUS	W 19-12	7,662
HUDDERSFIELD	23	05/08	GALPHARM STADIUM	L 18-36	
HULL FC	24	12/08	KC STADIUM	L 10-30	
LEEDS	25	18/08	GILBERT BRUTUS	W 38-34	10,269
CASTLEFORD	26	02/09	WHELDON ROAD	W 26-46	
BRADFORD	27	08/09	GILBERT BRUTUS	W 50-24	9,284
WIGAN	PO1	14/09	DW STADIUM	L 6-46	
LEEDS	PO2	21/09	GILBERT BRUTUS	L 20-27	(8,000)
				Total	140,108
				Regular season median:	9,156

SUPER LEAGUE: P27 W18 D 0 L 9 PTS 36 PF 812 PA 611 POS. 4TH
CHALLENGE CUP: P3 W2 L1
PLAY-OFFS: P2 W0 L2

2012	GAMES	TRIES	GOALS	POINTS
GREENSHIELDS	23	18		72
BLANCH	21	16		64
PRYCE	28	12		48
SA	20	9		36
STACUL	8	2		8
BOSC	20	9	2(1dg)	41
DUREAU	32	12	128(4dg)	308
FERRIOL	22			
HENDERSON	27	1		4
CASTY	32	9		36
MENZIES	22	9		36
ANDERSON	19	9		36
MOUNIS	22	2		8
RAGUIN	24	2		8
BAILE	6			
PELISSIER	17	2		8
GOSSARD	4			
MILLARD	30	14	1	58
SIMON	11	1		4
BOUSQUET	2			
FAKIR	28	1		4
PAEA	26	5		20
BAITIERI	31	4		16
DUPORT	32	19		76
FISHER	15	2		8
BARTHAU	1			
CARDACE	12	8		32
PALA	6			
MARIA	1			
LARROYER	2			
(30)				

Chapter 9

– A FRENCH CLUB –

Bit by bit Catalans were becoming more French orientated as time went on. Yes Guasch was always at the wheel from day one but other key positions at the club were held by overseas administrators, players and coaches. In 2013 though, the appointment of a French head coach in charge at the Dragons, was ground breaking. Laurent Frayssinous had been a classy, skilful stand-off for his home town club at Villeneuve-sur-Lot who had won everything in France as the century opened and to boot a French international representing the Tricolours at the 2000 World Cup. He played in the first ever Dragons team in that historical opener in February 2006 against Wigan. After one season only though the Australian connection of Potter and Waite had decided that Frayssinous would be better utilised in a coaching capacity at just 29 years of age and would start his long six year apprenticeship as assistant coach. Serving under, in turn Potter, Walters and Robinson before at last taking the helm in 2013. Frayssinous was to show his mettle and durability subsequently in key difficult moments at the club. By 2016 he would be the longest serving coach at the Dragons and with the most wins under his belt.

The French have a phrase *'franchir un palier,'* meaning something like going up a level. From day one of their existence the Dragons have been undertaking this journey. When they kicked off in season 2008 by still being there they had already passed the PSG stay of two Super League campaigns. Of course Catalans had always had a French owner in Guasch but antipodean accents predominated everywhere else in the early years. But bit by bit the club evolved into what everybody had hoped one day it would be, a predominantly continental operation from top to bottom.

An Australian and a Kiwi legend had led the charge from the off as CEO and skipper but that had changed by the time Trent Robinson had arrived with Christophe Jouffret from Provence in situ in the suit and the captain's arm band shared by Greg Mounis and Rémi Casty by then senior members of the squad. Casty had of course picked up the accolade of becoming the first ever Frenchman to be selected for the Dream Team at the conclusion of the previous campaign.

The Australian coaching guru David Waite who had been instrumental in the founding of the club, influenced the decision of Laurent Frayssinous to step down from playing after their debut season, to take up one of the assistant coaching posts at the side of Mick Potter in 2008. After six years in the post the former international stand-off originally from Villeneuve-sur-Lot had earned his spurs working under three Australian coaches and was Guasch's choice for head honcho going into their eighth campaign. Ironically, Waite who had been working for the NRL in a development role back in Australia later applied and landed Frayssinous's former post working in tandem with Jérôme Guisset for the 2013 season.

The wind of change was blowing elsewhere as Super League XVIII approached. The rise of the Australian dollar as well as the impending billion dollar television contract for the NRL was making the European game a less attractive proposition. Greenshield's impressive sojourn in Roussillon came to an end when he signed for North Queensland concluding his six year exile. The popular Australian set an overseas playing record of 146 games and registered 85 tries also a record for the club. The unpredictable Kiwi Sa also sought pastures a new switching to London Irish. A quartet of French regulars who had also served the club well, Ferriol, Raguin, Gossard and Stacul also bid their farewells after more than 450 appearances between them.

A fresh wind was heralding the arrival of a new guard of youngsters. Damien Cardace, Julian Bousquet, Antonio Maria and Kevin Larroyer all landed squad jumpers after debuting in 2012 with Mathias Pala and William Barthau also included in the 25 players originally listed. The only recruit from down under was the Cook Islander Zeb Taia from the Newcastle Knights while the big boots of Greenshields was filled by the emblematic Leeds Rhinos Kiwi star Brent Webb.

Bernard Guasch announced a challenging campaign ahead for the trail blazing Laurent Frayssinous. Would the debuting Frenchman be able to build on the success of Trent Robinson? Additionally the club President saw the autumn World Cup also a specific bridge to negotiate for the Catalans leading into 2014. Like all sides, keeping healthy is also a key factor, especially for Frayssinous's group with so many young new faces. The club set a goal of appearing at least in a major Semi-Final cup or league.

Unfortunately the Dragons hit choppy waters well before the off. Talisman half-back Dureau, Dream Team member in both the two previous campaigns complained of headaches in pre-season training before Christmas. Little did anyone know at the time how traumatic this episode would eventually play out. Dureau returned home to Newcastle for the festivities thinking nothing untowards. It was a routine visit to the opticians that revealed something more serious. In the end the half-back had to undergo a ten hour operation to remove a tumour behind the eyes. It was a seismic shock to all concerned with everybody's thoughts only on the long-term health of the player rather than foot-balling matters.

It cast a shadow on all pre-season build up. Thankfully the operation was a success and the hospital people eventually gave the little half-back a clean bill of health to resume playing after a three month break. But it would be springtime before Dureau trod the turf again. The former Newcastle player's heath and fitness issues would dominate the campaign like no other. Compounding Dureau's situation prop Paea reported back with a knee problem which had revealed itself the season before and led to an operation which would keep him out of action till April.

The pre-season shirt presentation evening has always been popular with the Dragons but in 2012 it took another dimension when it transferred up the road to Carcassonne a one hour drive from their Perpignan base. The Aude area including also Limoux and Lézignan had become part of the Dragons hinterland and where two of the *penyas* supporters groups where located. Around a thousand gathered at the Salle de Dome, the main municipal hall in the town for the occasion after the players had earlier taken part in a training session open to the public at the nearby Stade Domec.

Following the afternoon run-out at Stade Albert Domec in Carcassonne the squad along with local dignitaries and family paid tribute to Puig Aubert one of the greats of French rugby league and Catalan by birth (his statue adorns the perimeter of the ground). Later the new grandstand behind the posts at Brutus would also carry his name.

The first time the team presentation had been held outside the Roussillon region. The Salle de Dome being the municipal hall of Carcassonne welcomed a 1,000 fans and was superbly organised by the local penya Les Dragons du Lauquet. This supporters group take a bus load to Perpignan to all the Dragons home games.

A week or so later the cobwebs were blown away with the pre-season run out against the London Broncos at Stade Gilbert Brutus. A fresh winter's evening delivered a tough feisty workout for both sides remembered mostly for a bit of a free for all towards the end with four players sin-binned. Webb and Taia made their debuts with Bosc and Barthau sharing a half each along side Pryce in the halves.

The opening month of Super League action was going to be tough with three away games scheduled. Travelling outside of the peak season, flying time tables would be particularly challenging, with recovery time between games compromised. Even so, Catalans couldn't have been disappointed with the eventual outcome. Hull KR where brushed aside at New Craven Park on the first Sunday in February (32-24) with Webb showing up particularly well. The former Leeds player claimed a try on debut released splendidly by the young prop Bousquet with back-rower Taia first on the score sheet with try inside ten minutes. If the KC Stadium was an immovable object for the French, then East Hull had provided a lot more happy memories with this, their fifth success.

A Salford in free-fall were to be the opener at Brutus in 2013. The Lancastrians, struggling just to get a side out, following their ownership and money worries proved a desperate opposition. A reckless and clumsy tackle by Bousquet on a local boy Theo Fages was the unfortunate feature of the game. The former Lézignan youngster hit the Pia lad late and high with barely two minutes on the clock and was red carded while the Salford youngster was knocked out cold and needed hospital treatment. The only thing you could say was that it evened up the contest somewhat. Even with the one-man advantage Salford could hardly make a game of it and fell away sadly to a (40-6) defeat. Bousquet collected a five match ban and was the start of a turbulent season for the man-mountain. Injuries and further suspension would blight his progress as the year unfolded.

The Cup holders Warrington were next up at the HJ Stadium and the first televised game. In some ways it replicated the 2012 joust at the same place. Combative and fiery throughout. Webb yellow carded twice and the French side took a bit of a pasting from the media especially after the Bousquet incident. Some enjoyed it though as the Dragons wouldn't give an inch going down (16-24). It left however a legacy both physically and mentally which would plague them throughout 2013. Webb picked up a serious hernia injury which would blight his campaign while the refereeing and discipline issues would roll on and on.

Castleford at Wheldon Road without Chase should have been doable, especially after such a dominant opening period. They thought a Bosc drop goal had sealed it 7 minutes from the end but the Tigers grabbed one for themselves to tie it up at (17-17). Frayssinous lamented the point lost saying it could count at seasons end. How right he would be. Still at the end of February the Catalans found themselves 4th on the competition ladder with five points.

The other Rhubarb Triangle neighbours Wakefield were next up at Brutus with the first signs of spring in the air. This tranche of matches leading into Easter would really show where the Dragons were heading. Millard was moved to full-back for this encounter to plug the hole left by Webb. A terrible start ensued with Trinity 16-0 to the good early on before the locals got something back just before the break. At the end it was two points won but a real struggle to get the job done depending on a late penalty goal and one point drop from the right boot of Thomas Bosc (29-22). Wigan had been their real *bête noir* in 2012 with three conclusive victories against the French club. A huge improvement from their last run out a week earlier would be needed to get anywhere near the cherry and whites. The opening half-hour was competitive but they collapsed in a heap with seven uncontested tries and a (0-38) score line. It was disappointing that the envy and the durability shown at the HJ Stadium had evaporated by the time Wigan had finished with them. There were signs of wobbling then and still early doors.

Successive home games against teams below them on the ladder offered opportunities to redress the balance. Widnes though had already shown a different face to their calamitous efforts of the year before. Millard's tenure at full-back had not worked out so Bosc was shunted backwards with young William Barthau getting his first run out in ten months along side Pryce in the halves. Getting young Bousquet back after suspension was a bonus too. But as per Wakefield it was another slow unconvincing opening with the sprightly Vikings leading the way with a two point advantage heading into the break. Six tries rattled up in a much better second period with the visitors kept scoreless brought the two competitions points home (46-14) with Barthau and Pryce to the fore.

Elsewhere in Roussillon a certain slip of a lad from Salses by the name of Morgan Escare had been burning things up playing for feeder club St Estève in the local competition scoring tries for fun. The coaching team had been a bit reluctant to give him his head but the following week with Bradford in town he was given his debut at full-back when Barthau pulled out at the last moment with a muscle strain. The Bulls had, like Widnes, shown some progress from their previous campaign slowly getting over their financial and administrative problems. This turned out the best home performance so far against a combative

Yorkshire outfit who held the aces early on. Bousquet though was unstoppable from short range with his 117 kilos and got that all-important try just before the oranges. For the second successive home game the French side had kept the visitors scoreless and themselves clocking up five tries with debutant Escare celebrating by claiming one of them (30-10). Another one celebrating was Bosc on reaching his 150th appearance milestone following behind his golfing buddy Mounis.

The defining Easter programme saw Catalans crossing the Channel to London or more specifically to the Esher rugby union club in the leafy suburbs of the capital after their normal Stoop base was made unavailable. Again another edgy opening and Frayssinous's band didn't really seal it (30-24) until a late try double from Cook Islander Taia after Escare had got them off the mark earlier supporting Pryce's break out. That specific Thursday evening in London the French visitors were top of the pile.

It poured down early on Easter Monday which caused the schools rugby bonanza to be called off. Normally a thousand or so youngsters, coaches and parents pile into Brutus for this traditional festive occasion. An 11,000 crowd was in prospect for the clash with Super League title holders Leeds but the elements kept the numbers below the five figures expected. Crowds had been down on the previous year. The on-going recession had kept punters away especially visiting supporters while the Bein Sports live television coverage for all home games at an attractive price of just €11 per month had kept many locals too at home more so for those fans who would normally travel from further afield.

The Dragons wanted more than anything in 2013 to turn over the leading teams to confirm their rising aspirations. Already Warrington and Wigan had downed them across the Channel so would the Yorkshire side at Brutus offer something more productive, taking into account their indifferent season so far? By kick-off time the rain clouds had moved on leaving a sodden pitch on a day stalwart Fakir would be only the fourth Dragon hitting the 150 games tally. Leeds got a tentative grip on the encounter early on with the classy centre Moon opening their account, crossing for a converted try with Sinfield tagging on two penalties as well, to indicate that they would take anything offered them. By the break the locals had a blank sheet and in need of inspiration. The opening ten minutes of the second period appeared decisive when rough house forward Bailey was dismissed for a high and late challenge on Bosc and two quick-fire tries by the Dragons resulted. At 12-10 ahead for the first time they had the visitors, down to twelve men, where they wanted. Unfortunately they didn't have the wherewithal to close the game out with twenty minutes to go as Leeds showed their pedigree taking it with a late flurry (12-27).

Hull FC and the KC continued to be a no-go zone the following weekend as the French side suffered a second consecutive loss (8-28) with the only highlight being young Escare's bright career start with another try. Tongan prop Paea had made his first appearance of the year against Leeds after surgery on his knee but the Humberside episode then saw them lose Elima with a bad bicep injury which would see him disappear until August. The Dragons were facing the possibility of a third loss on the bounce when they travelled to Lancashire and St Helens next up. The Saints form though had been indifferent and their worst start in the Super League era and offered the visitors some hope especially after their scintillating victory the year before. Langtree Park continued to smile on the French visitors (22-12) with a Catalan's defence impregnable and they took their trying scoring opportunities when offered early on. Escare had exposure for the first time on Sky television leaving pundits duly impressed with another try and one disallowed. Ian Henderson steadied their nerves at the death though with a conclusive score.

Although St Helens were a scalp of sorts reverses against Warrington, Leeds and particularly the clouting they got at Wigan seemed to confirm already that Old Trafford still remained a bridge too far in the Catalans evolution. Wembley and the Cup on the other hand was always going to be more attainable. The events of 2007 had created something special in the psychic of the club regarding this particular challenge. They were desperate to repeat the exercise but this time to claim the prize.

In 2013 they were to be offered comfortable passages into the quarter-finals. Struggling Championship club Hunslet were met for the first time at their South Leeds Stadium in a 4th round tie on the last Sunday in April. An early lunch-time kick off was designated to allow the French team to catch an evening flight back out of Manchester. Although the win was comfortable (50-12) they had some hitches to navigate. Bousquet pulled up again in the warm up and had to pull out, Simon was knocked out in a tackle and Henderson sent-off before the interval. Baitieri and Mounis led from the front and steered them home with Barthau claiming a hat-trick of tries. Basement York were to be dispatched (92-8) three weeks later before the lowest ever crowd at Brutus. Records tumbled for the Dragons with sixteen tries racked up with Larroyer and Escare sharing seven between them.

Sandwiched between these Cup games the French side lost twice against Yorkshire opposition which kind of confirmed their present disposition. Huddersfield came to Perpignan in buoyant form running just behind the competitions leaders Wigan. A real novelty for the Giants visit was the inauguration of the giant video screen at the swimming pool end of the ground. This tussle replicated the Leeds game in that the locals couldn't win at home against twelve men. This time Luke Robinson was dismissed for a high challenge on Escare just before the hour mark when the Dragons were in front but they conceded two late tries just as they had done on Easter Monday going down (20-28). Additionally they lost Jason Baitieri for the season with a serious knee injury. 10th placed Wakefield away a week later and a Saturday Sky televised game was a debacle (12-30); their poorest of the campaign to date. They lost Vaccari early on and Baile and Pala struggled to contain the likes of Fox and Cockayne on the fringes. Larroyer's brace of tries was their only solace.

At the half way stage Frayssinous was struggling to keep his side in contention for a top 4 place although by the end of May his case would be strengthened as they picked up 5 points from three run outs against teams in the lower half of the table. Castleford with new coach Daryl Powell now on the bridge were beaten by half-time in the bright spring sunshine at Brutus with the local's already six tries to the good. The coach though was not happy with their defence inviting the Tigers back into the game late on. Still the durable Baixas lad Mounis would celebrate his 200th appearance in the sang-et-or – a club record with a win (39-30).

London as usual offered opposition in Manchester for the Magic weekend. Memorable in spades for the return at long last of the mesmeric scrum half Dureau after his tribulations. The double Dream Team nominee got a dream man of the match debut picking up an interception try for the opener and finished with an 18 point tally including six goals in a coasting (46-18) victory against the beleaguered Broncos. The injury curse though wouldn't abate unfortunately as Anderson's 2013 campaign came to grinding halt with a torn Achilles tendon. With Paea still struggling with a heavily strapped-up leg and now Anderson joining Baitieri out of the campaign it was becoming a bridge too far. Webb and Elima would only get back on the season's entrails to make any real difference. In a many ways their season was really cooked for certain when Anderson limped off the Etihad Stadium after half an hour.

If the Sky pictures had got tongues wagging about Escare's arrival at Langtree Park further confirmation regarding the '*Salse's moped*' sudden notoriety was established at Widnes the following weekend. Yes, for the young full-back to grab a try hat-trick against lowly York was one thing, but another repeat at the Stobart Stadium three weeks later was something different again. His first-half effort against the Vikings from under his own posts with a feint-and-go and a foot race untouched to go nearly the length of the field showed the lads rich potential. This second hat-trick though couldn't be celebrated with a win as the locals showed their new resolve to shared the points (32-32). What was more scary would be the images coming out of the Stobart of a staggering and forlorn Dureau. There had been nothing untowards regarding the Australian during the game until he fell back on his haunch's when about to convert a try. The distressing pictures fortunately did not precipitate any relapse in the player's overall health and subsequent visits to a specialist in Toulouse gave the player a green light fortunately to continue playing.

**STAR GAME 2013 SUPER LEAGUE XVIII ROUND 18 HULL FC
at Stade Gilbert Brutus on Saturday 8th June**

The former Newcastle Knights scrum half missed the Hull FC clash as a precaution but returned two weeks later for the visit of Hull KR. The Arlie Birds had a healthy record in Perpignan with just a couple of losses and bang in form too with just a single reverse in 10. Coach Frayssinous wanted to build on the recent results to keep his side on the shirt tails of the competition leaders but more so to dent the aspiration of the visitors who stood one place ahead. The Catalans coach wanted to see better defending than he'd seen at Widnes and additionally putting two decent halves together in the same game for the first time this campaign.

Vaccari got them off to a flyer with an opening try inside 5 minutes and although fellow wing Lineham countered with one for Hull FC the Dragons had a handle well on this affair by the break with two further tries by Escare and Duport with Bosc converting all three. The likes of Ellis, Westerman and Lynch in the visitors pack couldn't make headway against a watertight defence led impressively by Mounis, Casty and Henderson.

The Dragons here, patience personified, had a full set of cards. Larroyer got the all important early score in the second period and then locked the door shut. Duports second try was just the 'cerise sur le gateau' as the clock wound down. Bosc kicked impeccably with 5/5; all the points more particularly were posted by French players on the day the club celebrated its 100th Super League victory and in doing so climbed into the top 4.

Frayssinous was elated, "It's a good result for us. I'm very happy. I've been waiting for a big performance from us against a top-four side at home for a long time. Tonight we got it, especially defensively – we were pretty good with that. On attack we only needed around 50 minutes to achieve the win. Our bench is now becoming an impact for us like they were at the start of the season. Eloi (Pelissier), Morgan (Escare) and Kevin (Larroyer) have all stepped up in recent weeks but tonight we saw that they are becoming Super League players." The coach had been there back in 2006 and played in that memorable opening win again Wigan at Aime-Giral and eight years later as the first French coach in Super League he celebrated their century. Chapeau!

Catalans 30-4 Hull FC. HT:18-4. Weather: Fine & sunny. Attendance: 8,105 Referee: Richard Silverwood. For Catalans 5 tries from Vaccari (3), Escare (14), Duport (36,72), Larroyer (42) & 5 goals from Bosc. For Hull FC 1 try from Lineham
Catalans: Escare, Blanch, Duport, Millard, Vaccari, Pryce, Bosc, Casty ©, Henderson Simon, Taia, Menzies, Mounis Substitutes: Pelissier, Larroyer, Fakir, Paea
Hull FC: McDonnell, Lineham, Crooks, Yeaman, Crookes, Holdsworth, Heremaia Watts, Houghton, Green, Ellis ©, Westerman, Pitts Substitutes: Lynch, Whiting Johnson, Bowden

With two-thirds of the programme completed and a week of repos for the Exciles representative fixture, Catalans felt in a good position, especially when considering their long standing injury woes. Menzies yet again represented the club against England partnered by the Cook Islander Taia. Out of the blue though thunderstruck when it was announced that skipper Casty had engaged for the following two seasons with the NRL club Sydney Roosters. No doubt the link with Robinson was a major factor but the boy from Ornaisons up near Lézignan had harboured dreams down-under for a long time if the opportunity arose.

Although everybody around the club and supporters would be devastated to see him depart there was at the same time a huge amount of pride that the French game and Catalans in particular had created this move. Without Super League and what it had done for Casty's development it just wouldn't have happened. From 2014 there will be a real French rooster wearing the 'rouge, blanc et bleu' at Bondi Junction and thousands of fans this side of the Channel would have another side to follow. To soften this blow the club announced two young forward captures in Bradford Bulls promising back row forward Elliott Whitehead as well as Benjamin Garcia from Provence via Brisbane Broncos under 20's.

The following four weeks would though define the Catalans of 2013. Toulouse would host their Round 19 tie with Hull KR at the request of both the French Federations President Carlos Zalduendo and the local Toulouse Olympic club. After Barcelona, Beziers and Montpellier it would be the *Ville Rose* who would continue the 'on the road' tradition and what a splendid job this did in mobilising nearly 15,000 to the Stade Ernest Wallon home of Stade Toulousain the Catalans biggest crowd to date in France. A huge banner adorned an open terrace behind the posts with the words, "Super League en 2015 – here we come"!

It felt a festive occasion on a lovely early summer's afternoon by the Garonne. The Robins had picked up some form too after their clattering by Wigan at Easter time. Dureau returned on the bench after his scare at Widnes but Taia was missing with Larroyer stepping up in his home city. The start was incident per se. Did two Hull KR players knock on in the in-goal? All twenty five on the field thought so and stopped except full-back Eden who raced the full length of the field unhindered with neither the man in the middle or the video official seeing anything wrong. This set the tone of an exciting and fiercely fought encounter dripping in controversy. Larroyer had his best game with some stirring charges.

Escare had a try chalked off after a corkscrewing run to the posts for what appeared to most an insignificant push on a defender by Duport further out, well beyond the path taken by the elusive full-back. Yet, with all that going on, the locals were still able to regale their support with Bosc's drop goal just before the break edging them in front. They couldn't hold it though, as Eden went on to claim a hat-trick of tries sending the Rovers home happily with the two points (21-22) and a famous win; "Certain players failed mentally," confessed Frayssinous. The result, though disappointing, was tempered somewhat by the great success of staging the game in Toulouse, adding further impetus to the latter's Super League aspirations.

What happened at Huddersfield a week later could be contributed to the Toulouse venture, especially the late catastrophic collapse (60-16) to the competition's leading chasers. The first forty wasn't desperate with Brough feeling obliged to take the two points on offer as the bell sounded for the break. Duport had a try ruled out by the video official and then the Giants had a try confirmed by the same person when Taia looked to have been impeded in reaching an attacker. The perceived lack of 'fair play' was palpable here and what transpired in the last quarter at the John Smith's Stadium, maybe confirmed it for many across the Channel. It was the first time they'd conceded sixty points since Headingley on the last day of their debut season.

Two weeks before their best bet for a major Semi-Final in 2013 their hopes were melting away. London at Brutus showed even more of the local's state of mind as they just about crawled over the finishing line, eight days later against the season's no-hopers (34-28) with the Bradfordian Whitehead on debut and Duport reaching his 100th game for the club before the poorest turn out of the year. The Challenge Cup the following weekend against Hull FC turned into a tough, no holds barred quarter final, worthy of the competition with the home side showing some re-found pride and determination especially in defence but they still couldn't create enough to throw at the Airle Birds defence. Frayssinous again, "It's not only about selling your skin. You have to be intelligent at the right moments too." Hull FC just had too much to offer (13-24) and yet another Cup quarter final loss at Brutus in consecutive years after Warrington in 2012.

The Dragons had gone into the Cup tie below par and the defeat the following weekend at Salford (12-16) was part of where they were now with their seasons hopes evaporating in front of their very eyes. They seemed unable to put a stop to the tail-spin downwards. It all boiled over at Barton in the dying minutes with the team's exasperations, fermenting for weeks now, manifesting itself in a huge brawl. Skipper Casty landed a suspension for his involvement in the fracas. A resurgent St Helens a fortnight later were far too good (6-26) for the Dragons with a returning Pryce, against his former team, unable to lift them. A fractious encounter saw Maria yellow carded twice with Taia put on report for a late and high challenge on the Saints scrum half O'Brien. The Cook Islander received a three match ban for his indiscretion which the club appeared to accept but were raging with indignation regards punishment handed out or not to similar incidents to other players across the Channel. The Catalans responded by posting on their club web site a resumé of these images to support their case. Little good did it do them though as the RFL took umbrage and fined the club £1,500 for their troubles.

Bernard Guasch had been espousing in the local press the possibility that the Dragons after a promising start could well tumble out of the play-offs especially with the challenging run in. Indeed Frayssinous had said when the fixtures were originally issued that their play-off campaign would begin a month early when St Helens would arrive at Brutus the first weekend of August. With Saints departing then already with the two points it was looking contentious before the trip to Odsal to face the Bulls ahead of games against the serial big-hitters Wigan, Leeds and Warrington.

There was to be though the lift they would get when both Webb and Elima declared themselves fit to play after their prolonged absence with injuries. The former Leeds man had been out since February. Bradford had won a vital match at Wakefield the week before and were coming up fast on the rails with a play-off place in view. Interestingly the French side fielded five former Bulls in their line up in Elima, Henderson, Menzies, Pryce and Whitehead. If this was in anyway a bonus it was certainly not evident in the opening half with the home side pumped up and flying 18-4 to the good at the oranges and Catalans on the precipice. Staring into the abyss they stirred themselves. Fakir sounded the alarm with a charging try and Webb's class and experience showed what they had been missing. It was on a knife-edge and it was only a late Bosc drop goal that ended the Bulls season (23-22) to keep Catalans still engaged.

Wigan facing an impending Wembley trip arrived in Perpignan a week later, wanting to be anywhere but there. But exactly like Leeds a year earlier showed their credentials fielding a full strength team and not giving way till late on (22-6). The French sides defence won it for them as Wigan threw everything at them for a good hour. The cherry and whites for a long time had been the Dragons *bête noire* and the victory thus sweet and confirming finals football for the third consecutive year. Headingley was still the last bastion yet to fall to Catalans and so it proved again but Frayssinous's side went the nearest they'd ever been (12-20). McGuire's late converted try exaggerated the closeness and intensity of the encounter with Bosc missing a simple, vital late penalty. Young Bousquet who's season had been complicated with injuries and suspensions, immense in the confrontations with the hard men Peacock, Bailey et al.

The French side needed to win or draw their last home game to Warrington to secure 6th place on the ladder and permit them to host Hull FC in the first round of the play-offs. The Wire had already finished runners-up to Huddersfield but didn't take their foot off the pedal and arrived at Brutus with a full strength team. It was an emotional day as their two departing players of note Menzies and skipper Casty led out the team separately to a standing ovation with a special guard of honour for the Frenchman from the youngsters of his home village of Ornaisons. It turned into a mighty struggle in difficult, thundery conditions. The primrose and blue gained an early ascendency with two early tries but Dureau got an interception try from 80 metres out just before the break. The Australian half-back seemed to have won something back on the terrain towards the latterly end of the campaign. He had shown up present at Headingley and in the second half here his contribution would be significant. It was his little dabbed through kick which gave the maestro Menzies his last ever try at Brutus and put his side in front for the first time just after the hour mark. It wouldn't prove conclusive though as the visitors responded with their third try from wing Riley. Unfortunately just as at Leeds a week earlier a penalty more or less in front of the posts from short range was flunked this time by Dureau. So near yet so far (12-14).

Tony Smith the Warrington coach was first to shake hands with Menzies on the final whistle as the legend bid his farewells. Both sets of supporters applauded thunderously and all thirty three players formed a guard of honour on departure. The man from the Manly Peninsula had truly entered the Catalans and Brutus pantheon.

The play-off at Hull FC was an after thought. On another horrible wet night by the North Sea the visitors didn't respond (4-14). They couldn't lift themselves any more after the close shaves against Leeds and Warrington. In all honesty to finish in 7th position with all they had endured was a decent shout. With a French coach at the helm for the first time, lots would have settled with the final outcome. For some the arrival and progress of French youngsters like Bousquet, Escare, Larroyer and Pelissier was what lit up 2013. Escare finished top try scorer with 19 touchdowns in just twenty games following on from Duport with the same haul the previous year. Many of their victories were indeed 'Made in France' as the overseas contingent as a group struggled to play their hand. Millard and Blanch in the three-quarters couldn't find the form of the previous campaign – just 14 tries as a pair as against thirty in 2013 – as the side struggled to find a cutting edge. Only basement sides London and Salford scored fewer points than the Catalans.

( ) Denotes Challenge Cup games

2013 FIXTURES	RND	DATE	VENUE	RESULT	ATT
HULL KR	1	03/02	CRAVEN PARK	W 32-24	
SALFORD	2	09/02	GILBERT BRUTUS	W 40-6	6,872
WARRINGTON	3	15/02	HJ STADIUM	L 16-24	
CASTLEFORD	4	24/02	WHELDON ROAD	D 17-17	
WAKEFIELD	5	02/03	GILBERT BRUTUS	W 29-22	7,191
WIGAN	6	08/03	DW STADIUM	L 0-38	
WIDNES	7	16/03	GILBERT BRUTUS	W 46-14	7,357
BRADFORD	8	23/03	GILBERT BRUTUS	W 30-10	6,813
LONDON	9	28/03	ESHER	W 30-24	
LEEDS	10	01/04	GILBERT BRUTUS	L 12-27	9,465
HULL FC	11	07/04	KC STADIUM	L 18-20	
ST HELENS	12	12/04	LANGTREE PARK	W 22-12	
HUNSLET	CCR4	21/04	LEEDS CITY STADIUM	W 50-12	
HUDDERSFIELD	13	27/04	GILBERT BRUTUS	L 20-27	8,549
WAKEFIELD	14	04/05	BELLE VUE	L 12-30	
YORK	CCR5	12/05	GILBERT BRUTUS	W 92-8	(2,500)
CASTLEFORD	15	18/05	GILBERT BRUTUS	W 39-30	7,083
LONDON	16	25/05	MANCHESTER	W 46-18	
WIDNES	17	02/06	STOBART STADIUM	D 32-32	
HULL FC	18	08/06	GILBERT BRUTUS	W 13-10	8,105
HULL KR	19	22/06	TOULOUSE	L 21-22	14,858
HUDDERSFIELD	20	28/06	JOHN SMITH STADIUM	L 16-60	
LONDON	21	06/07	GILBERT BRUTUS	W 34-28	6,286
HULL FC	CCQF	13/07	GILBERT BRUTUS	L 13-24	(6,500)
SALFORD	22	19/07	SCC STADIUM	L 12-16	
ST HELENS	23	03/08	GILBERT BRUTUS	L 6-26	8,582
BRADFORD	24	11/08	ODSAL	W 23-22	
WIGAN	25	17/08	GILBERT BRUTUS	W 22-8	8,969
LEEDS	26	30/08	HEADINGLEY	L 12-20	
WARRINGTON	27	07/09	GILBERT BRUTUS	L 12-14	8,595
HULL FC	PO1	13/09	KC STADIUM	L 4-14	
				Total	117,725
				Regular season median:	8,105

SUPER LEAGUE: P27 W13 D2 L12 PTS 28 PF 619 PA 604 POS. 7TH
CHALLENGE CUP: P3 W2 L1
PLAY-OFFS: P1 W 0 L1

2013	GAMES	TRIES	GOALS	POINTS
WEBB	8	2		8
BLANCH	24	9		36
PRYCE	28	3		12
TAIA	25	12		48
BOSC	26	5	95(5dg)	215
DUREAU	9	3	13(1dg)	39
ELIMA	15	3		12
HENDERSON	30	3		12
CASTY	28	4		16
MENZIES	26	8		32
ANDERSON	12	4		16
MOUNIS	28	1	2	8
BARTHAU	5	5	6	32
MARIA	10			
PELISSIER	30	5		20
LARROYER	20	10		40
MILLARD	21	5		20
PALA	14	4		16
SIMON	20			
BOUSQUET	11	1		4
FAKIR	26	3		12
PAEA	18	1		4
BAITIERI	14	2		8
DUPORT	23	11		44
VACCARI	18	9		36
BAILE	6	3		12
ESCARE	20	19		76
GUASCH D	1			
MARGALET	1			
WHITEHEAD	8	1		4
GARCIA	2			
(31)				

Chapter 10
– HEADINGLEY FALLS –

Bernard Guasch had forewarned everyone that the season 2014 would be a difficult one for his club following on after the World Cup the previous autumn. The Catalans had provided more players than any other club side and the physical demands of fronting-up against the likes of New Zealand, Samoa and England would leave some traces behind. Whilst clubs such as Castleford would have everyone fresh as a daisy and on board for pre-season preparation by late October it was December before the Dragons were altogether.

The 9th campaign for the Perpignan outfit also corresponded with the return of relegation. The powers that be decided two sides would drop out of the Super League competition at the conclusion of 2015. For Catalans that set the alarm bells ringing; they had previously finished bottom of the pile twice – in their debut campaign 2006 and in 2010. For heartland clubs in the north a Championship place could be seen as recoverable but for the French entity a certain calamity.

Going into the new season coach Laurent Frayssinous recruited two Australian three-quarters in the Cronulla centre Ben Pomeroy and Sydney Roosters winger Michael Oldfield to add some thrust and pace in the backs something sadly lacking from 2013. The retirement of the irreplaceable Steve Menzies was softened somewhat by sound recruitment earlier of Elliott Whitehead mid-term the year before plus the ever reliable presences of Zeb Taia and Louis Anderson. If the back row looked more than solid the same couldn't be said for the props. Skipper Rémi Casty's move to Sydney and the NRL as well as the earlier loss of the no-nonsense David Ferriol had left huge holes difficult to fill. Jeff Lima had played much earlier in France at St Gaudens but since had made his mark on the game first at Melbourne and later at Wigan where he won medals and at Wembley, a Lance Todd Trophy winner too. His form earned him a return to the NRL with the emerging South Sydney and Michael McGuire. Lima's arrival in Perpignan was considered a real coup.

Injuries, illness and suspensions had been the lot of Frayssinous in his first year in charge and as the New Year beckoned he would have been hoping for better things. Unfortunately his luck wouldn't turn; well not initially, in fact it got worse. Scott Dureau and Lopini Paea had been two of Trent Robinson's key signings. The latter had played his last ever NRL game in the 2011 Grand Final for the Roosters and carried that form with him to Perpignan whilst the former an average Newcastle Knights performer turned into a double Dream Team selection.

Of course the popular 'Scotty' had been cursed with this tumour behind the eye at Christmas time 2012 and not surprisingly would struggle to make anything of the following campaign. Encouragingly he was back on the bridge for pre-season hoping for much better luck. Paea too had been struck by a knee injury the previous term but the medics seemed to be satisfied that everything would be OK going forward.

As usual London crossed the Channel to play ball and the first run out for the sang-et-or in 2014. On the last weekend of January the Broncos were at Brutus with a very limited line up after what can only be described as the most chaotic pre-season possible in the Super League era. Frayssinous played it right with the embattled Tony Rae and picked an 'A' team with lots promoted from Steve Deakin's St Estève. The Londoners had Sean Long pitch-side geeing them up and it worked at least till the break which had the visitors ahead. The only new face on show was wing Oldfield who grabbed a try and showed glimpses of what he had to offer. The locals won it (18-12) courtesy of Morgan Escaré's late incursion leaving the Dragons coach asking for more.

A week later Denis Bett's much improved Widnes made the trip over and would provide much tougher opposition. Frayssinous put out a strong formation with debuts too for Lima and Pomeroy. There were though still notable absentees with Duport continuing his recuperation from the shoulder injury incurred against England in the World Cup Quarter Final while both Paea and Anderson were back in Australasia for family and personal reasons. The latter was still struggling with the effects of his torn Achilles tendon the season before and asked for time away from the game to recuperate fully. The second warm-up game also left the coach dissatisfied. Like the week before they were behind on the score board at half-time. They didn't cross the whitewash until ten minutes from the end when a flurry of tries spared their blushes (18-16) with Escaré once again to the rescue.

The Super League fixtures didn't spare the Catalans either with four away games out of the opening five games starting on Humberside against Hull FC where they had concluded their previous season in the play-offs. Frayssinous had pulled off both Dureau and Webb early against Widnes with the hoped for response. A week later at the KC Stadium Escaré with a number 2 now on his back (he wore number 28 in 2013) was already in the full-back position and Bosc with Pryce paired at half-back. It was a roller coaster of an opener swinging one way and then the other; both sides had dominate passages but really failed to nail it.

Bosc's inclusion here appeared a master stroke with a sublime first-half, kicking Hull to death. His 40/20 set up field position for Escaré to chime into the line showing great footwork and a sublime pass to Cardace to cross in the corner. Bosc well-blooded literally by now then clacked a pinpoint kick to the posts plucked out of the night sky with aplomb by a leaping Whitehead and the visitors had the lead by just four going into the oranges. But the visitors couldn't hold on as their defence went missing dramatically on the return conceding five unanswered tries. Fortunately Westerman hadn't brought his kicking boots giving the French still a sniff and they finished with a fanfare with their own blitz of scores.

Tia picked up a brace and Cardace finished with a hat-trick of tries. If Bosc had converted from the touch line Escaré's first try of 2014 on the hooter they'd have shared the points. A tough way to miss out (34-36) with something to build on was the departing sentiment. The abiding memory though was Escaré's contribution creating tries and scoring them; already Salses's poster boy was putting down a marker that there would be no second season syndrome beside the Med for this lad.

It was back to Yorkshire a week later but to the west and Wheldon Road Castleford where the Tigers after an opening day win at Bradford where looking to confirm. Several casualties from Hull FC with Millard, Bosc and Fakir failing to make the *rendez-vous*; Cardace moved in from the wing with Escaré replacing him and Webb at full-back. Dureau was at scrum half with Bousquet and Antoni Maria taking over from Fakir and Elima in the forwards. The latter copping a hefty four match suspension for a challenge on Heremaia a week earlier. Places

Escaré's Star – really soared into the night sky as 2014 opened. The slip of a kid from the small Chateau town of Salses 10 kilometres or so up the road from Perpignan had been announced nine months before. On Humberside against the Airlie Birds on a dank, dreary February evening he was the shining light encapsulated in this picture here. He fixes Richard Horne stepping off his left foot, then dances around the Hull FC veteran on the outside to send wing Damien Cardace diving in at the corner, not once but twice showing he could create the openings as well as scoring them. It was marvelleous to see the Dragons producing such players as those who graced the French game with their pace and verve generations before such as Andre Carrere and Jackie Merquey. Escaré would go on to establish a new club try scoring record of 29 touchdowns in his first full season overtaking Justin Murphy's 27 haul in 2006.

like Castleford in the winters months were always special challenges with a tight pitch and passionate crowd close to. They hadn't lost there though since Robinson's first season in 2011 but this time they didn't measure up. It was tight up to the break but fell away rather worryingly after. Up the middle was holding but out wide they couldn't cope with the powerful Australian winger Carney running riot with a hat-trick of tries. Catalan possibly with the try of the match from Escaré after Dureau and Pryce had run from deep. If the heavy loss (6-32)) and the six tries conceded in itself wasn't bad enough Dureau suffered a severe bicep injury too; to add to the woe Bousquet also picked up a four match ban; the Lézignan youngster yet to throw a punch in anger not getting any favours from the disciplinary committee once again. The only bright spot was former skipper Casty being crowned World Champions with the Roosters in Sydney against mighty Wigan.

The imposing Leeds next up for the Dragons brought the first hit out of the season to Brutus. The Rhinos some peoples' favourites for 2014 had started well and possessed one if not the best backlines in the competition. On cue the Dragons backs were falling like toy soldiers, with by now Pomeroy and Cardace joining Millard injured plus a struggling Webb – fourth choice half-back Barthau got the call up too along with fringe selections Vaccari, Pala and Baile. It was men against boys even if the locals sprung a surprise crossing first with Oldfield opening his sang-et-or account sprinting clear from a nifty blind side break out. But it was just the lull before the storm as Leeds hit the throttle with three converted tries in a 10 minute spell before the break. It was a dull and dreary day weather-wise and Catalans were in no state to lighten it up. The final damage was (12-40) with another ten tries conceded. And yes another serious injury too to Henderson and a broken arm. If it doesn't rain it pours!

The 2013 opening was difficult but nothing like this with now 11 players unavailable for yet another trip to Yorkshire on the first weekend of March. The pressure was mounting on Frayssinous with Wakefield next up and knowing that after that St Helens, Huddersfield and Wigan were lined up. Unlike the first three encounters lovely early spring like weather and sunshine welcomed the Catalans to the old Belle Vue but such conditions didn't bring any relief or change of mood; talk of a false dawn was an under statement. Even though they were down on numbers there was still some quality and experience for Catalans to draw on but they would go from bad to worse and produce one of the most insipid efforts in the clubs history.

It was difficult to know where Webb was both physically and mentally that day. He was a shadow of the player who had won nearly everything at Leeds in a glittering career. Trinity peppered the Kiwi with high kicks all afternoon and found him wanting. It would be his last game in the Catalans colours and last game in Super League. Wakefield tore the French side apart with little resistance with five tries leaked by the break and a score line of 0-32. Another couple of converted tries brought more misery to the French visitors before a hint of resistance from Whitehead who would claim a couple of consolations in the shambles. He and the returning Anderson were the only ones to show up in the (14-56) thrashing.

Hardly before the first Dragons player had unfastened his boot laces in the sheds the alarm bells were already ringing loudly. The pre-match plan was that the team would stay in England after this Sunday fixture to prepare for St Helens the following Friday. However within minutes of the final whistle the coaching staff along with Bernard Guasch and Christophe Jouffret the CEO was already in a frenzied huddle on the team bus. There and then it was decided to abort the weeks scheduled stay across the Channel that very night and after a 12 hour journey via Barcelona returned back to Perpignan. As the President announced; "We'll go to wash our dirty linen in private at home in Perpignan. This match at Wakefield will permit the club to grow; we've been too lenient and soft. That's over now". On Monday evening Guasch along with Frayssinous would meet up with certain players to ascertain the reasons for the recent unsatisfactory performances. There was a palpable feeling that as a group the overseas players weren't pulling their weight. The fall out was

'Jaja' in happier times with his President Bernard Guasch embraced after their success in Montpellier against Wigan in 2011. It was a sad and abrupt departure for Fakir after 171 games in the sang-et-or without an Adieu merited such are the vagaries of professional sports. He did his bit in building the edifice.

quite dramatic as by the Tuesday Webb's time at Brutus was over and Fakir was excluded from the group and demoted to the clubs reserve team St Estève. A loyal and popular servant of the club since their UTC days, took the decision to heart and declined the offer and like Webb would not play for the club again. He would finish 2013 at Bradford before deciding to return to France and play at Lézignan. After 171 games for the Dragons it was an unsatisfactory ending for 'Jaja'. Years before in his pomp Brian Noble had tried to secure his services when the Bulls where top dog but for many the serious knee injury he suffered against Tonga at the conclusion of his first Super League campaign reduced his capacities considerably. He was never quite the same player again. Elsewhere both Pryce and Paea were given official warnings that things had to improve… and quickly.

The blood letting took its time to effect a change and not until leaders St Helens had ramped up a sizeable lead in the first half hour at Langtree Park the following Friday night. Escaré was back at full-back, Pala in the centres and Bosc at half-back with Simon replacing Anderson who had joined Elima and Bousquet in the dog house catching a one match suspension in the Belle Vue fiasco. A debut too for the imposing young Toulouse forward Gadwin Springer. Saints red hot and undefeated were mission impossible roaring out of the blocks with four converted tries. But something definitely clicked in the minutes leading into the break as they stared into the abyss; some inspiration and verve from two of their youngsters got Catalan starting at least the long climb out of their slumber. Garcia and then Pelissier squirmed there way over for two tries and at least some respectability.

The second period was more even with Oldfield flying over in the corner for a fine brace of tries for the visitors but the expected defeat (22-40) was far more honourable than a fifty point shellacking they had taken at lowly Wakefield five days previous. Still it was a loss and if one factored in the three final games of 2013 it represented 8 games lost on the bounce – the worst in the club's history.

With Huddersfield league leaders in the previous edition next up in Perpignan the stakes were already mounting for that first vital win. On a dreary damp evening in front of a crowd of 6,510 – a few thousand down on the corresponding fixture in 2013 the French side at last went into the green for go. A command performance led sumptuously by Anderson on his first game back at Brutus in ten months after a busted Achilles tendon with a brace of tries and supported well by fellow back-rowers Taia and Whitehead although here the Cook Islands skipper was in the centre. This trio though would prove the real lynch pin in the clubs renaissance in 2014 as the supporters at last had some thing to celebrate at last (30-14).

The change in mood was palpable as was witnessed even in the loss a week later (16-22) at the Super League champions Wigan. Shaun Wane's gang had inflicted serious damage on the Dragons for several years at the DW Stadium but this one wasn't going to be replicated on the last weekend of March. The dashing Escaré was to score one of his finest tries in an already blooming career this night. Clearing his line with the whole home side in front of him he combined superbly linking with first Pelissier, then Pryce and taking the return pass to saunter under the posts nearly 90 metres away from his initial touch. Breath taking. The little fella would get a second too as the Dragons went shoulder to shoulder in this one. It was level with hardly a minute to go when a poor last-play kick found the Wigan full-back Bowen too easily rather then finding the touch line, inexplicably allowing the Aborigine full-back to go the full length for the winner. Tough.

Still it left the club with only the beleaguered Bulls and London behind them on the ladder and with Easter already around the corner. Some journalists started twittering about the possibility of relegation already for the French club and its ramifications. The CEO Jouffret wasn't holding back either with his, "Catastrophic!" implications for Catalans in such an eventuality. Even so Frayssinous was under pressure from now on to turn things around; it would be his biggest challenge to date after taking over from Robinson the year before.

There was some respite on the first weekend of April when London Broncos travelled over again for a Challenge Cup 4th round tie. Notable in that it saw the debut of hooker Joan Guasch, the President's son, from the bench and international centre Duport returning after his pre-season shoulder operation. It was a game similar to countless others between these foes of late with the Dragons

Brothers in Arms! Mounis-Pelissier Catalans both. Here you would think they'd won the Cup! In reality just celebrating the flamboyant hookers first half try at Langtree Park against St Helens in March with the Saints already leading 24-0. The Dragons were at the bottom of a hole after what would be a record eight losses on the bounce with relegation staring them in the face. But this very moment it felt like some huge weight had lifted leading to better times ahead in 2014. Six months later they would be back at Langtree Park and just 80 minutes away from an Old Trafford Grand Final.

always struggling to completely dominate even if the result always came out their way; ten points between them at the break and 16 by its conclusion (40-24). The visitor's picking up three tries in the final quarter.

The Easter weekend is always seen as a bell-whether for the seasons outcomes and for Catalans this particular year even more so. Leading into the holiday period Denis Bett's Widnes outfit returned after their jaunt over in January and were by then turning a few peoples' heads up in 5th place with just two losses. The Vikings had been slowly improving and a far sterner opposition than the one who handed the Dragons their record ever win back in 2012 when wing Cardace on debut scored four tries. The former Lézignan junior who scored a hat-trick in the season opener at the KC Stadium was recalled too for this fixture in Mike Oldfield's absence.

Widnes showed their value matching the sang-et-or in a feisty opening period trading tries equally before Whitehead grabbed his second try of the half just before the break to give the home side an eight point cushion. One of the talking points up till then was Flynn overhauling Escaré after a length of the field chase; Salses pin-up boy was still much in evidence though picking up his customary four-pointer. With the warmer weather making its presence felt the sunshine was starting slowly to bring out the best of certain players. Whitehead who arrived mid-season the campaign before was starting to emerge as a real tour de force and grabbed his first hat-trick for the club in this encounter and with a brace too from right flank partner Pomeroy. The lanky Australian who had struggled with leg muscle strains earlier was gaining in confidence slowly but surely. It finished (42-20) with the visitors struggling at the end with injuries. If Bosc had had his kicking boots on the damage would have been worse too.

The big talking point around the game was the decision to join forces for the day with near neighbours USAP who were playing a drop kick away further down avenue Maréchal-Joffre at Aimé-Giral against Oyonnax in a Top 14 fixture later in the day. The two clubs management decided to offer access into both games for the price of one and the exercise proved a roaring success with the Dragons attracting their best turnout of the year with nearly 10,000 present including a decent representation from the union club's followers well evident.

The third meet up with the Broncos was on Maundy Thursday as the year before and again at a different ground. In 2013 it was out in the middle of nowhere at Esher rugby union and this time north of the Thames at The Hive in Barnet. It was a struggle against a game London side but the win (22-28) was secured on the back of early supremacy and a lead of four converted tries before falling away badly at the end. Hull KR on Easter Monday at Brutus was a first. The Holiday fixture has become a popular one in Perpignan even if the opposition seems to change annually. The club's best ever turn out at Brutus was on this day against Warrington in 2012 with over 11,500 present.

It turned out to be a humdinger of a tussle as the Robins buoyed by their success over the Airlie Birds in the Humberside derby days earlier arrived in fine fettle. It turned into a real cat and mouse affair as first the Dragons roared out of the blocks with three scores in the opening quarter of an hour from their trio try poachers par excellence Oldfield, Whitehead and the inevitable Escaré. Rovers though showed their colours replicating the locals surge with three converted tries of their own by the break to lead by just two. But the Dragons weren't to be denied as Oldfield and Whitehead each got across the whitewash again late on to steer their side over the winning line helped by a Bosc drop goal (37-24). The three games in eight days over the Festive period had well smiled on the Catalans with the six points picked up and a climb away from the bottom had begun. Their catharsis had worked for the time being and their own resurrection was now timely in place.

For the trip to Bradford the following Sunday for the Challenge Cup 5th round tie the club decided to travel by a charted plane direct from Perpignan airport. 2014 had proved a bit complicated in that the usual flights out of Gerona just across the border into Spain had been cut thus entailing extra mileage by the necessity to fly from Barcelona instead. The privately hired aircraft permitted the club to offer any spare capacity to sponsors as well as supporters.

The tie at Odsal though provided a hiccup as the doomed Bulls raised from their slumbers to give their embattled coach Francis Cummins a bit of a respite. Bosc missed out on this one but Barthau proved a more than capable replacement helping his side into a promising lead early on with three tries in the first quarter of an hour. Maybe the mind set drifted from that thinking it all too easy. If so they were to be proved horribly wrong as the Yorkshire side with a motivated Fakir on board roared back with three converted scores by the break to lead by a couple. The visitors just couldn't get back into it and the Wembley dreams drifted off for yet another year (20-33).

Dr. Koukash's Red Devils were next up as the fare changed to the league campaign and another challenge from a side close to the Dragons on the competition ladder. The Easter successes had been like a breath of fresh air and the Catalans were anxious of rowing on from there. The game mirrored the efforts of a week before, initially with the home side starting strongly, with Escaré scoring before most of the spectators had taken their seats. Millard followed soon after and by quarter time they were in exactly the same position at Bradford a week earlier as Escaré zipped over for his second of the evening. Again lackadaisical and some opportunism from Salford with Chase to the fore brought us déjà vu and Odsal re-visited. However this time fortunately we saw a responsive sang-et-or with Escaré claiming his first hat-trick of the year after drawing a blank the weekend before. With fringe lads like Bousquet, Simon and Barthau attracting the praises of the coach it was left to Pelissier to crown the win with a cheeky drop goal on the final whistle (37-24). For the first time in 2014 the French side started to look at those in front of them on the ladder rather than those behind.

A trip into Lancashire followed where Warrington had had an indifferent start compared to the previous campaign and were in the process of rebuilding. Not since their extravagant success over the old Wire on Easter Monday 2012 had the Catalans succeeded. If the Dragons had picked up five wins only one came on their travels and that at the hapless Broncos. There was going to be no respite this time either and with ample reason too. The French were holding just till quarter time but fell into a heap taking four converted tries without response leading up to the break. Within a minute of the restart Barthau had a kick charged down and a walk in for Bridge making it 30-0 and the match already over. Duport and the obvious Escaré got them mere consolation scores later – the full-backs effort worthy of note full of verve and opportunism. Frayssinous reflected, " The game, it is of being more patient with the ball. There is a series of things that have to happen before arriving there. The important thing now is to know how to bounce back. But this alternating between the hot and the cold is starting to tire me out."

The heavy defeat (10-42) had to be quickly put behind them and London for the fourth time in the Magic Weekend at the Etihad Stadium in Manchester would be the perfect opportunity. The year before against a much stronger Broncos line-up, they had made hay in the glorious May Midday sunshine, but in 2014 purgatory with one of the poorest efforts of all. The only positive was two competition points (24-22) as the Londoners, without a win to date were desperately unlucky not to break their duck. Magic Weekend always gets the Catalans best turn-out support-wise with the weather and the occasion being the key. They deserved better fare from their team. With the half-way house reached and perched 9th on the ladder at least considering their calamitous start, the Dragons had something at last to build on.

At least the calendar looked favourably on Catalans at this particular time with the other stragglers Bradford the following weekend in Perpignan. The home side embarrassed by their Cup exit earlier at Odsal had something to reddress for sure and found easy pickings against a Bulls side reeling from taking a century of points in the two preceding games. Escaré was over before the clock had done one full circle and his partners in crime Whitehead and Oldfield soon followed suit giving a clear three score advantage going into the break. Escaré repeated the dose straight away after registering his 15th touchdown of 2014 in just sixteen appearances and the game done and dusted as the visitors fell away badly (46-4).

The improving Widnes down at Lowerhouse Lane would be seen as a pivotal game in a crucial time of the campaign as summer started to show itself. The old Chemics were making a name for themselves in 2014 bidding for their first ever play-off qualification and going into this one locked side by side with the French. The Lancastrians had a chance here to make a statement and put a bit of clear water between themselves and a direct competitor. They had led at half-time the week before at in-form Castleford too and would have approached this one with confidence.

As in the earlier tussle across the Channel, the Frenchmen won the early challenges, taking the lead with Millard and Duport coming up trumps with tries but that too dissipated rapidly with the hosts claiming three tries of their own by the break and well set to claim their first ever success against Catalans. The cat and mouse struggle though continued as Frayssinous's team raised the stakes with a dominant third quarter with twin threats Escaré and Oldfield claiming touchdowns along with one from Pryce. From there you'd have thought their best win across *La Manche* to date was in the bag but you'd be wrong as the defensive frailties evident so long in this see-saw year would bite them on the proverbial. Widnes had it locked at (26-26) with minutes to go but Bosc missed drop goals attempts not once but twice inside the hosts 20 metres. Still the one point gained was enough to see the French entity at last lodged in 8th spot after Round 15 following their poorest ever opening.

With a weekend break for the Challenge Cup the club, its President and coach had time to mull over the present state of play especially after the earlier turmoil. The coaching staff including Frayssinous was in the final year of their contracts and it would soon be time to make a decision on their futures. It was accepted that June would be a crucial month with home games against high-flying St Helens and Hull FC followed by Leeds at Headingley where they had never won. Other news percolating around the club was the re-engaging of Saint-Paul-de-Fenouillet's finest Pelissier for a further two years. The 22 year old hooker was in line to become the youngest player at the club to complete a century of appearances. And continuing the theme the news broke of the clubs intention to run with an U19's Academy side in 2015 playing across the Channel – a momentous decision in the club's evolving story.

The competitions leaders Saints arrived on the hottest weekend of the year in Perpignan. In recent years the Lancastrians had found favour at Brutus in tough and often contentious situations. If the visitors had mauled the Dragons somewhat that night at Langtree Park back in March it also had corresponded with the first tiny sign of the Catalans revival. Ian Henderson back after his broken arm at Castleford early in the season was a good omen for the hosts having missed his leadership and experience around the ruck.

The huge hulk that is the Samoan Masoe had terrorised France in the World Cup at Brutus the autumn before but found the Catalans pack this time more feisty and impermeable with Elima on his 100th appearance for the club well fired-up. It was an almighty clash of wills in the opening half with just two unconverted tries from Duport and Oldfield separating the adversaries. But unrelenting pressure later broke the visitor's resolve and they imploded in the heat with the added loss of Lomax with a bad leg injury. Oldfield increasingly coming into his own, grabbed his first hat-trick in the sang-et-or as the Dragons created history with the biggest ever win over St Helens (42-0) with eight unanswered tries and as near a perfect performance as you could get. It was a seminal moment of their ninth campaign and individually a significant milestone too for Thomas Bosc when he became the first Dragons player in history to record 1,000 Super League points as well as the first Frenchman to do so when he crossed the whitewash for his side's fifth try in this sensational exploit. To cap it all, the march up the ladder continued now into 7th spot, overtaking Widnes for the first time.

Thomas Bosc with 210 run-outs for the Dragons had been there from the very start along with his mate Grégory Mounis. Both will share their savoir faire with the U19s Academy group in 2016. Utility back Bosc a hugely talented player who struggled at times to really believe in himself, especially in his early days. Who will ever forget the try he got at Brutus against Harlequins when he chipped the ball over the top of two defenders with alternative feet to score a wonder try.

Dureau's travails took an unexpected turn in June when it was decided to loan the Australian half-back to Trent Robinson's Roosters in Sydney for the remainder of the season. After a truncated campaign the year before, 2014 wasn't giving him any luck either, with an arm injury at Castleford back in February. As a replacement the Catalans picked up another Australian in Sam Williams from the St George Illawarra club while Dureau would subsequently get more game time at Newtown Jets, the feeder club of the Sydney Roosters in the NSW competition, pending a decision by the Dragons to honour the last year of the players contract in 2015.

Williams was thrown into his debut at Brutus the following weekend after the St Helens game for the visit of Hull FC, playing off the bench, covering for Pelissier who had copped a one match suspension. The Airlie Birds had had a turbulent season thus far with more downs than ups but arrived in Perpignan buoyed by a fifty point thumping of Widnes away the weekend before and their history so far across the Channel wasn't bad by any means; always competitive and troublesome. Nothing changed in 2014 either even after the locals carried on in the same vein as last time out with a couple of quick fired-up tries racked up in the opening phases from usual predators Escaré and Oldfield doing the damage. At 16-4 on the turn around it looked as if the Dragons would come home with a tail wind in their sails especially after Millard had got the locals further ahead with his side's 4th try. But it wasn't to be as the visitors fought back impressively with a couple of converted scores themselves to make for an exciting finale. The defensive effort shown seven days earlier was asked to turn up again and it did as the French side edged it (20-16). Poster boy Escaré's latest intervention took him to 15 Super League tries having drawn a blank against Saints the week before. He was at least over night anyway, alone on top of the try scoring chart before Saints wing flyer Makinson joined him by the end of Sunday afternoon with his contribution across at Wheldon Road.

Undefeated in their last five games after the Hull FC result saw the Dragons starting to consolidate their 7th ranking and the anonymity registered earlier now just a bad memory. Still with Leeds and Headingley facing them next the betting would be against a hold-up of sorts. The Rhinos in their den had always for the French side been a hurdle too far. To be fair you're talking about a golden generation striding the hollowed turf in blue & amber with titles to boot. Since their first sighting of Leeds and Headingley there'd been nothing but misery for Catalans with 16 defeats and some right thrashings. More especially across the Channel where they had never triumphed. It would be the last citadel for the French to claim on English soil.

Leeds still well placed sitting on St Helens heels in 2nd place were looking at their tenth straight home win on the last Sunday of June even if they had stuttered somewhat last time out there against neighbours Huddersfield. Catalans to be fair had been closing the gap to some degree since those sixty points shellackings in their early days. The season before, the Dragons had threatened to snatch it, but Bosc missed what looked like a simple penalty towards the end to hand back the initiative to the hosts with McGuire making them suffer the consequences yet again.

Leeds bedecked in a replica of the *maillot jaune* to commemorate the staging of the 2014 Tour de France in the city earlier had expected to confront their French visitors in their polka dot configuration but the organizers had screamed, *"Non, non c'est interdit!"* as some rights issue had been unfortunately transgressed by the manufacturer . Still it didn't stop the visitors from having a real go in this one with Escaré once again leading the charge with yet another try to his name with hardly a minute or so gone. They led at the break with Taia with a brace of tries to the fore and Williams kicking five goals. It was real nip and tuck after the oranges with Leeds unable to convert their tries with Sinfield absent. A late converted Millard try tied it up at 30 a piece and Escaré thought he may have pinched it at the death with a dramatic last minute drop goal from in front. With seconds remaining all the Dragons had to do was collect the kick re-start and play the ball a couple times. The difficult one taking the short kick off was secured, only for Pomeroy to subsequently run behind one his own players to concede an unforgiveable penalty straight in front of the posts which was converted leaving it agonisingly frustrating for the visitors (32-33). The Rhinos had got out of jail big time on this one for sure and would Catalans ever get a better chance to lay their bogey?

Although bitterly disappointed at missing out at Leeds, Bernard Guasch had seen sufficient progress there, and with the two successes against

St Helens and Hull FC enough to give the coaching staff a real vote of confidence for taking the club forward into their 10th campaign and beyond. Laurent Frayssinous's tenure along with his assistant Guisset was prolonged as far as 2016. For the head coach and the club it signified another major step forward as it meant the French born incumbent would be at the helm going into his third term, something the three previous Australian coaches had never achieved.

A return to the West Riding was programmed as July bloomed into view a week later and across to Odsal Top and the Bulls once again but not before the surprising news that former Bradford favourite Pryce was heading out of Perpignan to new pastures in 2015 having accepted an off from Hull FC. Although 32 year old Pryce had had an up and down sort of three year stay he had in 2014 shown signs of his old self and was maybe looking for a contract extension. Whatever was discussed didn't change the clubs stance that they had not seen their hopes of silverware materialise during Leon's time and along with Brent Webb – both winners at their previous clubs – it was now not going to happen and the Dragons were looking to put that sizeable element of the salary cap elsewhere as developments were to later reveal.

Even if Bradford had offered little in Perpignan earlier there was the question of the Cup elimination to digest. After coming so close at Leeds it was imperative that the Dragons kept pushing on and certainly taking maximum points from the bottom two stragglers was a given. It proved to be another close one with the ten tries registered shared equally, with Bradford ahead by the break; Williams for the second successive week kicked impeccably including a late penalty to add to Whitehead's late crucial try being the difference (32-30) on a day the Tour de France cycle race passed by just a stones throw away from Odsal Top.

The redoubtable Wigan next came calling to Brutus with the locals more than eager to make up for their narrow loss at the DW Stadium back in March. With a late 9pm kick off favouring the Lancastrians in the heat it turned into a more than feisty affair – indeed sour and some bad blood spilling over. There was a feeling that Wane's side played too close to the margins of legality and the locals reacted in kind; two Dragons players Duport and Garcia in the bin in the second period. "It was necessary to respond to their aggression", claimed Frayssinous post match. The English press rounded on the French for their indiscipline and Wane didn't help matters with his call to arms the next time Elima and crew arrived in Wigan. That said the visitors, smarter with the ball in hand with Bowen again causing the French side trouble all evening, won more than comfortably (16-37).

Wakefield's visit was like the exorcism of all the malcontent of Belle Vue on the first Sunday in March. It rested a date ingrained in the minds of those who had suffered that day and Round 21 was to be their redemption. The Dragons got most of it out of their systems by the break at 28-0 winning in a canter (40-6) notable for Whitehead's second hat-trick of tries giving the second rower his 17th of the campaign and the best tally of any forward in the comp.

If Wigan was a real set back they had picked up the two points against Trinity and still felt a chance to move up further at this critical phase in the competition with Round 22 next up and the home straight pending. But if it was to materialize the next two games against the two sides directly in front of them would tell us the reality. There was fall out after the Wigan match with Duport and Garcia suspended and Elima injured so they travelled light to the John Smith Stadium on the last weekend of July. Huddersfield had supplied Catalans first win of 2014 and had run up fifty points at home the week before against the struggling Bulls. The season before the Dragons had suffered one of their heaviest ever defeats leaking 60 points against the Giants. It never promised to get anywhere like that but three early tries conceded revealed that an away win against anyone but the two relegated sides wasn't going to come here either. A stroppy effort and eventual loss (16-38) had the coaching staff still scratching their heads. The line of thought was; what was the point of just making the Top 8 if they couldn't win away come play-off time. As usual the sight of Escaré grabbing another try was the only solace but for him his star was still rising as he registered his 6th try in as many games.

In its own way the loss at the Giants was going to prove for the Catalans the start of their second hiatus of 2014. Not content to prove their critics wrong about holding on to their Super League status in a relegation year they had by now got themselves into a reasonable position to qualify for the end of season play-offs and those in charge at Brutus were adamant that the side secure this goal and more. Warrington arrived in Perpignan stinging from a shock home defeat to Wakefield and one week before their Cup Semi-Final date with Leeds.

A weakened Wolves team made the crossing but that made no difference as the visitors proved again too strong (24-26) to claim the second double over the French side in successive campaigns. Amazing similarity, in that the last two editions were both played under thundery skies in Perpignan, with again just a penalty goal making the difference. This time Bridge's penalty goal was sufficient whereas in 2013 Dureau's late effort drifted wide. The positive in the downpour was wing Oldfield's second hat-trick of tries; strange that of the three major overseas recruits it was the former Manly and Roosters flyer, who had been playing mostly NSW Cup the year before, was by then the one claiming the accolades.

After Leeds it was the turn of both Wigan and Warrington to claim the spoils in France, with the turgid away form persisting, Guasch wasn't content. They had a week off to re-charge their batteries before going to the improving Salford as the run-in commenced knowing now holding their 7th spot was their only goal with the Red Devils, Widnes and Hull KR all in contention. The new AJ Bell Stadium had thus far been impregnable to Catalans on earlier visits and the sequence this time didn't change either (22-34). From Red Devils to red warning lights flashing was the Dragons mode. Only superior point difference separated them from a late calamity again. With a week to ponder and reflect the club took another major decision, cutting both Pryce and Paea from the squad in the lead up to the London game.

Both had been summoned earlier at the time Webb and Fakir faced the chop back in March. After Pryce had announced his decision to leave at the end of the campaign a month or so early he said, "I've really loved my three years in France – it's been a fantastic experience. I would like to thank Catalans fans for their support and now want to finish the season in the best possible way". Maybe not too obvious but something seemed to drift away from Leon's persona and certainly Frayssinous detected it too. The separation caused an immediate rupture and, clearing his locker abruptly Leon was gone. It's a shame he didn't give himself the opportunity to say his farewells on the pitch in the way Paea was accorded at seasons end. Both had written something of the Catalans story in their time by the Mediterranean. The Hull FC bound stand-off had a fan in Frayssinous throughout his time in Perpignan even if the eventual parting was difficult. The popular Tongan Paea had his best years under Robinson but seemed to struggle afterwards following knee surgery.

Round 25 turned out to be decisive. The French side after three reverses drew a trump card with the luckless London in Perpignan for the third time in 2014. On the eve of this tussle two other ties elsewhere would start to confirm final standings. Widnes shocked high-flying Wigan on the Friday night while over on Humberside the Airlie Birds ran the 9th placed Robins ragged. The twenty-eight unanswered points there and then marked Rovers card because it gave a significant point aggregate cushion to the Dragons going into their last away fixture at Hull KR the following Sunday. A clear victory against the Broncos would more or less guarantee their qualification. Of course the Londoners arrived all-bouncing after their famous victory over Leeds; their only win of the campaign at the Hive the previous weekend. Catalans made everything safe as one expected early on with three quick fire tries and a 34-0 score at the break. The Broncos made a game of it on the return playing for pride but ultimately out-classed (46-4); while Escaré claimed his second try hat-trick of the season putting him level at the top of the try scoring charts with 24 in his first full campaign alongside Makinson and Monaghan. The war-horse that was Henderson too shared a glass of bubbly on becoming only the second overseas player to wear the sang-et-or jumper, other than Greenshields, for the 100th time.

Since Pryce's departure the tandem Williams-Bosc in the halves proved to be a winner and the Australian helped the French side to eventually come home with a tail wind in their sails.

A man of the match performance from him at Craven Park the week after in their convincing win (32-14) with two crucial tries late on. Oldfield too was finishing his first year in Perpignan all guns blazing with his third hat-trick of tries. This win was heralded as the first away success of note and sent them into the grand finale against Castleford at Brutus on the last weekend of the regular season feeling on top of the world. Above everything it vindicated the two tough decisions they felt they had to make at different stages of the season to get the necessary response. One felt that Frayssinous, under pressure throughout the year, had held his nerve not once but twice and grew subsequently in stature.

Of course Castleford came with historic intentions seeking a first ever possible top of the table finish while the locals played their *"trouble-fête"* perfectly. Catalans had been well and truly towelled at Wheldon Road back in the winter months but here with the sun on their backs they were as good as they'd been all year. The dark days well and truly behind them including that record losing streak now full of the *joie de vivre* and wanting to send the Brutus faithfull away buoyant and content on their last home appearance. In front of their sixth 9,000 plus crowd of 2014 they took the Tigers apart slowly but surely to deny the Yorkshiremen their prize (28-6) after a titanic opening half-hour nip and tuck before Escaré, who else, unlatched the door with a brace of tries before the break.

Similarities with 2009 abounded. A turbulent year under Kevin Walters, they made it to the play-offs with a victory on the very last weekend of the regular season at St Helens where they'd never won before, to land the final 8th spot. With a grand Greg Bird in-tow they charged past both Wakefield's and Huddersfield's resistance across the water in Yorkshire and onto Headingley for their first ever Semi-Final against the Rhinos, who would go on to be acclaimed Super League Champions that year. Leeds would be there again in 2014 but this time finals football from the off.

STAR GAME 2014 SUPER LEAGUE XIX PLAY OFF 1 LEEDS RHINOS at Headingley on Saturday 20th September

The local rag *L'Indépendant* screamed it loud, "HISTORIQUE!" on its front page of their Sunday edition 21st September 2014. Leeds and Headingley had been the bench mark for the French club since their entry in 2006. The Rhinos had ruled the roost after all since nearly a decade with those five Grand Final victories and four Wembley visits. Catalans had taken some hammerings certainly in the early years 58-10, 60-12, 54-8 and 53-6 amongst them with the win-loss deficit still monstrous at 4-17. Headingley was the very last bastion to be conquered. They got incredibly close in late June in Round 18. But, but they were not going to be denied this time. Their defining Headingley moment had come at last.

Assistant coach Guisset echoed the words of Robinson in the build up," That to beat Leeds you had to achieve four things: To block their speed, block their space, block their off-loads and block their kicking game".

Leeds, after their Challenge Cup success had backed pedalled but on their last appearance at Headingley, had pushed St Helens all the way playing with 12 men. They were still eyeing a first ever Cup and Super League double. The Dragons arrived with a bit of form behind them and lots of desire. 14-6 behind at the break and all to do. Two of their stalwarts in their campaign's transformation Taia and Anderson played important roles here with a try apiece. The latter converted to the front row powered through leaving Hardaker in a heap to put them in the lead for the first time just before the hour mark. The Rhinos roared back however with a response from Jones-Buchanan and at 20-18 the locals though they'd done enough.

The stroke of luck denied them on the 29th June this time turned their way dramatically with virtually seconds remaining. Hardaker seemed to have done the right thing clearing his line and getting back into the field of play only for Sinfield's pass to the wing Briscoe to incredibly go astray and the hero of the hour for the visitors Williams to swoop, gather and dive over for the winning score with the sounds of "Catalans!, Catalans!" descending down from the main stand from a small band of supporters, who had travelled over on the chartered flight with the team, ecstatic.

An elated Bernard Guasch responded, "This team is magnificent; entering into history. They have beaten a grand Leeds today, beaten also Mr Bentham the referee and the public. It has been necessary to be very courageous, very solid and they needed to keep a cool head for the whole 80 minutes. Leeds is the Mecca of rugby league and I'm very happy for the coach Laurent Frayssinous who has known how to impose his personality; he has known how to take difficult decisions when it was necessary in order that the group of players finally unified and became extraordinary!"

Leeds 20-24 Catalans. HT: 14-6. Weather: Overcast. Attendance: 7,000 est. Referee: Phil Bentham. For Leeds 3 tries from Ablett (16), Watkins (40) Jones-Buchanan (69) & 4 goals from Sinfield (3) & Hardaker (1). For Catalans 4 tries from Williams (25, 79). Taia (46), Anderson (57) & 4 goals from Bosc

Leeds: Hardaker, Briscoe, Watkins, Moon, Hall, McGuire, Sinfield © Leuluai, Burrow, Peacock, Jones-Buchanan, Ablett, Delaney Substitutes: Aiton, Bailey, Achurch, Sutcliffe

Catalans: Escaré, Oldfield, Pomeroy, Duport, Millard, Bosc, Williams, Elima Henderson, Anderson, Taia, Whitehead, Mounis © Substitutes: Lima Bousquet, Pelissier, Garcia

The scenes were delirious at Perpignan airport hours later with several hundred fans gathering at 1am early Sunday morning to welcome their favourites home victorious with an impromptu rendering of *'Els Segadors'*. The Dragons, if still ignored in France nationally, at least in this southern enclave the local paper led with the Catalans escapades on three successive days setting a new all time high. Guasch's mobile nearly in melt-down after the final whistle with the congratulations tumbling in and on social media over 100,000 hits on the clubs Facebook page on the post-match celebrations in the Catalan's changing rooms.

Of course Leeds, unlike 2009, was not a gateway direct to Old Trafford but to the John Smith Stadium Huddersfield and home of the Giants who the Dragons also collided with five years back in the second week of the play-offs. Huddersfield had finished in a respectful 3rd slot and had themselves turned over the Rhinos home and away in 2014. However the Giants had crumbled disastrously a week before the Dragons came calling again, 57-4 at Wigan. The French side knew from experience how difficult it was to be able to respond to crushing early losses in the play-offs losing heavily themselves at the DW Stadium to the Warriors in 2012. The big issue in this quarter-final tie was centred on Danny Brough's availability having missed the shellacking across the Pennines. The Catalans had only lost once in the first week of the play-offs – that away at Hull FC the year before – in six attempts. Strangely in the years they were best placed, they didn't deliver whereas their best effort to date had been in Kevin Walter's debut season nearly making the holy grail from last place.

Well, the news for Giants fans was promising, with their talisman Brough back in harness for the eliminating tie while the few niggling injury worries for the Dragons dissipated. Live wire hooker Pelissier would become the tenth Frenchman and the youngest to play his 100th game in the Dragons shirt. The first major hurdle to get over was whether the match would indeed take place. Some major electrical malfunction had completely immobilised two of the four giant floodlight pylons. The pressures were on for the officials to do everything to get the fixture played recognising the time constraints. The lighting affected one of the major stands too so everyone present was ushered into one area. It was decided to press on utilising the two functioning pylons and just hoped that things could only improve. They managed the first quarter in less than perfecting conditions before normal service was resumed.

By the time the engineers had put things in order it was a try a piece from opposing wingers Broughton and Millard. It was locked 10-10 at the break. The second period absorbing with nothing taken or given as the two slogged it out. It wasn't pretty but tight as a drum. Robinson's try from Brough's little dink had the home faithful hoping. The visitors looked out on their legs at times but somehow mustered one last charge to turn it around. Bosc's delicate punt to the corner saw Oldfield palm the ball back to Whitehead who's basketball type flick put lurking Pomeroy over in the corner for the clincher (18-16). There was till more than 10 minutes left and it took a mighty rearguard action to keep a lid on it. Anderson mentioned in dispatches heroic in the call of duty arrived on the eve of the match after staying back in Perpignan for the birth of his fifth child. Escaré's cameo piece at the death to diffuse Brough's kick and deny the Giants territory and possession timely and crucial showing awareness and composure was significant – a class act.

You'd have thought St Helens a week later to be more accommodating! After all, courtesy of the last weekend demolition of Castleford by the Dragons in the regular season, had handed the Lancastrians the League Leaders Shield without lifting a finger. The same said Tigers who had suffered the ignominy of a crushing defeat 41-0 at Saints the week before and doing to the other West Riding outfit what the Dragons came up with at Huddersfield. Nathan Brown's lot were always going to choose Catalans in the Club Call palaver as the lowest ranked outfit still standing. The standing bit proved apt too. The French side showed desire and guts to get past the Giants but with the travelling to and fro across the Channel even with the club pulling out all the stops to ease their recuperation it was going to be a tall order. With just the one training session in between the two games the Dragons had to hope lady luck would come calling to give them either the right bounce of the ball or/and the fifty-fifty refereeing decisions going their way to stand a chance. The miracle just didn't happen for them (12-30). Took a sucker punch try going into the break to give the hosts a one score cushion; but energy was draining them and a couple of tries around the hour sealed their fate. Heads still held high at the end; they'd given everything they had.

The curtain had come down on one of the most eventful episodes in the clubs young history. From near oblivion to the *"remparts"* of the Theatre of Dreams all in the course of a few fascinating months. They had arrested the perceived decline of the Robinson legacy finishing in the same position as the year before 7th but more impressively finished with all guns blazing in the play-offs something even the Australian failed to achieve. What was bizarre was the inability to succeed on their travels in the regular season. You'd have thought the effort the club had made to ease their travels arrangements would have paid off; maybe cosseted too much! Only the proverbial doomed duo Bradford and London had conceded, otherwise it was only on the penultimate weekend of the campaign when they won on the road at Hull KR did they register their third victory. In a season where they equalled their best ever results in France with 11 wins – same as Trent Robinson's best year when they finished in the Top 4 – they registered their 2nd worst away results; identical to that in Kevin Walters calamitous 2010 when they finished bottom of the pile.

If the defence was thought as their Achilles heel the offence was second to none; in fact their 132 try haul had only once in nine campaigns been bettered, the 142 in Robinson's last season. Key to that collection was the confirmation and the upward trajectory of Escaré after a dazzling debut the year before. The lad from Salses is in many ways a real throw back to days gone by when France confounded the wider rugby world – both codes – with little light-footed guys playing with panache and élan. In his first full year in the sang-et-or he would set a new club try scoring record of 29 tries taking over from the previous incumbent Australian wing flyer Justin Murphy in the club's debutant year.

The young full-back thought wasn't alone ably abetted by wing Oldfield who got better and better as the season unfolded as well as the former Bradford back-rower Whitehead's blooming form which brought him 19 tries; the best in the competition for a forward. This trio with 70 tries between them was in many ways what 2014 was mostly all about. The other was the growing in stature of French coach Frayssinous who had been tested to the limits in his second year in charge at Stade Gilbert Brutus but had come through the fire intact and strengthened.

The doyen of league writers Dave Hadfield summed up the Catalans latest edition, "Well the departing David Waite has just told me that the Dragons are 'only going to get stronger' and if so a strong Catalans makes the competition that much more convincing". Amen to that.

( ) Denotes Challenge Cup game

2014 FIXTURES	ROUND	DATE	VENUE	RESULT	ATT
HULL FC	R1	14/02	KC STADIUM	L 34-36	
CASTLEFORD	R2	23/02	WHELDON ROAD	L 6-32	
LEEDS	R3	28/02	GILBERT BRUTUS	L 12-40	8,500
WAKEFIELD	R4	09/03	BELLE VUE	L 14-56	
ST HELENS	R5	14/03	LANGTREE PARK	L 22-40	
HUDDERSFIELD	R6	22/03	GILBERT BRUTUS	W 30-14	6,150
WIGAN	R7	28/03	DW STADIUM	L 16-22	
LONDON	CC4	04/04	GILBERT BRUTUS	W 40-24	(3,834)
WIDNES	R8	12/04	GILBERT BRUTUS	W 42-20	9,588
LONDON	R9	17/04	THE HIVE	W 28-22	
HULL KR	R10	21/04	GILBERT BRUTUS	W 37-24	9,863
BRADFORD	CC5	27/04	ODSAL	L 20-33	
SALFORD	R11	03/05	GILBERT BRUTUS	W 37-24	7,862
WARRINGTON	R12	09/05	HJ STADIUM	L 10-42	
LONDON	R13	17/05	ETIHAD STADIUM	W 24-22	
BRADFORD	R14	24/05	GILBERT BRUTUS	W 46-4	6,438
WIDNES	R15	30/05	HALTON STADIUM	D 26-26	
ST HELENS	R16	14/06	GILBERT BRUTUS	W 42-0	9,864
HULL FC	R17	21/06	GILBERT BRUTUS	W 20-16	9,000
LEEDS	R18	29/06	HEADINGLEY	L 31-32	
BRADFORD	R19	06/07	ODSAL STADIUM	W 32-30	
WIGAN	R20	12/07	GILBERT BRUTUS	L 16-37	9,505
WAKEFIELD	R21	19/07	GILBERT BRUTUS	W 40-6	8,256
HUDDERSFIELD	R22	27/07	JS STADIUM	L 16-38	
WARRINGTON	R23	01/08	GILBERT BRUTUS	L 24-26	7,858
SALFORD	R24	15/08	BARTON STADIUM	L 22-34	
LONDON	R25	30/08	GILBERT BRUTUS	W 46-4	7,076
HULL KR	R26	07/09	NEW CRAVEN PARK	W 32-14	
CASTLEFORD	R27	13/09	GILBERT BRUTUS	W 28-6	9,223
LEEDS	PO1	20/09	HEADINGLEY	W 24-20	
HUDDERSFIELD	PO2	26/09	JS STADIUM	W 18-16	
ST HELENS	SF	02/10	LANGTREE PARK	L 12-30	
				Total	109,543

Regular season median : 8,500

SUPER LEAGUE: P27 W14 D1 L12 PTS29 PF733 PA667 POS. 7TH
CHALLENGE CUP: P2 W1 L1
PLAY-OFFS: P3 W2 L1

2014	GAMES	TRIES	GOALS	POINTS
WEBB	2			
ESCARE	32	29	1 (1dg)	119
PRYCE	25	5		20
POMPEROY	29	7		28
OLDFIELD	31	22		88
BOSC	21	2	83 (1 dg)	175
DUREAU	1		1	2
ELIMA	22	1		4
HENDERSON	18	3		12
LIMA	25	1		4
TAIA	32	12		48
ANDERSON	23	5		20
MOUNIS	19	2		8
BARTHAU	6	1	12	28
MARIA	10	1		4
PELISSIER	30	4	(1 dg)	17
WHITEHEAD	28	19		76
MILLARD	25	13		52
PALA	6			
SIMON	12	1		4
BOUSQUET	19	1		4
FAKIR	3			
PAEA	23			
BAITIERI	23			
DUPORT	22	11		44
CARDACE	4	4		16
BAILE	7	1		4
VACCARI	3			
GARCIA	22	2		8
SPRINGER	1			
J GUASCH	6			
MARGALET	1			
WILLIAMS	12	4	21	58

(33)

Chapter 11

– WILL CARNEY PLAY –

The club would celebrate its 10th anniversary in 2015 and wanted to do it style. After their semi-final finish the year before, expectations had soared especially when it was revealed that the Australian prodigy Todd Carney had signed a three year contract. The former Kangaroo and Dally M Medal winner was considered the Catalan's biggest ever capture even if he had some off the field issues as part of his baggage. Stacey Jones and Steve Menzies had graced the club with their presence but both had had their best years behind them by the time they landed beside the Mediterranean. Carney at 28 years old was considered at his peak and more particularly a genuine world class stand-off which the club had never had.

With Rémi Casty returning after his sojourn in Australia with the Sydney Roosters, and another former Kangaroo in centre Willie Tonga also on board, the club believed now they had assembled their strongest squad since they arrived on the scene in 2006. Reaching either Wembley or Old Trafford was now in their sights. The bookies still had them at 11/1 behind Wigan and St Helens for the Grand Final, but had Carney down already as favourite for the Man of Steel!

A fourth arrival was a change in the coach staff with the appointment of the recently retired Warrington hooker Michael Monaghan as one of the two assistants to Laurent Frayssinous, following the return home of the incumbent David Waite after loyal and valued service – in two stints – in Perpignan. Frayssinous was keen to secure the Australian Monaghan because of his recent playing experience.

To make way for the newcomers the club let go ten players from the original 2014 squad. Webb and Fakir had departed early, followed later by Pryce and Paea in that infamous second purge. Millard was keen to stay but the overseas quota was full and he would go on to join South Sydney. Interestingly, of the French lads who left, three landed professional contracts across the Channel with Barthau joining London Broncos, Baile went to Bradford and Simon to Wakefield. It was surprising the number of changes Frayssinous sought. Since Robinson's term, the French coach had secured two 7th placed rankings. Mick Potter put the brush through them after that first year and bottom place when fourteen moved on and after Walter's calamitous second season and bottom of the pile again in 2010, a dozen were let go. The perception around Brutus was the club was maturing and expectations rising. The club off the field was improving with the success of the newly named Puig Aubert stand behind the posts with its bars and boutique generating extra income.

Co-captain Greg Mounis the boy from Baixas approaching his 30th birthday with more than 230 appearances to his name, had seen it all from the very start, "The first match versus Wigan, the final of the Cup in 2007 and landing that qualification at Leeds." In reference to the play-off success at Headingley the previous September, "My adversaries respect me. They know what type of player I am. Since I started playing as a boy I always wanted to make the game my job and become a professional – what better for a Catalan club *de cœur*!"

"I remember it as if it was yesterday. We were so excited to be able to tangle with the best in Europe. And then there had been this victory (Wigan) and this immense joy. Yes after we took some right thrashings, the season had been long and difficult but a group had been born after this first season. We finished last but we had learnt".

"We started training first at St Estève – it was epic! It's incredible when I think back there, all these changes; this evolution in the club and in the mentalities. We have the level of infrastructures and management equal with the Top 4 of Super League. We have nothing to envy of the others now."

Finishing in the play-offs places was now the expectation year on year. Since 2008 they had only missed out once and further had reached the semi-final stages on two occasions. The bar was being raised consistently. Whereas the first five years proved spectacular with that Wembley appearance in year two followed by a 3rd place finish the year following they were, as an organisation on and off the field, still very fragile as 2010 would prove.

By the time Frayssinous had taken over, the club had moved on appreciably, and why the French coach was under pressure from the off. Finishing in the top half of the competition was now a given; the key now was to challenge for a Top 4 place amongst the best. These development's encouraged Frayssinous to put the pressure on local players at the Dragons to push on or move out. That's what he appeared to be doing after 2014 knowing that the much awaited U19s Academy was going to become a reality. He would announce the smallest Super League squad of just 23 players going into their tenth campaign so as to keep his options open and everybody on their toes. The club's "Dream Together" catch phrase caught the mood. The stakes stacked high as the Dragons locally sought to become sports "standard-bearer" for Perpignan and Roussillon ahead of USAP, unimaginable when Guasch had had that birthday 'Do' as the century turned.

If Carney's arrival had been the really big headline story around Roussillon possibly in tandem could be included the news of the formation of an U19s Academy side which would play against other Super League formations starting from 2015. The first year would be a dummy run playing up to 15 friendly fixtures with the majority across the Channel and full integration into the system the following year. Bernard Guasch had invited both Leeds and Wigan over in 2014 for a one-off triangular U19s tournament pre-season and was envious of what the top clubs in Super League were producing regarding young local talent. The announcement that the Dragons were looking to annually spend up to £500,000 over the next five years to develop their youth strategy was a revelation. To follow on would be an U16s Academy and a developing coach education programme to raise the levels across all the schools of rugby from primary level upwards across the region.

It's been evident for some time that the quality of the young French players has been on the rise, most notably with the arrival on the scene of the likes of Morgan Escaré. The full-back was developed through the St Estève set-up which had been progressing all the time from its inception back in 2006. Even taking into account the lowering of standards across the French competition, it was still impressive to see how a young all-French side with an average age of not much more than 21 years, could more than hold its own against other more experienced formations including overseas players. It would have been inconceivable a decade back.

Pre-season preparation had its best start aided by a tranche of the best French players, for the first time, giving the Tricolours autumn programme a miss. Elima decided to retire from the international scene and the others to decline invitations were Escaré, Bosc, Mounis, Casty and Duport. Freshness would be a point of order with a thirty game Super League schedule announced. Frayssinous wanted certainly a better start than the previous one and would be helped by a kinder programming with three games consecutively at home early on – the inverse of the year before.

Those initial run-outs though always come with a proviso. Nothing ever runs completely smoothly with a hitch in cold windy weather even in the South of France. Carney, who earlier had been welcomed by the most attended press conference ever seen at Brutus, with London based Australian journalists travelling over and followed by the first training run-out in front of several hundred captivated fans, was one of the first sufferers with muscle pulls and strains. A sign of things to come.

The coach couldn't secure any Super League home opposition for their regular two pre-season run-outs having to be satisfied with the demoted London Broncos and more interestingly a French Selection up at Carcassonne on the last two weekends of January. The Aude area just north of Perpignan with its three semi-professional set ups in the French competition put together a joint initiative under the Chevaliers Cathares banner. Before that the Broncos not for the first time willing opponents pre-season.

Referee Tim Roby was in charge as he would be for the Cathares game too spending a week in the Dragons camp observing and ironing out any rule changes and interpretations. Both first choice half-backs Carney and Dureau gave this one a miss with Frayssinous giving a group of 19 a first gallop. The Londoners looked in better shape than they did the year before and gave Catalans a decent opposition going down (32-16). Seven days later on a bitterly cold day at Stade Domec in Carcassonne a crowd of over 5,000 turned up to see Carney make his entrance against the regional selection. The newcomer didn't disappoint with a couple of tries and several assists before departing after an hour. The part-timers of this new entity didn't embarrass themselves either in the loss (58-24) in what was a thoroughly enjoyable occasion despite the inclement weather.

All attention was now turned to the Super League season opener at Langtree Park less than two weeks away – a repeat of last years play-off semi-final defeat on the same ground. Having assembled your possible best ever squad to celebrate your tenth year is one thing but getting them all available and fighting fit is another. The gremlins were already on the prowl that first weekend of February with snow in the air. Both first choice half-backs would disappointingly miss this opening rendezvous with leg injuries. Ian Henderson moved back from hooker to scrum half partnering Thomas Bosc in a patched-up combination. The opening salvos couldn't possibly have been more problematic. Inside one minute the Australian debutant in the centres Tonga was being carried off on a stretcher having got his head on the wrong side of opposition prop Walmsley on the very first collision. Fortunately for the former Kangaroo the injury wasn't serious but he would play no further part in this opener.

Within minutes it got worse when Bosc, the only genuine half-back fielded took a high shot and left the scene momentarily. Against all the odds against the reigning champions, Bosc returned and struck a sweet one-pointer with last action of the first period, to give his side the narrowest of leads with a score line of 7-6. Saints had taken an early lead with a converted score before Eloi Pelissier found some space around the play-the-ball after the locals conceded a succession of penalties to bring the foes level. It was encouragingly a more than decent opening half considering their mishaps. After the break though the hosts were too strong as the French side struggled to hold the line with the title holders adding a further three unconverted tries in an opening day defeat (7-18) for the visitors. Some distress left in the wind after this one with the returning Casty breaking a bone in his hand. Earlier a bit of history was in the making when Catalans U19s Academy made their first ever sortie losing 4-26 in the curtain raiser with Carpentras's Arthur Romano scoring their first ever try.

Castleford would have the honour of opening the show at Brutus the following Saturday, highly motivated, after the Dragons had spoiled their party on the last day of the regular season the previous September denying the Tigers that historic top of the pile finish. There was a lot of feeling here, delivering a real gladiatorial contest in the best coliseum tradition, with Brutus as a back drop keeping referee James Child on his toes throughout. As things got heated the whistler distributed his retribution with three yellow cards with a double for the home side in Elima and Pelissier. 11 v 12 was tough but the locals would hold their nerve after the bulldozer wing Carney got the visitors off to a flyer with a fine try, while his name sake Todd was still in civvies high in the grandstand watching on unfortunately.

On the plus side though was that Dureau would play his first game back on home terra firma since 2013. His *'annus horribilis'* had started at Castleford twelve months before with that ruptured bicep injury. He was keen here to make up for lost time with a man of the match performance reminding us of pomp years 2011-12 with his unique double Dream Team nominations. He took some contentious heavy treatment too from Tigers defenders but came through with flying colours creating both the Catalans tries in the second period for Escaré with an exquisite reverse kick and the try scoring pass for Elliott Whitehead to edge his side in front. The score would have had more of a taste if the man of the moment Dureau hadn't had a try wiped out by the video official after an interception, brushing the side line by centimetres after a 60 metre race. It was a nervy finish though as the Tigers responded well with an equalising score of their own before 'Biscuit', as the popular scrum half is known, sealed it with a late drop goal (13-12).

The Dragons felt aggrieved only responding to perceived aggressive play from their opponents. But the disciplinary committee hadn't seen it that way and not for the first time. The Dragons duo of Elima and Pelissier would have to sit out three matches between them for their indiscretions. After such an abrasive entrée having the following week off was no bad thing with the new expanded World Club Challenge taking centre stage. Warrington next up at Brutus on the last weekend of February would offer up a major challenge and more so after their more-than-honourable narrow loss to the down under Dragons of St George Illawarra a week earlier.

The really big news around this Round 3 affair was the grand debut of Carney at last after his recurring leg muscle problems. It couldn't have been a better opener for him regaling the expectant crowd with all his talent. Leading, cajoling, he was everywhere and distributing with precision. 18-0 at the break said it all. The old Wire, back in the frame as a champion side would be, registered two converted tries early in the second period before the Dragons finally killed them off with a Zeb Taia double, his second coming from Carney's break out and putting the Cook Islands skipper sailing between the posts unhindered. A reference performance against one of the leaders of the pack (36-18) and the first time the primrose and blue had conceded to Catalans in nearly three years and a first for coach Frayssinous since his time on the bridge. Regarding Carney the coach enthused, "The best is yet to come. I haven't any doubt about his capacity to create something individually. But the positive from this afternoon comes from him influencing the combinations around him with dexterity and security."

The French coach wasn't getting carried away reminding his charges the Dragons can often get themselves up for the big matches but then stumble in front of the minnows. Salford would be the third game on the bounce in Perpignan and the locals really wanted to finish this opening home tranche on the front with a third success. The Red Devils though with Rangi Chase would always offer a challenge of weight. Salford aspirations rising by the season under their dynamic patron Dr Koukash looked up for it from the intensity of the pre-match warm up and one wasn't misplaced at all by their intentions as they grabbed the locals by the throat and shook them. 22-0 it was as the hosts caved in by quarter time! Like the proverbial rabbit in the cars headlights – frozen. Shaken the Dragons lifted themselves from their slumber and fortunately got themselves back into it by the break with three converted tries.

In one of the crazies encounters in the Catalans story so far as another 40 plus points were racked up after the turn-round with defences now a peripheral option. Amazingly, the locals got themselves in front for the first time swopping tries by the score with less than ten minutes on the clock. They even got a seventh try from Henderson to give them a two score cushion at 40-32 but it still wasn't enough as the Red Devils grabbed a late converted try. All the hosts had to do was clean up an-up-and-under close to their own posts, which little Escaré performed admirably with the final siren just seconds away.

Yet this game still had a sting in its tail when referee Phil Bentham surprisingly penalised the full-back for not playing the ball, believing the tackle had been completed. Salford kicked the penalty to tie it (40-40)! The normal rational and temperate Frayssinous stormed on to the pitch to confront the official believing his side had had a point stolen illegitimately by Bentham's decision. The coach would be fined £500 half of which suspended till the end of the season for his actions. In the days to follow former RFL refereeing boss Stuart Cummings believed that the official in this instant had called it wrong. His view was that the Salford player who had brought Escaré to the ground didn't have hold of the player, so the tackle was not completed. For Catalans this certainly felt like a point lost and on top of this discontent they lost Carney late on with a cracked rib from a tackle they believed to be both late and from behind.

Still, the five competition points picked up early, represented an adequate debut and something to build upon as their Humberside tour loomed in view. A week stay-over culminating with games against the Robins and the Airlie Birds was programmed. The initial injury prognosis for Carney was possibly a month side lined while the news was better concerning co-skipper Casty getting the green light for the New Craven Park bash. Hull KR had recruited strongly in Australia in the close season with some choice recruits in Campese, Kelly and Blair. Rovers had turned over Wigan in their last home game and a week before had been more than credible, running Warrington away close.

The French side though had an excellent record in East Hull with their last loss there way back in 2010. Bosc would replace Carney, while as well as Casty returning, Pelissier was back after his suspension. Everything seemed to be going swimmingly well with Tonga scoring a try in the first minute to be followed by three more and a score line of 20-4 heading for the break. The Robins did though through Cockayne pull six points back on the siren giving them a sniff to get back into it. What unfolded couldn't have been imagined! Forty points without a single response was the verdict as the Dragons imploded with seven tries conceded at a point a minute leaving them colossally adrift at the conclusion (20-50).

The softness, defensively as against Salford earlier, reared its ugly head once more. Fortunately they didn't have to return home to face the music. Together as a group they could mull over their shortcomings and try and get themselves sorted before heading west across the city the following Friday and Hull FC with a certain Leon Pryce on board. Frayssinous livid with their comportment against the Robins wanted if nothing else a whole-hearted effort from everyone against the struggling Airlie Birds then languishing in bottom place. The big surprise selection-wise was the rapid response from Carney to get himself to the starting gate, probably all strapped up around his middle. The coach couldn't hide from the primordial role he had bestowed on the Australian play-maker from the start of the campaign.

Alas it went worryingly wrong virtually from the off as the star signing hobbled off on the half hour mark clutching his leg again. As the week before, they drew first blood with a Duport try but then fell away all too easily conceding four unanswered tries before the break. The effort seemed to be there this time but not the execution especially once again completing a match with only one play-maker making it to the end. Taia as his way, never a backward step, earned a last minute try but they weren't really in it, permitting the hosts to rise off the bottom (22-33).

It had been a dispiriting stay across the Channel and hardly a way of preparing to tangle with the runaway leaders Leeds at Brutus a week later and worse was the news that not only Carney would be missing again but Oldfield too, with Duport picking up a serious shoulder injury which would see his 2015 term terminated, all too prematurely. Behind the scrum was increasingly looking thread bare now. The best bit, of news from the stay beside the North Sea was the first ever success of the Academy U19s against their Hull FC counterparts (46-20).

An inform Leeds side with pace to burn would offer a monumental challenge eight days later in Perpignan against a stuttering Dragons outfit struggling to get their best side out. They would be smarting too remembering the famous win the French had had at Headingley back in September which dumped the Rhino's out of the play-offs. The first half was nip and tuck with the Yorkshire side just edging it with Ward's try just before the break. Then a real 13 minute purple patch for the sang-et-or from the restart with three tries registered. Whitehead got his second score from Bousquet's exquisitely timed pass, quickly followed by Pelissier and then Cardace from Pomeroy's delicate flip.

Suddenly up by two scores and time to consolidate with cool heads. Instead they showed the complete opposite. Direct from the kick restart prop Lima somehow got himself bundled into touch and from that cheap possession conceded Leeds were under the posts just moments latter. This error compounded by Dureau's kick re-start sailing out on the full and Leeds through a Hall and McGuire combination saw the latter stroll over by the uprights and the sides were tied just 5 minutes after the hosts had got a real foothold in the contest. Catalans still had time and opportunities but were far too impatient in pushing passes and losing possession. They lost the plot alarmingly and the

Rhino's came home with wind in their sails (22-38), sending them top and the Dragons in the opposite direction down from fourth to 10th in the log jam mid-table. Again solace elsewhere as the Academy U19s hosting for the first time the redoubtable Leeds youngsters showed their potential, going down by just a few points 28-35. Notably in the Super League game played after this curtain raiser that three of the visitor's tries came from Ward, Singleton and Sutcliffe all who had progressed from their youth programme in recent times and why the French intend in time to hope to follow that same path.

The promising start in 2015 looked already a distant memory after a winless March. However with Easter beckoning and spring time around the corner a reawakening was hoped for especially with Wakefield and Widnes next up all in the space of five days. Maundy Thursday and a Trinity side in crisis would surely provide a first win away win across the Channel since the previous September. If not the Catalans could well be rock bottom and any high fluting ideas of silverware later merely candy floss. It had to start in the engine room with the prop forwards imposing and enforcing. The blokes touching the ball the most just weren't advancing enough – against Leeds none of them recording a100 metres gained.

Trinity at Belle Vue had caused heartache the year before but in 2015 going backwards at a great rate of knots after a promising opening were an offering just at the right moment for the Dragons. There was a hint that Wakefield were targeting the French sides visit though and had rested key players a week earlier at Wigan where they took a 50 point hammering. It didn't accrue though as Catalans romped it (40-4) their best ever result at the old stadium with the game gone by the break with already four unanswered tries registered augmented later by a hat-trick from Cardace. Stanislav Robin originally from Villeneuve-sur-Lot became the 94th Catalans player to debut for the club here and the fiftieth Frenchmen to do so filling in for Escaré who copped a one match suspension following the Rhinos game.

Widnes arrived Easter Monday buoyed hugely by their success over arch rivals Warrington down in Lowerhouse Lane earlier. Coach Betts was happy to leave out players of note ahead of a Thursday game four days later. The sizeable Chemics contingent who had made the trip over was already in party mood and would be well satisfied with what unfolded. The holiday fixture attracted the best turn out of the year so far helped as usual by the hundreds of children from the annual rugby festival earlier in the day. An average of 9,075 had attended the first five home fixtures, the best ever recorded for that time of the year. The winter months are less popular for visiting fans and French support can be compromised with the local competition still ongoing.

It was sealed by the Dragons as a contest in the first ten minutes with three converted tries. After the loss of Pomeroy with a knock to the head the hosts seemed to settle for conservation. The second period pretty even with two tries each as both camps content with the proceeds as the game meandered to its conclusion (32-16), the best result by Widnes in Perpignan and light years from their debut back in 2012. Maximum points then taken from the holiday jaunts with a 6th place on the competition ladder when 12th spot was a possibility at the start of the week. Seeing the Dragons joining the then top four placed sides Leeds St Helens, Salford and Hull KR as the only teams successful in both holiday games perked them up for the immediately major challenges ahead starting with Wigan away.

Losing the injured Pomeroy on top of Duport reduced their options in the centres with Whitehead dropping back to plug the hole wasn't the best preparation against the cherry and whites on what would be a damp and rainy day in Lancashire. Wane's side redoubtable and so far unbeaten at the DW Stadium won in a canter and Catalans never remotely threatened (0-34).

The French side didn't really get off the bus or plane in this one. If Hampshire had had his kicking boots on it would have been a massacre as the home side gorged on eight unanswered tries. In the decade of Catalans if Leeds had been their bête noire east of the Pennines, over the top, Wigan ruled supreme handing out a fair bit of sorrow with 0-30, 0-58, 0-44 and 0-38 score lines on top of the latest zero.

The second weekend of April would see the club take a few hits. After the Wigan no-show their reserve team St Estève lost to Lézignan in the final of the Lord Derby Cup Final in Carcassonne (25-27) in front of 4,124 spectators and shown live by the public France 3 Television. Additionally it was announced that Whitehead would not be renewing his contract with the club and after three years in Roussillon would be seeking pastures anew in 2016 down under with Canberra in the NRL. He would be missed.

Coach Frayssinous wasn't happy after Wigan; "There are some players who give and have a hunger of winning and others who say they want to win. There's a difference". Huddersfield the following Sunday in Yorkshire would mark the end of the first phase of the competition with the Giants their last opponents before the return fixtures commenced. The claret and gold at home had only once ever offered themselves up against Catalans in the regular season (8 wins-1loss) whereas the play-offs against the Giants were a different kettle of fish. A subdued Escaré was left out for the first time for this one with Robin again deputising. The first twenty was close, a converted try apiece, but after the Dragons resistance melted away quickly finding it difficult to contain Brough's kicking game with three tries in the last ten minutes of the half, the key. Tonga's sin-binning didn't help matters as the hosts capitalised on it after the hour mark with a couple of tries bringing it to seven conceded in total which now seemed to be the norm on their travels. The loss (14-38) saw them yo-yo back to 10th on the ladder exactly where they were before Easter.

At the half way stage of the first phase of the 2015 campaign Catalans found themselves in a hard place and far from their pre-season aspirations with just four wins and Carney only featuring in three of the games thus far. The Robins of Hull KR would come to Perpignan on the last weekend of April after having torn the French side apart at New Craven Park earlier in what was a seminal moment of the year. A twenty point lead whittled away and half a century of unanswered points conceded. Frayssinous decided to forego his earlier selections of firstly Whitehead and then Taia plugging the hole left by the still absent Pomeroy in the centres. Gadwin Springer a young French forward who had been outstanding in the recent French Cup Final would make his home debut while wing Fouad Yaha would become the first ever player to be promoted from the newly formed Academy set-up, and at 18 years and six months the youngest player to feature for the club. Yaha a big powerful teenager from the Avignon area has some pedigree too in that his uncle appeared for Paris St Germain in the Super League twenty years earlier.

Carney appearing again after his month out of action was still troubled by his hamstring problems following his cracked ribs against Salford. He was obviously still not the player who turned out so impressively against Warrington on his debut and played well within himself against Hull KR, easing team mates into space and distributing passes cleverly. It turned out to be a less than convincing win (32-24) with the visitors very much in the contest up to the break with on loan Catalans French international second-rower Larroyer much in view; a good contribution though from a quartet of young French forwards in Pelissier, Garcia, Bousquet and Springer with the latter scoring his first ever try in the sang-et-or.

The month of May though always looked like it would determine the Dragons season with St Helens and Wigan crossing the Channel and well-placed Huddersfield to be met at Newcastles's St James Park in the Magic weekend. First up though would be at the revitalised Castleford at Wheldon Road where the French side had an average record with three wins and a draw on their eight previous visits. It was a milestone day too for Catalans third musketeer Thomas Bosc, celebrating his 200th game in the sang-et-or following in turn from the other two locals Mounis and Casty, with all three having been there from day one of this glorious adventure. Alas it wouldn't smile on the amiable utility back filling in for Carney yet again unavailable. A horrible opening half saw them twenty points down before Yaha gave them some hope just before the break with his first ever try at this level. Garcia who finished up in the centres claimed an impressive hat-trick of tries in the second period and if Escaré hadn't flunked his pass to unmarked Taia late on, maybe the loss (28-33) could have been avoided.

Reining champions St Helens would be formidable opponents six days later and everybody behind the scenes was working hard to get Carney back on the pitch in time. It was now or never for the Dragons if they really wanted to confirm their pre-season aspirations of reaching Old Trafford or Wembley to celebrate their tenth year. Frayssinous's side had been combative at Langtree Park in the cold of February battling against the odds. A perfect spring like day presented itself and delivered a near perfect timely result (33-26) for the French side lifting their moral to the heavens. *"Même quand Carney boite (he limps), tout va!,"* summed it all up.

Yes Carney was present but hardly on one leg and never threatening to take on the defensive line. However his leadership and ball distribution were nigh-on perfect. It didn't start well with the Lancastrians over in the opening minute but Garcia continued where he left off the week before claiming a brace of tries. Saints edged it by the break a goal difference. Escaré a sumptuous score scorching away freed by Carney's deft inside ball put them in front but the visitors wouldn't relinquish with the wing Swift flying and a fourth individual try. Everybody on their feet for a grandstand finish delivered perfectly by Taia for the locals slaloming away from a clutch of St Helens defenders to register a famous victory confirmed with Dureau's last second drop goal.

Featherstone in the Challenge Cup 5th round would be next up at Brutus and the third time the sides had be drawn against each other in the knockout competition. Rovers had been well beaten in Perpignan back in 2007 when the

Zeb Taia on song again with a devastating finish against St Helens at Brutus skipping past four defenders in the process, to win the match. The Australian born Cook Islander, an unheralded signing from Newcastle Knights became simply one of their best ever signings. Consistent performer of the highest order with 37 tries from 81 games. Merited his Super League Dream Team nomination in 2015.

Dragons against all the odds went on to claim a Wembley Final place in only their second year of existence. The Yorkshire side this time round though a much stronger Championship set-up than the earlier edition even if half of them stayed at home. It turned into a bizarre, underwhelming spectacle with the Catalans claiming their quarter-final place by the narrowest of margins (37-34), when for big parts of the contest, looked decidedly second best with Lima sent-off for a high tackle on the only Catalan in blue and white, Marginet.

STAR GAME 2015 SUPER LEAGUE XX ROUND 15 WIGAN WARRIORS at Stade Gilbert Brutus on Saturday 23rd May

A sole victory in nine encounters against the cherry and whites including a right 34-0 thumping at the DW Stadium earlier was part of the pretext leading into this game. Heckles were further raised by a comment coach Shaun Wane made about the Dragons not succeeding away from home which irked Frayssinous somewhat.

The visit of Wigan though in their 10th season was dripping with resonance. The Lancashire giants had even played in Perpignan at Aimé-Giral against the UTC before that momentous Super League opening back in February 2006. Only a year later another momentous happening with the new boys from across the Channel dumped Wigan out of the Challenge Cup in the Semi Final at Warrington. When Catalans wanted to impress up in the regional capital at Montpellier it was Wigan who got the invite, not once, but twice.

In reality the locals had been preparing this one from the final whistle against St Helens a fortnight before. The win against Saints had put a spring back in their step. Carney with that game under his belt was better prepared and laid in wait. It was sensational stuff. "Le vrai visage (real face..) des Dragons", proudly announced L'Indépendant the morning after ten tries racked up and nearly sixty points registered with a double hat-trick of tries from Taia and the returning Gigot, a revelation in the centres after four years in the wilderness.

Carney was just fabulous on one leg and a bit but slowly getting there. His leadership and ball distribution top notch with teenage wing Yaha grabbing a brace of scores before the break from the Australian's timely interventions. 34-10 at the turn-round already and even the local support couldn't believe what was unfolding in front of their very eyes. Yes a win was hoped for but not by any means this margin. The second period was just more of the same with the visitors shell-shocked and unable to respond. Escare's little gem of a try with a pick up and chip over the top and acrobatic dive in celebration was the proverbial 'cerise sur le gateau'. The festival started long before the end with the biggest crowd of the year enraptured. Twenty minutes after the final whistle the home players had still not returned to the changing rooms.

The joy was palpable everywhere around the club and the French game after this success. The performance and result just epitomised everything Catalans believed they were capable of in 2015. If Carney could reach his full fitness and stay there in tandem with Taia all was still possible and a real lift going into the Magic weekend and the Huddersfield Giants. But without doubt this game will go down in the annals of one of the magic moments of a still young club emerging. And to cap it all on a memorable weekend the embryo U19s Academy side beat Wigan too (28-26) with the performance from a slip of a lad from Carcassonne 16 year old Lucas Albert catching everybody's attention with a try and six goals.

Catalans 58-16 Wigan. HT: 34-10. Weather: Cool and windy. Attendance: 10,423. Referee: James Childs. For Catalans 10 tries from Yaha (10,40), Gigot (15,37,70) Taia (26,33,60), Oldfield (49), Escaré (63) & 9 goals from Dureau. For Wigan 3 tries from Charnley (7), Sarginson (29), Burgess (44) & 2 goals from Smith

Catalans: Escare, Oldfield, Gigot, Tonga, Yaha, Carney, Dureau, Elima, Henderson Casty ©, Taia, Whitehead, Baitieri Substitutes: Anderson, Mounis, Pelissier Bousquet.

Wigan: Bowen, Charnley, J Tomkins, Sarginson, Burgess, Powell, Smith, Crosby McIlorum, Mossop, Bateman, Patrick, O'Loughlin © Substitutes: Williams, Tautai Sutton, Lloyd.

May had smiled on the Dragons with the exception of that below average effort at Castleford on the opening weekend which they could well have won. But the last day of the month would determine their season 2015 significantly. At the splendid St James Park in Newcastle on the Magic Weekend the Dragons would celebrate their 300th game against high-flying Huddersfield and wanted to show case their credentials in front of a crowd of 26,917.

In damp condition the opening period hadn't done anything for them, behind on the score board 10-0 and spluttering. Carney playing his third consecutive game for the first time since his arrival in Roussillon, had started slowly but suddenly exploded into life, putting the 4th ranked Giants to the sword. All his passing skills and distribution we'd seen, but not since Warrington back in March, had we seen him really taking on the defensive line. In a ten minute spell after the hour mark he turned the contest on its head with a brace of tries – his first in the sang-et-or.

His second score came after Dureau had been man-handled by McGillvary centimetres from the try line. Still ruffled by the challenge, the former Newcastle Knights player fluffed the conversion from near in front, denying his side a lead of 24-18 with less than 5 minutes to play. The miscreant McGillvary who some believe shouldn't have been still on the field for his challenge on Dureau earlier went on unbelievably to grab a try on the very last play of the game and converted from the side line by the ecstatic Brough to tie it up (22-22). It didn't end there though for the French side; in the time between scoring his second try and the last score Carney tore his pectoral muscle and had to depart dumbfounded. In all the commotion the end result was that the Dragons lost a valuable competition point against one of their close challengers but more importantly Carney would be side-lined for two months as would Tonga who played on with a broken jaw. No wonder *L'Indépendant* newspaper headlined it, *"Magie Noire!"*. The blackness didn't stop there either as Frayssinous's post-match comments slating the officiating saw him land his second £500 fine of the campaign from the RFL for his troubles.

"L'enfant terrible" didn't show up in Roussillon but Carney's problem in France was just getting out there, in one piece, on the pitch. But when he did . Watch out. He played half-cock for many of those dozen appearances but still imposed himself with his sleight of hand. He rarely ran with the ball, but when fit enough proved a handful as here on the Magiuc weekend, opening his account.

Catalans found it difficult to readdress this major mishap and it showed at Warrington the following Friday. Pomeroy was back after an absence of two months in the centre with young Robin at stand-off for Carney. The Wire had collapsed in the second half against Saints at Newcastle and were off-key in this one in a rather tepid affair. The Dragons led at the break with the rejuvenated Gigot a try scorer yet again and had missed opportunities in the second half to win it but fell away badly towards the end (18-26).

More bad news came with Oldfield's previous knee problem flaring up again; the former Maly wing, a real success in his first season in 2014 with twenty-two tries, wouldn't play for the club again. These proved turbulent times around Brutus as in the same week three young French players announced their departure. Utility back Pala who had struggled to impose himself in his five seasons at the Dragons signed for Leigh while promising forward Springer with just three Super League run outs surprisingly went to Castleford – both taking immediate effect. Garcia their rookie of the year in 2014 shocked the club with his announcement that he intended to take up a contract with Penrith in the NRL from 2016. Bernard Guasch was disappointed with the former Avignon junior's decision; allowing for the fact that the back-rower had already played Holden Cup football with Brisbane earlier. The President believed his best time to return Down-Under would have been in his mid 20s with by then an established Super League career behind him. To compensate for these losses the club quickly announced that two of their reserve team forwards – Thibaut Margalet and Ugo Perez – had signed professional contracts.

With still the sole away win at Belle Vue to their tally, home wins became even more crucial as summer came over the horizon. Flaming June would bring some respite with two home games in consecutive weekends at Brutus with Hull FC and Wakefield Trinity as visitors. The Airlie Birds were always scrappers especially in Perpignan and never easy beats. They were in form too after winning the derby game against the Robins at St James Park and turning over Widnes on their artificial pitch – no easy feat. More worryingly, they'd leap-frogged Catalans on the competition ladder, pushing the French side into the last qualifying 8th place. Somehow the locals found the wherewithall to land the win (20-14) after a really exciting struggle. Although the visitors scored first the locals were in the ascendency by the break with three unanswered tries and showed some resilience late on to withstand an Airlie Bird fight back despite seeing the mainstay Taia hobbling off with a leg injury.

The Cook Islands World Cup skipper missed out a week later when Brian Smih's revitalized Trinity side arrived. In the frantic comings and goings the former Kiwi and NRL wing Krisnan Inu landed in Perpignan after a winter spent in Paris with union Champions Stade Francais and took his place on the right flank against Wakefield. He showed up well too with a fine early try before Catalans fell back and were made to work very hard to get the result and the two points (32-12). What one certainly didn't envisage though on the third weekend of June that these 20 points secured would be the sum total for the Dragons during the first phase of the competition. Would it be enough to give them their minimum expectation for 2015 a place in the so-called Super 8s?

If doubts were already being felt internally about any possible charge to Old Trafford they still had the Challenge Cup to go at and Hull KR away, not insurmountable, especially with the Robins by then a little depleted with Campese the fulcrum of their attack out for the duration. On a grey damp Thursday evening beside the docks in East Hull the Dragons imploded in the first quarter with a pumped-up Robins believing this was their year taking a stranglehold on it with three converted tries. At 4-26 by the break the mass was about to be said. Inu continued to show his attacking prowess with a brace of tries on the return but they had left themselves too much leeway to catch up (26-32). The effort was there but not the application. The abiding memory is of a forlorn Taia, after giving his all yet again for the sang-et-or cause, huddled-up pitch side in the drizzle with an ice pack clutched to his lower leg.

The team was truly between the proverbial rock and a hard place as July dawned. Dumped out of the Cup, could they respond and get themselves out of this tail-spin and downward spiral? The news about Taia wasn't good. A confirmed fibula stress fracture which would keep him out for six weeks was a bombshell. The Dragons would go into the last month without their two best players by far in Carney and the Cook Islander. Taia since his arrival in 2013 had proved one of the top ten overseas players to have deposited their suit cases beside the Mediterranean. Up until New Craven Park he had missed only a handful of games and was an ever present last term. Casty and Mounis may wear the captain's armbands but the real leaders out there who provide the savoir faire would be sitting it out when they were most needed.

Carney in cameo mode in contrast to the durable, persistent performing Taia had proved the Catalans fulcrum around which everything turned. When they turn up together the Dragons are switched on as Wigan and others found out in 2015 but as Wakefield and Hull KR showed, devoid of their involvement, they lacked purpose and direction. July saw possibly a glimmer of hope on their travels against sides below them on the competition ladder in Salford and Widnes; the latter had never beaten the Catalans in eight match-ups and lost recently twice at home leading into this match while the Red Devils were topsy-turvy to say the least.

In both games the French side led early on by 12-0 but in both couldn't hold the route. The dramatic and gut-wrenching Cup exit seemed the last straw and what confidence was left draining swiftly away. They led Salford up till the last five minutes before former Dragons old boy Dobson picked their pocket and the two points with a converted try (14-18). It seemed only Anderson was turning up and after his try just after quarter of an hour of play they came up with zilch for the remaining hour.

On the eve of the Widnes trip another set-back with teenage wing Yaha dislocating his shoulder at the ultimate training session and was replaced by a former USAP union club junior in Jordan Sigismeau, with another debutant Lucas Albert promoted from the clubs U19s Academy set-up. The latter would be the fourth choice stand off used in 2015 and at barely 17 years old the youngest ever to wear the sang-et-or. All a bit poignant on a weekend when another Catalans player the eloquent and durable toiler co-skipper Grégory Mounis celebrated his 250th appearance in these colours too. Widnes well deserved their victory (22-29) with a couple of late consolation scores from the Dragons conveying yet another lack-lustre performance.

In the lead-up to the Widnes game the direction the club was heading would start to unfold with the announcements that the former Wigan star Pat Richards would make a surprising return to Super League by joining the Perpignan club from 2016, along with Warrington's international half-back Richie Myler. Heading out and back to Australia would be Scott Dureau after five up and down years beside the Mediterranean.

The scalp of Huddersfield in Perpignan on the last home match of the first phase would have been well savoured after the goings on from the Magic Weekend affair. There proved to be no justice, and for hardly ten minutes into this encounter the Dragons were well and truly emasculated, with Whitehead left in a heap and carried off on a stretcher unconscious and whisked off to hospital after an accidental head clash with a Giants player. Minutes later co-skipper Casty was crunched in a tackle and hobbled off with his ligaments shredded. They were game as hell and gave it their all but not enough valid troops to make the difference. They ran the 4th placed Giants right down to the wire and believed they had a raw deal from officialdom yet again on the deciding score but it was not to be (12-14). Bernard Guasch had seen enough and let fly. His tirade against perceived injustices poured forth for which he was handed a £1,000 fine from Red Hall pending an appeal.

Leeds at Headingley would bring the curtain down on the first phase of the season a week later. Fortunately for Catalans in a campaign where 'every minute counted' their qualification for the new 'Super 8s' was already assured before they left home base on the Saturday when nearest challengers Hull KR went down at St Helens the night before. Good news though was that both Tonga and Carney were declared fit and possibly Taia and Bosc too in the next week or so. The Dragons of course had broken their Headingley hoodoo a year before winning there for the first time. They wouldn't do it again (22-36) but gave a decent account of themselves in a tough encounter against the competition leaders, ahead leading into the break, but ultimately killed off by three tries conceded in a 6 minute spell around the hour mark. Gigot continued to show up with a brace of tries; the Avignon wanderer with 7 tries to his tally in just ten run-outs was having an impact whereas his early spell in Perpignan trawled just a single try in 25 appearances.

The overall sentiment around Brutus at this stage was real disappointment and under achievement remembering where their aspirations laid. However they had indeed qualified yet again to do battle with the competition big-hitters as they had done for each of the previous five years; in total they had not reached this stage only three times in their first decade. No mean achievement. In 2010 they had landed up in bottom place in the Super League after playing at Wembley two years earlier and an incredible 3rd ranking in the league the year after. By 2015 Catalans expectations had soared; that meant being with the 'big boys' year in and year out and pushing forward relentlessly. Nothing else would suffice.

Before the second phase got under way the club made real waves with the signing of the giant Queenslander Dave Taylor from the Gold Coast Titans and quickly followed by the Leeds PNG hooker Paul Aiton and Manly's Kiwi back-rower Justin Horo. All three were internationals and first-choice selections by their respective clubs. Heading out of Brutus though would be the mercurial Zeb Taia, a major loss, after an outstanding three-year term and returning to the NRL as would be the toiler Ian Henderson after a five year stint of note. The musical chairs of player movement was nearly completed with the Giants wing flyer Jodie Broughton packing his bucket and spade for Canet Plage to replace the injured Mike Oldfield who was Sydney bound.

The new end of season 'Super 8s' though would prove a different and difficult challenge for the 8th ranked Dragons. Unlike the previous year when they could navigate the play-offs on a straight knockout basis from 7th place and reach the Semi-Finals courtesy of this route, this time taking their league points with them meant they were really too far behind the field to get back into contention from the off. It would be a very tall order especially on the back of five successive losses dating back to the Hull KR Cup exit in late June. It meant that they could only reach the Semi-Finals with a near perfect set of 7 wins from 7 – with four ties away it was mission impossible. They had just left themselves with far too much to do. One immediately thinks of those defensive lapses at home to Salford and then away at Hull KR when 20 points ahead. Late on two scores up early away at both Salford and Widnes couldn't be navigated successfully. That's where they lost it.

Frayssinous wouldn't throw in the towel and the club would at least be content with the schedule which would give them two home fixtures out of the first three to keep them hoping. A huge eight point difference behind the Giants in 4th spot before the kick off meant they were in 'the last place saloon' mode with no respite. St Helens comfortably placed in 3rd spot would be first up at Brutus in early August. The locals consoled by the return of Bosc, Anderson and more importantly Taia where going to be up for this one particularly, knowing that the Saints had lost the week before in the Cup semi-final against Leeds in what had been an epic energy sapping encounter. Catalans at least would get off to a good start with a well merited win (26-16) against the title holders more remarkably so as they played nearly half the match down to twelve men after Pomeroy had been dismissed for a shoulder charge on Jones. In rainy conditions Escaré's 80 metre gallop was just the tonic going into the break. Within minutes of the turn around the former Cronulla centre was gone and it would take a herculean defensive effort from that moment on to secure the points.

If wayward Salford had been a fly in the ointment denying the Dragons a win in 2015 it would be the Giants from over the hill who would eventually deflate their balloon and thwart all hopes of reaching Old Trafford. Thus four matches were scheduled, including for the first time, a Magic Weekend fixture in Newcastle if both the sides qualified for the Super 8s. If the first hit-up was a cake-walk for Paul Anderson's men, the other two a sliver between the protagonists with Catalans, desperately unlucky at St James Park, denied a late win with Dureau inexplicably failing to convert Carney's second try next to the uprights. The game at Brutus with the locals on their knees, losing Whitehead and Casty injured, was also as tight as a drum with a late contentious try awarded to the visitors.

In August the Catalans would go to Huddersfield with some intent, especially with Carney and Taia in harness once again. The Giants 10-6 up going into the break when a catastrophic blunder by Willie Tonga handed the initiative to the hosts in the blink of an eye and the visitors resolve ebbed away at that moment. Brough added two penalties later and it finished (12-24) although it felt closer. Tonga would not play for the club again. A forlorn character who never showed any form that won him Kangaroo representation and Origin status back home in Australia. He had that knockout blow within seconds of his debut at St Helens and broke his jaw against Huddersfield in Newcastle. He didn't have much luck.

Frayssinous was pleased with their effort overall in Yorkshire and was determined to get as much out of the new competition as possible starting with Castleford the following Saturday. There was something left over here from the earlier game against the Tigers on the opening weekend of the season. It certainly had them fired up and they tore the visitors apart spectacularly (44-26) and amazingly had Pomeroy sent-off once again for a dangerous tackle with hardly half an hour gone. They had roared out of the blocks and leading 20-0 when the Australian centre saw red. But it hardly mattered with Carney pulling the strings they racked up a further three converted tries with Gigot claiming a second try hat-trick since his return from anonymity.

There followed a week off for the Wembley Cup Final. Of course they'd had dreams themselves of a return to Wembley Way but the Robins had proved too good for them. Catalans though would play in London in 2015 but at The Den; home of Millwall FC. Wigan had decided to play far away from Lancashire to display their brand and keep Super League alive in the capital following London Broncos departure. It sounded like a thrashing (16-42) but the French side were in the contest up till near the hour mark before subsiding. Frayssinous, pleased with Inu's contribution, wasn't too disappointed ahead of the last home game of the year.

Leeds are always an attraction at Brutus, more so when top of the pile and recent Cup winners. The club after a term of disappointments handled the back end rather well. The trickle of headline signings for 2016 made-up for the ennui as did the last two heroic performances at Brutus – when down to twelve men. With few travelling across the Channel a near 9,000 turn-out was encouraging for the final hurrah. The five departing Dureau, Garcia, Henderson, Taia and Whitehead led the team out on their last outings. The Rhinos were never in this one, still coming down from their Wembley triumph and maybe, believing they still had enough leeway to land top spot on the ladder. Catalans wanted to send their Australian bound quintet away happy as well as their supporters. They would do it too and with the grand manner. Carney, at last putting a run of games together, was in his element well supported by Inu and Whitehead celebrating with the last try of the game and his sides eighth in their biggest ever win over the Yorkshire juggernauts (46-16).

The night before a depleted Hull FC full of youngsters pushed high flying Wigan all the way as teams out of contention for the premier standings had showed up playing for pride and all wanting to go out on highs. Frayssinous was pleased that they could finish with such a flourish at Brutus and then turned to his last fortnight on the road to salvage their abysmal away record. Neither Taia or Carney would play again in 2015 after the Leeds game and they were down to the bare minimum seven days later at Warrington where the young Catalan forward Ugo Perez would become their 100th player to wear the sang-et-or in their penultimate fixture of their tenth campaign. It would turn out an inglorious occasion for the visitors who seemed quite content to allow the Wire to give their retiring players a warm send off, including Catalans bound Richie Myler scoring their last try in a (6-48) stroll in the sun.

The following weekend though they would have a last chance to redeem themselves travelling to Humberside where they hadn't won at the Airlie Birds since 2008. It was much the same side which travelled to Hull FC but Henderson particularly was spitting feathers after their no-show at the HJ Stadium. The Scottish international would score a try in a man of the match winning performance (28-24) sending him out on a high after a five year stint in France never lacking in endeavour or commitment. The popular Whitehead another try scorer on his farewell game. Inu too would grab a try, his seventh in just 13 run outs, which would convince Frayssinous to extend his stay at Brutus for another twelve months at least.

The Supers 8s had indeed been well managed by Frayssinous's boys winning four games, a tally only bettered by Wigan and the Giants. After 30 Rounds Catalans finished in 7th spot identical to their previous two campaigns. Their home record was as good as any in their ten years equalling the eleven wins in 2012 when they finished 4th on the ladder and one more than Potter's side in 2008 with ten successes at Brutus and a 3rd placed finish. Walter's team of 2009 and Robinson's side of 2011 both won more Super League games on their travels across the Channel than in France. The French coach going forward into their next decade would need to improve greatly if the club's rising aspirations were to be realised after their meagre away returns of 2015, with just a couple of successes which was the poorest return since their debut year of 2006.

In all that though, they would land a double success against St Helens for the first time and the biggest ever wins over both Leeds and Wigan. On the debit side they couldn't beat the floundering Salford home or away. Whenever Carney and Taia appeared together on the same team sheet you knew they'd have a chance of winning but Carney played a dozen games in total and Taia missed half a dozen games late in the campaign. Their first choice back line was

The homespun lad from Bradford had really matured like a good Roussillon wine in his 2 years plus spent on the Mediterranean coast, both as a player and a person, possibly giving him the confidence and assurance he needed to take on the new challenges awaiting him in Australia's capital Canberra in 2016. The season before he was the highest try scoring forward in the competition (19) and became simultaneously the first English player to win an international cap when playing in Perpignan as well as the first Englishman to be nomination for the Dream Team from across the Channel.

decimated from early on while the front row armoury as a unit couldn't impose themselves sufficiently.

The end of their first decade felt like another page had turned. Trent Robinson's side had evolved but under Frayssinous guidance hadn't brought the hoped-for results. Leon Pryce and Brent Webb, champions elsewhere, didn't deliver. Losing both Taia and Whitehead to the NRL at the seasons end would be difficult to bridge for sure. But going forward the recruitment seems to be still impressive and showing ambition. That and a nucleus of French players gaining in experience year-on-year will keep the Dragons moving forward and reaching for the stars.

( ) Denotes Challenge Cup game

2015 FIXTURES	ROUND	DATE	VENUE	RESULT	ATT
ST HELENS	R1	06/02/15	LANGTREE PARK	L 7-18	
CASTLEFORD	R2	14/02/15	GILBERT BRUTUS	W 13-12	9,169
WARRINGTON	R3	28/02/15	GILBERT BRUTUS	W 38-18	8,782
SALFORD	R4	07/03/15	GILBERT BRUTUS	D 40-40	8,864
HULL KR	R5	15/03/15	NEW CRAVEN PARK	L 20-50	
HULL FC	R6	20/03/15	KC STADIUM	L 22-33	
LEEDS	R7	28/03/15	GILBERT BRUTUS	L 22-38	8,876
WAKEFIELD	R8	02/04/15	BELLE VUE	W 40-4	
WIDNES	R9	06/04/15	GILBERT BRUTUS	W 32-16	9,683
WIGAN	R10	12/04/15	DW STADIUM	L 0-34	
HUDDERSFIELD	R11	19/04/15	JS STADIUM	L 14-38	
HULL KR	R12	25/04/15	GILBERT BRUTUS	W 32-24	7,938
CASTLEFORD	R13	03/05/15	WHELDON ROAD	L 28-36	
ST HELENS	R14	09/05/15	GILBERT BRUTUS	W 33-26	8,886
FEATHERSTONE	CC5	16/05/15	GILBERT BRUTUS	W 37-34	(3,500)
WIGAN	R15	23/05/15	GILBERT BRUTUS	W 58-16	10,423
HUDDERSFIELD	R16	30/05/15	NEWCASTLE UTD	D 22-22	
WARRINGTON	R17	07/06/15	HJ STADIUM	L 16-28	
HULL FC	R18	13/06/15	GILBERT BRUTUS	W 20-14	7,956
WAKEFIELD	R19	20/06/15	GILBERT BRUTUS	W 32-12	7,834
HULL KR	CCQF	25/06/15	NEW CRAVEN PARK	L 26-32	
SALFORD	R20	05/07/15	BARTON STADIUM	L 14-18	
WIDNES	R21	12/07/15	HALTON STADIUM	L 22-29	
HUDDERSFIELD	R22	18/07/15	GILBERT BRUTUS	L 12-14	9,761
LEEDS	R23	26/07/15	HEADINGLEY	L 36-22	
ST HELENS	R24	08/08/15	GILBERT BRUTUS	W 26-16	7,392
HUDDERSFIELD	R25	14/08/15	JS STADIUM	L 12-24	
CASTLEFORD	R26	22/08/15	GILBERT BRUTUS	W 44-26	7,473
WIGAN	R27	05/09/15	LONDON THE DEN	L 16-42	
LEEDS	R28	12/09/15	GILBERT BRUTUS	W 46-16	8,851
WARRINGTON	R29	19/09/15	HJ STADIUM	L 6-48	
HULL FC	R30	25/09/15	KC STADIUM	W 28-24	
				Total	125,388
				Regular season median:	8,864

SUPER LEAGUE P23 W9 D2 L12
SUPER 8S P7 W4 L3 POS. 7TH
CHALLENGE CUP P2 W1 L1

2015	GAMES	TRIES	GOALS	POINTS
ESCARE	29	12		48
DUPORT	6	3		12
POMEROY	17	4		16
TONGA	19	6		24
OLDFIELD	14	7		28
CARNEY	12	5		20
DUREAU	27	3	95 (2 dg)	204
ELIMA	24			
HENDERSON	29	3		12
CASTY	21	2		8
TAIA	24	13		52
ANDERSON	27	4		16
MOUNIS	18	1		4
BOSC	21	6	24 (1 dg)	73
LIMA	21	2	1	10
PELISSIER	24	9		36
WHITEHEAD	32	13		52
GARCIA	25	8		32
PALA	4	1		4
CARDACE	11	5		20
BOUSQUET	29	2		8
SPRINGER	3	1		4
MARIA	8			
BAITIERI	29	1		4
GUASCH J	3			
ROBIN	9	2	(1 dg)	9
YAHA	11	3		12
GIGOT	18	11		44
MARGALET	3			
INU	13	7	3	34
SIGISMEAU	8	3		12
ALBERT	2			
PEREZ	2			

(33)

Chapter 12
– WHERE NOW –

Catalans Dragons have without doubt been one of the great success stories of the Super League era. After Paris Saint-Germain's early demise they have re-integrated the French presence giving the competition the wider geographical and cultural profile it deserves. A fabulous roller-coaster of a ride beyond every ones dreams became reality. From obscurity to a Wembley appearance secured in only their second term and subsequently played finals football in every season bar two of their first decade. Exactly 100 players had worn the sang-et-or colours between 2006-2015, fifty-five Frenchmen and 45 overseas players. The latter consisting of a good dozen or so who had either worn the Kiwi shirt or the Kangaroos green and gold. Two Englishmen from Bradford both internationals represented them too. Yes they acquired two wooden spoons, but each time they showed the wherewithal to get themselves back up off the floor with aplomb.

Bernard Guasch has turned the Dragons into possibly the biggest club in the history of the French game even without winning a trophy. Crowds of over one million have poured onto *les tribunes* since February 2006, numbers unheard of this side of the Channel. They dragged the old crumbling Brutus back from obscurity to the use it was originally created for half a century before and filled it regularly with passion and colour. Visiting fans loved it and came in numbers supporting their teams creating a new and quite unique atmosphere never realised before.

It was a steep learning curve for sure navigating the fortnightly trips across the Channel and developing the French players to the required level. The club would grow though year-on-year both on and off the pitch. Mounis, Bosc and Casty would mature from young striplings into experienced Super League regulars with 200 plus games under their belts. The latter would play alongside Sonny Bill Williams in the NRL in 2014 and would be followed later by the youngster Garcia heading to Penrith; testament to the clubs growing status. As is the trend of Dragons players securing professional contracts with English clubs with Gadwin Springer being an example, joining Castleford after only three run-outs for the French side. Also lots of lads who experienced life at the Dragons would go on to share their experiences with French clubs. Aurélien

Cologni (Lézignan and France), Cyrille Gossard (St Estève), Renaud Guigue (Avignon), David Berthezene (Palau) and Younis Khattabi (Carpentras) all took up coaching opportunities later.

Of course Frayssinous would become the first Frenchman to coach in Super League in 2013 as the club continued to evolve as a real French entity. CEO Christophe Jouffret would bring continuity after some turbulent times at the out-set and Guasch involved other former players appropriately with Raguin as football manager and Ferriol as club ambassador. Off the field the club emerged as a real power-house commercially with Christophe Levy taking the reins post 2010 when the second phase of the stadium had been completed. This put the club on the front foot recruitment wise as it appeared to strengthen as the years passed. The location helped too as did their connections with previous down under personnel and coaches.

If top Origin and Kangaroo players heading to Roussillon became headline news the formation of local players was gaining in ascendency. Todd Carney may have been one of their biggest headline ever signings for the Dragons but just as importantly his arrival coincided with the major announcement of the official launch of the clubs U19's Academy set-up to debut across the Channel in 2016. €2.5 million will be invested in this project over the next five years as the club moves forward on all fronts including raising coaching levels across the board.

Where once the French contingent consisted of players being pulled from the French Elite1 competition alone there is now the prospect of players arriving much earlier and better equipped with the competitiveness the new U19s Academy structure will facilitate. Already a couple of teenagers have debuted with the Dragons and the hope will be that that will proliferate in the years ahead. The club had not just taken the Sky monies and sat on it but used it to prime the pump. From a starting budget of around €2M they have seen it rise year on year to now approaching €10M. The investment by the municipal authorities to develop the new Puig Aubert stand has been a winner on all fronts enabling the club to access various new income streams including a vibrant and profitable boutique.

Media wise the club has made in-roads certainly locally with the popular regional daily, *L'Indépendant*; at the out-set USAP completely dominated the sporting scene. Today the Dragons are right up there with them. The popularity of local newspapers in France negates against sporting entities from different regions having exposure and why the Toulouse based *La Depeche du Midi* rarely mention them in their main sports section. Only joined up involvement would prise the door open. By 2015 three local radio stations cover all the Catalans games homes games while *Radio Bleu Roussillon* provide regular match commentaries from England. Television coverage has been excellent from the start but Bein Sports recent involvement has taken it to another level. Maybe the Dragons are the most televised rugby club of either code this side of the Channel as presently all their home games are shown live in France, England and Australia.

Just having France involved in the race line-up leading to Wembley and Old Trafford is everything; the footprint going forward though must be deeper and wider. The dream of playing at these mythical venues in front of 70,000 fans is what inspires the *treizistes* across the Channel and for them keeps the game alive. They feel connected with that bridge and it has to be strengthened. The game both sides of the Channel need to be joined at the hip. If recent changes in the games structures don't easily accommodate such advancement, nonetheless 2016 will witness for the first time ever three French entities playing week in-week out across the Channel with Catalans Dragons, their U19's Academy side and Toulouse Olympique in Ligue 1.

But somebody has to arrive on the scene to broaden the Super League profile. A game locked away in the M62 closet is too limited. There has to be a challenge to the Lancashire and Yorkshire hegemony from somewhere. The Winfield Cup of Sydney acceded to the NRL and Melbourne, Auckland and Queensland joined the party. The London of Tony Currie fleetingly threatened to change the order of things with their runners-up spot in Super League II and later a Wembley visit while Brian Noble gave Wales a brief look-in securing a play-off place in 2010. Both though were shooting stars, far too quickly disappeared from view. The emerging Catalans Dragons, entering their second decade at the top table, must offer the best bet yet to re-arrange the Super League furniture some time soon. Remember Old Trafford and her Theatre of Dreams was not built by Busby and others to stay local but to stretch out to new and distant horizons. Continental Europe and Real Madrid and Barcelona would be where it manifested itself. Super League needs big clubs and more of them and in the right places too. Rugby league fans everywhere who wish to see the game in Europe extend its reach will but hope, cherish the idea, embrace it, will it to happen. A Latin touch that John Wilson would have appreciated (NDLR the RFL Secretary 1922-46) *Vive la différence!*

CEO Christophe Jouffret arrived from Avignon where he played the game via the French Federation and during his tenure both stability and rapid growth has been established.

"Catalan people are very passionate and proud. After ten years we can say it was the right decision to have the Super League franchise here. Although the competition is extremely strong in France from rugby union and football the spectacle that Super League provides with its passion and commitment has enabled us to succeed, and win over doubters. It was difficult initially to win over sponsors as a club basically playing in an English competition limited to the North of England and us being located at the bottom of France."

"There were many challenges. Not least the logistics or travelling across the Channel every other week not helped by frequent changes in the airline schedules year on year. Our recent link up with Hop! an Air France subsidiary has benefitted us by enabling the team to travel direct from Perpignan and saving on overnight accommodation."

"Our U19's Academy will be in the main competition in 2016 after a year of friendly-matches. This will represent a major innovation for our club. We are thinking of playing again an 'on-the road' fixture in 2016, maybe in a city in the South of France or Paris. Everybody has to buy into this de-location, choosing the right club and liaising closely with the RFL."

"Regarding the television rights between Sky Sports and Bein Sports; this is a RFL responsibility in conjunction with the Super League clubs. We have a close relationship with Bein and can influence them to some degree but ultimately it's not in our hands. If one day however Toulouse joined us in Super League it would be advantageous to everybody in France. We would have a derby fixture to promote and Super League could be exposed here every weekend rather than every other week."

"40% of our income is commercially driven including merchandising, 20% via our public partners at local, departmental and regional levels (NDLR the 'Sud de France' branding on the team jersey is a promotional tool of the Languedoc-Roussillon Regional Council), 20% television rights and just 20% from gate receipts, season tickets and match day activities."

The Dragons Business Club was founded in 2010 coinciding with the opening of the new Puig Aubert stand and commenced with 60 members; by 2016 the numbers had more than trebled. They have their own executive, their own distinctive blazers and polos, meet five times a year with the last rendez-vous chartering a plane to Manchester for the Super League Grand Final. Their motto is: passion, quality and conviviality. They are an integral part of the clubs success.

Christophe Levy, the Dragons Commercial Director ; "The Dragons represent a network of over 400 enterprises and partners, 5000 season ticket holders and 9000 spectators reunited at Stade Gilbert Brutus. *We propose today to our partners a range of presentations, varied and adaptable to their needs so as to maximise the impact of their communications. We offer equally a visibility important with all our home games televised live on Bein Sports and Sky Sports (NLDR viewed in France, England and Australia)."*

The French coach entering new territory with his fourth year at the helm in 2016 – a first for the Dragons. Already with more wins under his belt than any of those preceding him. The huge challenge now is getting his team to a Final.

2016 – "This will be a new group with numerous recruits. And it will take some time for it to gel. After, we will have a group of quality, hoping it will have the least injuries as possible.

We will have for sure, new ambitions once again and I'll need time to re-assess our present situation. We will all be very motivated because the club has provided us with the means of putting together a group of real quality. Even if it is only our eleventh season this club merits having the recognition that it must have and we will do everything to make that happen."

"The Academy set-up is a real bonus for us with our proper entry from 2016. It will be good too for our reserve team St Estève being fed by this new entity becoming more or less our U23's. I remember when I was young how difficult it was to find good images of the game. Even just being able to see recordings of the Wembley Challenge Cup games or NRL Finals was a challenge. Todays kids here grow-up watching the Dragons and other Super League games every week courtesy of Bein Sports television coverage; their appreciation of the game has been enhanced, the mentality and game sense too."

"It will take time for Toulouse to arrive in Super League. I see us working closely with them in the meantime. Previously we have sent them players such as Barthau and Gigot when they played in the Championship before. It was difficult the last time because we had our own problems and Trent had to resolve them more importantly and where his emphasis was. Hopefully in the near future we can strike a good synergy between us so to take both of us forward. We have a real problem with our fringe players for instance after the S t Esteve season finishes in May. So establishing a productive dual-registration link-up could well aid both of us."

"The changing scene down-under will propose to us challenges too and why again the Academy side will be in the long term so important. We definitely need to raise the bar to develop French players of higher quality. I see a near future where we have 4-6 marquee overseas players and French players of a higher standard than in the past. But we won't win a trophy with 17 French players in the next five years! Ten years a possibility – it would be a good objective. But what I know is that I wouldn't be scared in say 5 years time playing with 17 French players. If Lucas Albert and Fouad Yaha are examples of what are to come we will be in a stronger position further down the line for sure."

"I think the French competition will continue to improve. As Toulouse establish themselves playing in England once again it will be an opportunity for their U23s to forge a new path in Elite 1 (Something which Toulouse weren't able to do last time out 2009-11). Teams like Lézignan and Carcassonne want to continue improving themselves. I have been impressed by the standard of play presently; well sure it would be better if we could find a few more teams of the same level. The profile of the game though across the board has improved with the arrival of the Dragons."

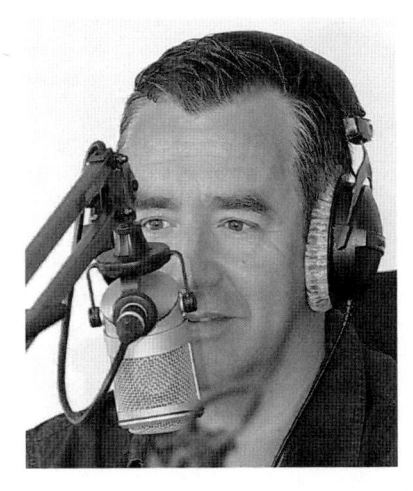

Bruno Onteniente has been the rugby league writer for the Perpignan based daily L'Indépendant since 2009. He also doubles up as the voice of Radio Bleu Roussillon providing full commentaries on all the Dragons games home and away.

"Going forward the club has to win something. The fans expected to win something in 2015. And the President said they would win a trophy and they haven't delivered.

Now it's a must to satisfy our passionate supporters. If they don't win a trophy in the next five years it will be difficult to progress. Wembley arrived very early for the fans and their appetites wetted. The club thought that the recruitment for 2015 was of the calibre to land a trophy but injuries got in the way. Again for 2016 the quality signings have raised expectations even further."

"Laurent Frayssinous has been able to use his connections with Trent Robinson, Kevin Walters and Mick Potter to attract the calibre of players they pick-up; Michael Monaghan too with both his links to Canberra and Manly facilitate the arrival of Carney, Horo and Stewart. They are real pluses."

"The Academy set-up has achieved a category 1 rating from the RFL after just a dozen friendly fixtures. A lot of quality and technically good players are being formed there. Thomas Bosc and Greg Mounis are mentoring these players and they have said to me that these youngsters are superior to them in their development at the same age. They work all day on the skills and they will progress a lot quicker than French players in the past."

"I think we should start looking at more English players as recruitments in the future. As well as the money available in the NRL there are the added problems that the Australians with families in tow have additional responsibilities. Both Taia and Henderson were hoping to stay longer but the pull of home for their partners and kids has to be factored in. Broughton and Myler the way to go; not too far from family and they know also the competition they play in."

"With the French team the constant changes over the years doesn't build stability. We've had Cologni, Goulding and now Agar in quick succession plus the Dragons connection with Guisset cutting his ties. Agar is now looking towards the 2017 World Cup and bringing on the young players who want to play for the national team. I think there's a need to develop a stronger link between Laurent Frayssinous and the French coach."

"Pia when winning the French competition in 2012/2014 had 9-10 overseas players and far too many for the good of the Elite 1. Maybe 2-3 at most is more acceptable. Bringing in more, younger French players is better. I prefer to see a local competition of 6-8 competitive clubs to prevent blow-outs. The present standards need to be maintained and improved."

– POSTCRIPTS –
A - World Cups 2008-2013

Just prior to the launch of the Super League in 1996 France lost narrowly to England at Gateshead (19-16); they still hadn't won across the Channel since Headingley in 1990 or indeed on home soil since Marseille in1981. The hope was with the new era of full-time professionalism and a French presence in the capital with Paris St Germain at least the game in France would be caught in the slip stream of developments across *la Manche*. Unfortunately that didn't transpire as the French project bit the dust within two years. By the 2000 World Cup the Tricolours would have to cut their cloth accordingly while the game's traditional power base in England and Australasia would zoom up to a new plateau.

The 12th WC though was a damp squib after the euphoria of 1995 except to a degree surprisingly across the Channel where the Tricolours were well supported with a 10,000 crowd in Carcassonne for their (28-8) win against Tonga. Of course the *treizistes* had a strong attachment to the international game and were the originators of the first World Cup back in 1954 led by their charismatic and visionary Federation President Paul Barriere. Gilles Dumas's side qualified for the quarter-finals before losing heavily to the Auckland Warriors dominated New Zealand side (6-54) at Castleford.

With Catalans Dragons accession to the Super League in 2006 the hope was that the bridge between France and their competitors at international level would be reduced. It would prove far more difficult to achieve than many hoped for or expected. In the build up to the 2008 event in Australia the job of rekindling the Tricolours embers was given to the urbane, hugely experienced and successful John Monie. The Australian had a CV to wish for from Parramatta to Wigan. With the Dragons assistant coach Laurent Frayssinous along side it looked the perfect tandem to take the international side forward. The year before the event, Tony Smith's England would be met at Headingley in mid-season. Whereas the English coach could select totally from the Super League, the Australian had to dip into the French competition for more than half his line-up. A respectable 12,685 crowd saw the Tricolours hold their own in the opening half 10-16 before falling away later on to concede (14-42).

The back end of 2007 in Paris the Tricolours showed up well against a New Zealand side of Mannering, Jeff Lima, Louis Anderson, Thomas Leuluai and Asotasi two of which Lima and Anderson would go on later to wear the sang-et-or in Perpignan. Indeed on the cusp of a first win against the Kiwis in 27 years; denied a try by the video referee and caught out by a late try from the influential Leuluai did for the Tricolours in a tight hard fought encounter (14-22). The performance impressed coach Monie and similarly impressed the crowd of 6,791. At Stade Jean-Bouin, home of Stade Francais, was the Government's Sports Minister Bernard Laporte formerly the coach of the French rugby union side.

With Potter's Catalans side surprisingly knocking everybody over in 2008 the joust with Smith's England selection in Toulouse in June was eagerly awaited. Two Australians scrum half Wynne and full-back Clayton from the French competition featured along with other local semi pros Sadaoui, Anselme, Carrasco, Sabatie and Planas. Again a case of *déjà-vu* with France holding their own in the opening phases but Burgess's try hurt them leading into the break. After it was just a procession as they leaked seven second half tries to fall in a heap (8-56) before a crowd of 8,123 at Stade Ernest Wallon who left wanting more from their favourites. Sydney was 120 days away and the building site had much work to do.

There were four refugees from the 2000 World Cup which travelled to Australia eight years later. Guisset, Rinaldi who was then playing at Harlequins, the St Gaudens forward Borlin and Frayssinous who was there in his coaching capacity. The party included a dozen Dragons players and eight from the local French competition four of which had spent part of the summer in Brisbane at the Broncos on the instigation of coach Monie; Fellous like Rinaldi had left the Catalans was also included in a party which comprised of a quartet of Australians qualified on residential grounds.

Their opener was against Scotland at the Bruce Stadium on a hot day on the 26th October before a shirt sleeved crowd of 9,287. The Bravehearts included half a dozen Australian raised players including the three Henderson brothers of whom Ian at hooker would also later carry the Catalan sang-et-or colours. The Englishman Brough, then of Wakefield Trinity, would skipper the team. It was a testy opening with both teams grabbing tries. Lézignan full-back Taylor first for the French and wing Steel, a former union international for the Scots. France would secure the win though before the break with two converted tries from back-rower Guisset and centre Wilson opening up a two score lead. Scotland valiantly tried to peg it back but fell short. Two late scores from Guisset again and Carcassonne's Moly sealed a convincing win for the French (36-18) in the capital and all looked well for then on in.

If only. The vagaries of the competition meant that there was little room for manoeuvre and each game would count. Five days later it was over for the Tricolours. At the WIN Stadium in Wollongong Fiji would take them apart. A combination with ten NRL aligned players would just be too quick and too strong. A decade earlier or so maybe with NSW bush players in tow but not with the likes of Hayne and Uate who would both later play Origin and become Kangaroos. Play maker Wynn's dislocated elbow didn't help the French cause early on but the pace and vivacity of the Pacific Islanders was too much. Hayne at full-back was untenable in the opening half leading them into the break at 18-6 with just Wilson's try for the French. After the oranges Fiji just went into over drive with sprinter Uate completing his hat-trick of tries. The *'ampleur'* was hard to take (6-42) regardless. There was little to cheer for the fifty or so French supporters present in the crowd of 9,213. Arnaud Hingray writing for *L'Indépendant* screamed, *"La France humilée"*. Coach Monie commented, "It's a great disappointment. We wanted to show another face than was evident today. We lacked enthusiasm and the defence which had shown itself on the first game hasn't responded today. We have lost the battle up front. Until the time France can field a second Super League team we will not be able to rival certain nations". He will not be the first or last to utter such sentiments.

France took the defeat badly especially when Scotland had turned over the Fijians (18-16) four days later. They were in no fit state to tackle Samoa a week later out west at Penrith for the 9th place. They couldn't get themselves up for it taking five unanswered tries in the opening half. A couple of tries on the hour mark from Guisset and Planas salvaged a bit of pride but not much against a side littered with names who would distinguish themselves in Super League such as Meli, Pulueta, Carmont, Hansen, Leuluai, and Lauiti'iti. A (10-42) loss which would see them occupying last place on the standings. A part-time France had well beaten Tonga in 2000 but development of the Pacific Island nations was on a steep upward curve as Papua New Guinea's performance up in Townsville against England had indicated. This was a trend which would have some wind behind it and change the world game like never before.

*All players Catalans Dragons unless indicated

France v Scotland

1 Taylor (Lézignan), 2 Murphy, 3 Wilson, 4 Raguin, 5 Sadaoui (Carcassonne) 6 Bosc, 7 Greseque (Pia), 8 Fellous (Widnes), 9 Rinaldi (Harlequins), 10 Elima 11 Guisset, 12 Anselme (Albi), 13 Mounis Substitutes: 14 Moly (Carcassonne) 15 Wynne (Toulouse Olympique), 16 Casty, 17 Fakir

France v Fiji

1 Taylor (Lézignan), 2 Murphy, 3 Wilson, 4 Raguin, 5 Pelo, 6 Bosc 7 Moly (Carcassonne), 8 Borlin (St Gaudens), 9 Wynne (Toulouse Olympique), 10 Elima, 11 Guisset , 12 Sadaoui (Carcassonne), 13 Mounis Substitutes: 14 Casty, 15 Fakir, 16 Baile, 17 Greseque (Pia)

France v Samoa

1 Taylor (Lézignan), 2 Planas (Toulouse Olympique), 3 Sadaoui (Carcassonne) 4 Raguin, 5 Pelo, 6 Wilson, 7 Bosc, 8 Fellous (Widnes), 9 Moly (Carcassonne) 10 Guisset, 11 Fakir, 12 Anselme (Albi), 13 Mounis Substitutes: 14 Elima 15 Carrasco (Toulouse Olympique), 16 Griffi, 17 Baile

None Catalans Dragons players used: 41%

By the time of the 14th World Cup 2013 Catalans Dragons were eight years old; a certain maturity about the place and no longer the proverbial new boys on the block. Going into the previous edition in Australia five years earlier the French club had benefitted from a degree of success un-hoped for under the sure guiding hands of coach Potter but none of it translated into a credible outcome in and around Sydney under the tandem Monie-Frayssinous in 2008.

After that the French Federation President Nicolas Larrat demanded changes. And how. The decision to appoint Bobby Goulding as the new coach was right outside the box. Goulding an outstanding international player in his day hadn't achieved anything of note outside coaching at Rochdale in the lower leagues. From Monie to Goulding took some understanding to many in the game. Larrat had hoped to keep Frayssinous involved but the Dragons assistant coach declined the invitation.

It was to prove a volatile period in the Tricolours history. Although the World Cup had been a huge disappointment the French side had a real opportunity the following year to redress the situation quickly with their participation in the newly inaugurated Four Nations tournament, pitting themselves against the games major powers Australia, England and New Zealand. The mid-season game against England up in Paris would be Goulding's baptism in 2009. It would be a reminder of the huge task facing the young inexperienced English coach.

A French side which gave a debut to the experienced Limoux scrum half Murcia. England and more so half-back Myler ran the Tricolours ragged at Stade Jean-Bouin before a crowd of 7,369 with the Warrington player claiming a personal haul of thirty points in a (12-66) romp.

Goulding's arrival at the helm of the French game also coincided with Kevin Walters taking over in Perpignan after Potter's move to St Helens. After Paris, Goulding would have realised if need be, the challenge in front of him going into the Four Nations in the autumn. It wasn't to be a seamless transition down in Roussillon for the former Kangaroo half-back as the Dragons struggled early on to maintain the standards of the previous campaign. By September though fortunes had turned somewhat, with that Greg Bird inspired charge to Old Trafford thwarted narrowly at Headingley on the penultimate weekend.

The mood around Perpignan was on the up that September and Goulding found it possible to make a fist of his first real challenge. England at Doncaster would be a testing opener. Greenshields made his debut in blue after his three years spent in France. The Australian full-back would give confidence to those in front of him as the Tricolours gave the best performance against a major international side in years. Leading at the break 12-4 and muscling up against an England side which fielded a bench of Graham, Roby, Eastmond and Westwood. A couple of late converted tries did for the French as they fell away a bit (12-34) before a respectable crowd of 11,529 but the feeling was definitely upbeat.

The Kiwis who had surprised the rugby league world a year earlier winning the world cup for the first time would be formidable opponents next up in Toulouse. Buoyed somewhat by the Doncaster performance and a decent 12,869 turn out at

Stade Ernest Wallon, the Tricolours were not intimidated by the giants in black in the early stages. On 39 minutes only a converted try separated the protagonists. After the break though it turned into a procession as the mighty visitors hit their straps scoring 24 points in an eight minute spell as the absence of heavy-weights Greenshields and Ferriol really started to tell (12-62).

The mighty Kangaroos lay in wait in Paris the week after. Even with Greenshields and Ferriol returning it was an uphill climb. Again a decent first forty with just two tries conceded but peppered from the restart with three touchdowns in a 5 minute spell undid the hosts. Skipper Elima got their only points with a try on the hour as their only consolation (4-48). Bernard Laporte now managing the Stade Francais union outfit alongside marketing guru Max Guazzzini was present along with Richard Lewis from the RFL, in the modest attendance of around 3,000 at Stade Charlety out on the capitals periphery. The talk was of a possible interest in SF attaching a Super League entity to its sporting portfolio.

Goulding would not be judged by his debut season in charge of the Tricolours but pivotal would be 2010. Not a lot would have been expected in their results against the major nations but the forthcoming Alitalia European Cup in the autumn would decide his future and legacy. Qualification from this tournament against the four home nations was mandatory as it opened the doors to the Four Nations of 2011. Unfortunately for the Englishman the fortunes of the Dragons that year nose-dived. By the time they played England in the mid-season Test Catalan where bottom of the league with a bare two wins from 16 games played and confidence shattered. An England of Tomkins and Widdop behind and a pack of Burgess, Graham and Ellis et al up-front pummelled them at Leigh (6-60) before a crowd of 7,951.

By September Goulding must have been wandering what state his players would be in, assembling for the fast approaching EC after their most calamitous campaign since their entry. But hope springs eternal; well it did in Avignon on the second weekend of October. With all the tribulations that had unfolded in Perpignan over the summer it defied belief that the game across the Channel at that particular moment in time had the audacity and wherewithal to raise themselves. Incredibly the Federation where able to mobilize its support; 14,552 poured into Parc des Sports to see their favourites pulverise Andy Kelly's Ireland (58-24).

A week later at Albi against Scotland it was more subdued with 7,150 in attendance but the Tricolours still had enough to land the victory (26-12) which would enable them to return to the Tarn and the same stadium for the tournaments clincher with the Wales the following weekend. Its was damp and overcast against the Scots but a lovely sunny autumnal day for the crunch match to decide a place amongst the games best in 2011. Wales with Harris at the helm and Thomas in the centres had some gravitas about them. Federation President Larrat had invited the Government's Sports Minister Madame Rama Yade as guest of honour as well as Richard Lewis. The scene was set perfectly with 10,450 present.

It was as tight as a drum as one would expect with the stakes at play. France led by a single unconverted try at the break. On the turn round the Welsh went in front with a converted try and that lead was extended when Thomas crossed for a second. The French cheered on by the vocal crowd grabbed an equalising score and it was locked with hardly ten minutes on the clock. A drop goal edged the hosts ahead again and it looked like they would hold out until a French forward put in a high tackle in front of the posts from barely 30 metres out to gift the game to the visitors at the death (11-12). So close and yet so far. Truly 2010 had been the treizistes *annus horribilis* and left their national coach now with nowhere to go.

Not sure who pulled the plug on the mid-season Test but Guasch at the Catalans was not complaining in 2011. It was just too big of an ask for the Dragons to front-up alone against the rest of the Super League especially by now with additional NRL recruits too. Goulding was content to see out his contract even if he had thin pickings to look forward to when the main action was elsewhere. They would become England's sparring partners preparing for the Four Nations on successive weekends in October. At Leigh Sports Village they went down to the England Knights (18-38) before a crowd of just 2,071. Team Manager Guy Lafforgue was disappointed, "The players have sold their skin, the same if three or four are below the level of others in this type of match. I'm disappointed by this twenty point difference – this wasn't to me the real gap between these sides."

A week later in Avignon France again showed its colours and its potential. Any game against England raises the heckles even in a year *"blanchi"* by the events of 2010 and the Welsh result. The love affair of the Tricolours with Avignon continued unabated with another super following of 16,866 at the Parc des Sports against a strong England side containing Australian reared lads like Reed, Widdop and Heightington. New coach at Brutus Robinson had dramatically turned the Dragons fortunes around and the feel good factor had quickly returned but as this only manifested in small incremental improvements for the national team; England were accelerating. Staying in their slipstream was increasingly a hard task as long as the present status quo continued. It was an entertaining free flowing encounter with England taking the spoils (18-32). They tagged on a couple of games against other home nations too beating Scotland at Brutus (46-10) before an impressive 10,313 crowd and on the first weekend of November crossed the Irish Sea to Limerick to beat Ireland (34-16). As well as the attendances across the Channel the arrival on the international scene of youngsters Pelissier, Bousquet and Cardace offered some solace and room for optimism further down the line.

It was time to move on and Goulding was thanked for his contributions; it had been a strange journey. Bobby admitted himself that he had been genuinely surprised to be given the job in the first place but threw himself into the fray as only he could. He was popular with the players but lacked the real experience and know how at this level to make a real difference. Maybe some of his personal problems too were being played out at this time. It was transition time too for Larrat as President of the Federation who wasn't seeking another term in charge. The following year would see changes at the top of the Federation with the Toulouse Olympique's President Carlos Zalduendo taking the reins and a new coach for the Tricolours. Aurélien Cologni who had played alongside the likes of Frayssinous and Guisset at the Dragons in their debut year had been making a name for himself coaching at Lézignan and was given the national team job for 2012.

In the year leading up to the 14th World Cup England, Wales and France would play a Triangular tournament. With a blank weekend allocated in the Super League schedule the Welsh would host France at Wrexham in June in preparation for the autumn event. Just over 2,000 turned up at the Racecourse ground to see France succeed (28-16) where they had failed two years earlier at Albi the last time the two had met. Cologni's big challenge though would come later in the year starting with a re-match with the Welsh at FC Lens soccer ground in northern France well away from its traditional bases. Luc Dayan was the President of the club and was a fan of the game and an acquaintance of Charles Bietry at Bein Sports – the French television broadcaster who were covering both the NRL and Super League including Catalans Dragons home games. A hard fought second win against Wales (20-6) in late October before yet another impressive turn out of 11,628 in alien territory gave the Tricolours a lift before the huge challenge against the English. The result at Lens qualified France for the Final against England after the Welsh defeat (80-12) at Wrexham a week later.

The England side under McNamara had shown real signs of progress with the governing body making serious resources available. The two games played that November where further evidence of the Tricolours plight. More or less identical results and score lines accrued; (6-44) at Hull's Craven Park (7,000) and (4-48) at Salford's Barton stadium (11,456). In both games the hosts had it in the bag after just half an hours play and the Tricolours conceded 8 tries in each. The French back line exposed, lacking both pace and size. Coach Cologni had his finger on the pulse, "It's very difficult to accept such score lines but I'm proud of the team as they never let their guard down. Mentally we have been present but we have also players fatigued by their Super League campaign. At least we have seen some players like Bousquet, Barthau, Soubeyras and Larroyer show their worth. It's necessary now to raise the level of our wingers and centres especially defensively because we've taken too many tries on the exteriors." It would be a recurring theme which wouldn't go away any time soon.

Zalduendo wanted quick results and saw only a Super League coach to take the Tricolours into their World Cup year. Wakefield Trinity's man Richard Agar was the man to put his hand up for the cause; he had a soft spot for the French and had developed a good working relationship with Robinson in his time at Perpignan. His appointment early in 2013 didn't give him too much time to prepare his side unlike the competitions organisational arrangements which were all well in place. Avignon and Perpignan were to prove ideal venues to receive two of the three French qualifying matches to be held that autumn.

Agar was able to arrange a couple of get-togethers throughout the season and the group was in camp for the whole duration of the tournament spending time in Toulouse, Avignon and Perpignan. As across the Channel the promotion and marketing of the event crossed new boundaries with the famous old World Cup Trophy commissioned by Paul Barrière all those years before touring all the *treize* bastions of the Midi. It was all quite magnificent.

The Tricolour squad, as expected, was dominated by Catalans Dragons players. Indeed of the 23 selected teenager Theo Fages of Salford was the only player who had not worn the sang- et-or in Super League. Half a dozen players were trawled up from the French competition including Sébastien Raguin who combined the duties of Catalans club manager and part-time player at St Estève. Other than Fages the only none-French based selection was Clint Greenshields then of North Queensland Cowboys. Catalans Dragons fielded more players (20) than any other club in the 14th World Cup and intriguingly just ahead of Trent Robinson's Sydney Roosters outfit with sixteen.

Half a century since crowds like this attended French internationals as the World Cup 2013 euphoria crossed the Channel in style. Avignon and the Vaucluse a real rugby league pocket yet to be developed as their youngsters travel far to be appreciated.

Coach Agar arranged for the Tricolours to have one pre-tournament run out against the USA at Toulouse's Stade des Minimes nine days before their opener at Hull KR's Craven Park. France had been placed in a tough four team group alongside the holders New Zealand, their nemesis Samoa who had walloped them twice in recent World Cups in Cardiff 1995 and Sydney in 2008, plus Papua New Guinea who had brought them to boot in Paris in 2000. The USA warm up had proved a bit of a calamity; the loss (16-18) dampened spirits somewhat leading into the opener.

A horrible cold, wet and windy day adjacent to the North Sea welcomed them, not improved by a hostile local crowd of 7,481 getting behind the Kumuls courtesy of Stanley Gene. Fortunately the Tricolours got off to a flying start with Bosc sneaking over for a converted try. Little did one realise at the time how important that six point cushion would prove. Young Fages nearly got them another try after a snipping run but was just held short. Papua New Guinea responded with two unconverted scores to edge them in front in a tight contest in tough conditions before, on the hour mark, Bosc landed a penalty goal to tie it up.

It was left to the trusted right boot of half-back Barthau to seal the win with a fine drop goal from 30 metres out to win the game for France. The Tricolours had to battle hard and defend well in the last quarter of an hour to hold out although they the had the luck of a missed penalty goal by the Kumuls from straight in front. They had made a winning (9-8) start and two vital points towards a quarter final place their hoped for goal.

The charismatic Rodolphe Pires here interviewing Sonny Bill Williams prior to the kick off against the Kiwis. Pires the voice behind the microphone of Bein Sports; adored by the treizistes. Passionate, energetic and approachable – the man from the Tarn has it all.

Without doubt the real success in the World Cup in France was what was achieved up in Provence at Avignon. The game in those parts had receded somewhat from its earlier hiatus. The local club though had rebuilt and had won the Lord Derby Cup in 2013; their first major success in decades. Five figure crowds had been recorded at the cities major stadium for recent games against Ireland and England but the demand for tickets for the plumb tie against the title holders New Zealand went through the roof. Also this was not the case of hundreds of tickets freely handed out either as has been the case in the past. Incredibly the ground was sold out a week before the game; possibly a first across the Channel with 17,518 takers and a ground record to boot.

With Greenshields and Pelissier absent France struggled against the size, power and pace of the Kiwis wanting to make up for an indifferent performance against Samoa. The two Bentley brothers born in New Zealand but reared in France both featured. The Tricolours conceded their third try just on the half-time bell which hurt them. They committed too many faults and gave up too much possession. After fifty minutes or so they were a busted flush as the score rolled out to a (0-48) thrashing as some had feared. Everybody around the camp just put their hands up and honestly accepted that the Kiwis were just too good. New Zealand had enjoyed their cross Channel jaunt and their skipper Mannering appreciated their reception. Post match the conquerors swept into the conquered changing rooms bringing beers with them and had a sing song with the customary exchange of shirts plus photos taken especially with the competitions celebrity, Sonny Bill Williams.

Everybody knew that the Samoa clash next up was the big one for France. There was history with it too. Tuigamala's side had destroyed the Tricolours in Cardiff in 1995 by (14-62) and it got no easier in Sydney last time out (10-42). The Diaspora of Polynesians and Melanesians had accelerated considerably in the last few decades with many settling in both New Zealand and Australia. Many of their finest athletes landed up playing in the NRL and many of them spilling out into the jumpers of Samoa, PNG, Tonga, Cook Islands and Tonga come World Cup 2014. Stade Gilbert Brutus in Perpignan like Avignon was packed to the rafters with another ground record of 11,576 for this titanic show-down. The Pacific Islanders steam-rollered the French by all means possible, fair or foul, to get the result (6-22); they had some class too in full-back Milford which counted but the Tricolours showed up courageous in the battle and the crowd showed its appreciation especially when Escaré secured their six points.

Defeat meant that England at Wigan rather than Fiji at Warrington in the knock out stages. As for the Samoa game the team line up against England would be the first time the Tricolours in the World Cup fielded a side of present or former Catalans Dragons players only. It was a tight turn around for Agar's side after the Monday night in Perpignan against Samoa for the quarter final at the DW Stadium on the Saturday. The mauling by the Kiwis followed by the physical battering by Samoa could have left France empty handed. Instead they turned up at Wigan and against the odds showed lots of bottle and fervour. Yes, they again displayed their weakness in attack, lacking a real cutting edge but they pestered and annoyed England all night. They even had the temerity to take the lead early on with a converted try by Duport. But the Tricolours wouldn't be undone down the middle but on the fringes where England's wingers proliferated. In the second half the French resisted even knowing the cause was gone but only two further tries conceded in their elimination (6-34) in front of 22,276, the biggest for a match against the old enemy in half a century.

The French press were impressed; the *L'Indépendant* headlined it with, *"Les Bleus tête haute, with the honour saved by a courageous French team"*. Remarkably with just a sole victory as eight years earlier in Australia the French experienced it this time completely differently, lifted hugely by the home support received in Avignon and Perpignan. They recognised the difference in class especially when up against New Zealand and England and took pleasure in the Tricolours commitment and spirit against the odds. Manager Dumas lamented, *"Le XIII de France n'a pas de Dureau,"* to lead them around the field. Just three tries registered in the whole tournament from Bosc, Escare and Duport, the latter possibly the most consistent Tricolours performer. Skipper Elima remarked on the odds stacked against his side in the major confrontations; " England can identify 40-50 possible selections from the top four or so sides of Super League while we struggle with not many more than a dozen."

*All players Catalans Dragons unless indicated

France v Papua New Guinea

1 Escare, 2 Vaccari, 3 Baile, 4 Duport, 5 Greenshields (North Queensland) 6 Bosc, 7 Barthau, 8 Fakir, 9 Pelissier, 10 Casty, 11 Larroyer 12 Raguin (St Estève), 13 Mounis Substitutes: 14 Fages (Salford), 15 Elima 16 Garcia, 17 Simon

France v New Zealand

1 Escare, 2 Vaccari, 3 Baile, 4 Duport, 5 Stacul (Lézignan), 6 Bosc 7 Fages (Salford), 8 Elima, 9 K Bentley (Toulouse Olympique), 10 Casty 11 Larroyer, 12 Raguin (St Estève), 13 A Bentley (Toulouse Olympique) Substitutes: 14 Mounis, 15 Fakir, 16 Garcia, 17 Simon

France v Samoa

1 Escare, 2 Vaccari, 3 Baile, 4 Duport, 5 Greenshields (North Queensland) 6 Bosc, 7 Barthau, 8 Fakir, 9 Pelissier, 10 Casty, 11 Larroyer 12 Raguin (St Estève), 13 Mounis Substitutes: 14 Gigot (Avignon), 15 Maria 16 Garcia, 17 Simon

France v England

1 Escare, 2 Cardace, 3 Baile, 4 Duport, 5 Greenshields (North Queensland) 6 Bosc, 7 Barthau, 8 Fakir, 9 K Bentley (Toulouse Olympique) 10 Casty, 11 Elima, 12 Raguin (St Estève), 13 Mounis Substitutes: 14 Pelissier, 15 Khattabi (Carcassonne), 16 Maria, 17 Simon None Catalans Dragons players : 28%

(All 22 players selected had played Super League at the Dragons except for Fages).

POST 2013

At the end of Richard Agar's third year in charge of the French team serious questions were being asked about the coach's ability to turn the Tricolours flaying fortunes around. Following the 2013 World Cup France finished runners-up in the two subsequent European Championships. In 2014 they lost out to Scotland and the year later to Wales. The former had real repercussions though as it would deprive the Tricolours of playing in the 2016 Four Nations against Australia, England and New Zealand. This would represent France's second successive failure to qualify in this event after they lost out to Wales in 2010. Regardless some felt there had been sufficient talent in the young and inexperienced squads announced in both 2014/2015 to do the business against opposition similarly placed. But the results and performances just didn't come to fruition.

Following the 2013 World Cup it appeared that there was disquiet in the Tricolours camp possibly about remuneration. What did transpire though was that senior players such as Olivier Elima, Greg Mounis and Thomas Bosc would terminate their international careers. Losing the experience of a trio of players all at the same time with over 700 Super League appearances between them would be a problem for Agar and the French Federation to come to terms with. Simultaneously Bernard Guasch was airing the view that the Dragons fortunes in Super League were being hindered by the over reliance of his club in providing players for the national team remembering that in the 2013 World Cup the Dragons had supplied more players than any other club side (20). Catalans start to their 2014 Super League campaign would be their worst ever. This year on, involvement he believed had to be re-addressed so as to permit sufficient recuperation prior to pre-season preparation.

In an ideal world the French Federation and the Dragons should be working together hand in glove but unfortunately to date that hasn't been the case. The vital coaching link between the two was broken after the 2008 World Cup and never re-instated. You never got the impression that the two parties were communicating to each other regarding scheduling of international fixtures and how it would affect the Super League club. It was reported for example that a New Zealand tour was being envisaged for the autumn of 2015 before the Kiwis decided otherwise and chose instead maybe a more lucrative trip to England. If that had materialised though what would the results have been on and off the field for the Tricolours knowing what state they were in? Other stuff emerged too around the Federation's less than enthusiastic stance on the Dragons launch of their U19s Academy across the Channel – a project that previous coaches such as Mick Potter and Trent Robinson had advocated strongly.

With the RFL's new clarion call 'jeopardy' ringing in his ears Bernard Guasch would more than ever ring fence his clubs needs and aspirations above all else. With the club healthy off the field he would search everywhere to bring in the best players he could find to Perpignan to stay in front of the competition. The Tricolours like New Zealand would have to share the load. (NDRL the New Zealand Warriors provided just two players out of the 23 man Kiwi squad who played in England during 2015) Fages at St Helens, Springer at Castleford and Garcia at Penrith in the NRL will have to be the template from now on awaiting a second or indeed 3rd Super League presence further down the line.

B - French Elite 1 Competition

How the local French competition fared after the arrival in Super League of the Catalans was always going to be challenging. The focus had moved eastwards from the Atlantic and Villeneuve Sur-Lot to the Mediterranean and Perpignan at the turn of the century even if Toulouse Olympique under Justin Morgan had had their moments in 2005 and their incredible Challenge Cup run across the Channel. It was decided that when the Dragons kicked off in 2006 that their presence in the local league would be maintained with the inclusion of the Union Treize Catalans (UTC).

That first year there were 12 clubs in Elite 1 with the reappearance after a long sabbatical of Marseille and with the Bentley brothers Valu, Andrew and Kane signed up along with the young Younes Khattabi from Entraigues looked a promising proposition. Unfortunately with off-field financial problems quickly materialising they proved just a shooting star and folded before the season was out. With Justin Morgan by then embedded across the Channel at Hull KR it was the Donkeys of Pia who would take over from the UTC winning a cup and league double and thus keeping the silverware in Roussillon. Pia beat Toulouse in the Championship Final at Stade Ernest Wallon home of Stade Toulousain with a certain Trent Robinson in charge of the losers that May weekend.

The following year they ran with the same 11 teams who had competed in 2006 and the same results as Pia claimed an impressive league and cup back-to-back double as the codes power base consolidated around Perpignan. By 2008 though they had lost Villefranche, who where replaced in turn by Albi, still retaining 11 clubs. Both these clubs were from the same Midi Pyrenean region and from the Aveyron and Tarn *departments* respectively. It was important that the game achieved as wide a footprint as possible and doubly disappointing that by seasons end both had been lost. To add insult to injury Albi reached the Final of the Lord Derby Cup that year, losing to Limoux at Carcassonne with a good following from the Tarn. Whereas Villefranche suffered from their relative isolation Albi still had a discernable league following with a cluster of active juniors clubs in support.

By this time the accolade of top dog had edged north to the Aude area just north of Perpignan. Here, regardless of the success of its three very well established clubs Carcassonne, Lézignan and Limoux, the game has resonance. Close proximity and six annual derbies feeds the interest perpetually. If elsewhere crowds numbered only in their hundreds in the Aude the clashes between the local sides pull 2,000 plus on a regular basis. In 2008 Aurélien Cologni who was part of the Potter's initial Dragons squad in their debut season was installed as player-coach at Lézignan and he would take the *FeuCeuLeu* to a Championship title for the first time in 30 years.

2009 was a significant year in that the Toulouse club had followed the Dragons across the Channel and had integrated the Co-operative Championship. The hope was that the Olympique club would still keep a presence in the French competition but this didn't transpire in the way the Federation hoped for and instead TO XIII adopted St Gaudens as their partner club in Elite 1 utilising Gilles Dumas connections at both clubs. With Albi gone after just one term and Toulouse not doubling up as the Dragons had done with UTC, the competition was looking at only nine sides, but fortunately Avignon rebounded and moved up.

At the beginning of the decade there had been automatic promotion and relegation between Elite1 and Elite 2 but increasingly the second tier couldn't compete with the wealthier clubs who not only had the better local players but the means to draft in overseas players too. The clubs behind had had enough and preferred to compete at a level commensurate with their resources. On the field Lézignan retained the Championship title, beating neighbours Limoux in Carcassonne in front of an impressive 11,263 turn out, while up at Albi in the Tarn Carcassonne won its first bit of silverware in nearly twenty years picking up the Lord Derby Cup.

The reality was that with the Dragons still in their infancy, the French Elite were still taking time to come to terms with their arrival in Super League and its implications. With all the best players in Perpignan it was a new world which had opened up. There was still though the sight of French players who had played Super League dropping down and returning to the local competition bringing that professionalism with them. Internationals Aurélien Cologni and Renaud Guigue who played under Potter in the Catalans debut year, went on to be player coaches subsequently at Limoux and Avignon respectively while Younes Khattabi, the first ever French player to score a try at Wembley in a Challenge Cup Final returned to his roots up in Provence and would six years later play against England in a World Cup quarter-final. Rubbing shoulders with the like of Kiwi legend Stacey Jones et al was only to benefit the French game in its totality long-term. But this transition and journey was only just beginning.

From 2010 onwards the local competition would continue to lose stability and direction. When the Dragons entered Super League four years earlier there were 12 teams in Elite 1 but that had now dropped to only nine. There was still no sign of promotion and relegation returning as the Elite 2 clubs still hadn't the means to compete with the stronger clubs. The end of the previous decade had seen the Lézignan club dominate with their first Championship success in thirty years and their superiority had legs too as their winning streak would stretch to four with two further national titles in 2010 and 2011, the latter against neighbours Limoux before 11,874 at nearby Narbonne. That victory also historic in that it equalled the record of XIII Catalan back in the 1980's with four successive triumphs. And on top of that these last two achievements could be added wins in the Lord Derby Cup against Pia at Montpellier in 2010 and in 2011 against Limoux at Avignon.

By the following season the competition re-claimed Toulouse Olympique after their three year stay across the Channel was terminated. That first year back for them was compromised by having to back up between summer and winter competitions though it was evident that they'd achieved a certain toughness and durability from that experience in England. 2012 would be the year of the Canary and Carcassonne with a first league and cup double in more than forty years led inspirationally by the former Penrith and Salford player Luke Swain. The following year the Aude hegemony was over with the league title heading south for the year when Pia triumphed against neighbours St Estève-XIII Catalan in Perpignan. The fragility of the competition showed itself again as the holders of the Max Roussie Shield folded in months when the municipal authorities refused to bankroll the village outfit any further. Founded in 1960 and with seven Elite 1 titles to their name, Pia Salanque were no more.

St Estève-XIII Catalans continued to evolve under the returning Steve Deakin. Formerly known as the UTC the all French line-ups of mostly youngsters continued to evolve under the tutelage of the Englishman and later of the former Dragons player Cyrille Gossard. Players such as Escaré, Pelissier and Bousquet were being developed and soon to be promoted into the ranks of the Dragons in Super League. The sudden demise of Pia, successful on the field courtesy of heavy overseas recruitment but poorly supported, was hardly missed. Into their place jumped another Catalans minnow in Palau but more favourably, looked on as a club dependant on local talent. Very quickly the Perpignan clubs of the Elite 1 had turned their focus to development and recognising their supporting status in relation to the Dragons. At the beginning of the century the four local Elite1 clubs in the Perpignan area could muster up to 25 antipodean players, but by 2014 none would be turning out at Elite 1 level whereas the contingent over at Stade Gilbert Brutus was the calibre of Stacey Jones, Greg Bird, Steve Menzies and later Todd Carney, world class.

In 2014 the new in-coming Federation President Carlos Zaduendo introduced a new Championship format integrating Elite 1 and Elite 2 in a desperate attempt to create a viable competition The introduction was hardly a qualified success as the difference in levels between the two was still too great. This disparity even between such a hand-full of clubs encapsulated the ongoing state of play in France. The new structure didn't last with Zalduendo scurrying around trying to get former Elite 1 notables Lyon and Albi back at the top level by the autumn of 2015. He would have some luck with the Tarn club but not the Rhone side. They decided to go back to a simple *aller-retour* structure, as before, with a top division of nine sides. Even then they would be troubled by the financial woes up at Villeneuve-sur-Lot. Fortunately their future was guaranteed at the very last moment to enable one of founder clubs, celebrating their 80th year, to continue. Toulouse had been disappointed by their exclusion from the English game but it didn't diminish their long term goal to return yet again but this time stronger and wiser than before.

Under a new President, Bernard Sarrazain the Garonne club started to rebuild on and off the field with the Federation's President totally in support. In 2014 they would claim their first ever cup-league double in more than 70 years of trying, defeating Carcassonne at Stade Domec for the Lord Derby

Cup and Lézignan in Perpignan for the Championship title. The following year they defended the Championship title, successfully beating Carcassonne at Colomiers.

Toulouse, the 4th city of France, hosted an array of major sporting clubs playing at the top level in competitions with both a national and international dimension. It was why Toulouse Olympique viewed the domestic game, consisting mostly of clubs from small towns and villages in the South inappropriate to their needs, and why since the beginning of the century had sought a presence in a European Super League. They felt that it was the only way the code could make headway in the city and prosper. The RFL's Ralph Rimmer was on the Stade Ernest Wallon pitch in Toulouse in 2013 alongside Zalduendo for the Dragons-Hull KR game, where banners announcing TO XIII's accession to Super League in 2015 would be unfolded. However the new changes in the games structure initiated by the RFL later would though scupper that aspiration. To some it was incredulous to imagine that they would be invited back to a lower division than the one they departed in 2011 but that was what would be offered to them. The fact that they would be playing some teams initially not at the level of the Elite 1 didn't dissuade them. If that was the only way to eventually reach the holy grail of Super League so be it. Their intention would be to access the Championship in year one and that's where they were as 2016 beckoned. Toulouse Olympique, unlike 2009, would run with a reserve side in the Elite 1 competition incorporating the local Broncos set-up who previously had played in Elite 2. The road back for Toulouse was on track once again.

Perpignan has shown the way for others to follow. The locomotive TGV *haute de gamme* was pulling the rest of the game along in its slip stream. But on its own, insufficient to make the break through nationally and internationally, and why Toulouse's full participation is crucial. Avignon is another potential major hub further down the line building on the huge support they generate for international fixtures up in the Provence region, backed up by an endless seam of local talent. In the meantime players aspiring to become full-time professionals are looking increasingly elsewhere than the Elite 1. At a time when England are losing players to the NRL, young French players in increasing numbers are joining Super League clubs across the Channel as an alternative to Catalans. Simultaneously the penny seems to have dropped regarding French teams with French players. The season 2015-16 has seen all but the odd club fielding all local players something not seen in decades.

A decade earlier Mick Aldous the Australian who previously coached the Tricolours briefly had advised that the French Federation and the clubs to concentrate on the U14s, U16s and U18s age groups as a priority so as to make the senior pool bigger. The French competition just needs to find its true level with predominately local players. If they did it's possible that clubs, who in the past played in the top tier, could once again move up to join Elite 1 even if the standards dipped a bit initially. The over reliance on overseas players has artificially inflated the standard of play. Possibly they have to let this go. In some ways it has to start again from the bottom up with a serious emphasis on formation involving schools of rugby, U14s,U16s, Juniors, Masters, Touch, Women's teams et al.

After a decade of the Catalans Dragons traversing the Channel the game below is still coming to terms with its implication. Until the major building blocks at the apex are in place it is eternally treading water. In Ireland at the start of professionalism in rugby union they had a once and for all chance to change over night. What emerged was that four new full-time professional super regions, Connaught, Leinster, Munster and Ulster were formed which subsequently became the driving force for the national teams development and success. Maybe French rugby league can imitate something along those lines. In 1958 long before the Heineken Cup was thought of, Carcassonne and Albi played-off for the equivalent of that in the thirteen man code against England's best that year Hull and Halifax when the respective domestic competitions were on the same footing. Its inconceivable today of imagining that returning but the code has possibilities where it still has a discernable presence in Perpignan, Toulouse, the Aude and up in Provence around Avignon. The real challenge would be replicating the Catalans Dragons success story elsewhere.

Appendices
– FACTS & FIGURES –

PLAYER ROSTER - CHRONOLOGICAL 2006-15

The list of Catalans Dragons having played for the club since their debut against Wigan on 11th February 2006

Year	No.	Player	Opposition	Data	Venue	Result
2006	1	Laurent Frayssinous	Wigan	Feb-11	Aimé-Giral	W 38-30
2006	2	Justin Murphy	Wigan	Feb-11	Aimé-Giral	W 38-30
2006	3	Teddy Sadaoui	Wigan	Feb-11	Aimé-Giral	W 38-30
2006	4	John Wilson	Wigan	Feb-11	Aimé-Giral	W 38-30
2006	5	Mark Hughes	Wigan	Feb-11	Aimé-Giral	W 38-30
2006	6	Sean Rudder	Wigan	Feb-11	Aimé-Giral	W 38-30
2006	7	Stacey Jones	Wigan	Feb-11	Aimé-Giral	W 38-30
2006	8	Chris Beattie	Wigan	Feb-11	Aimé-Giral	W 38-30
2006	9	Julien Rinaldi	Wigan	Feb-11	Aimé-Giral	W 38-30
2006	10	Adel Fellous	Wigan	Feb-11	Aimé-Giral	W 38-30
2006	11	Jérôme Guisset	Wigan	Feb-11	Aimé-Giral	W 38-30
2006	12	Jamal Fakir	Wigan	Feb-11	Aimé-Giral	W 38-30
2006	13	Ian Hindmarsh	Wigan	Feb-11	Aimé-Giral	W 38-30
2006	14	Pascal Jampy	Wigan	Feb-11	Aimé-Giral	W 38-30
2006	15	Grégory Mounis	Wigan	Feb-11	Aimé-Giral	W 38-30
2006	16	Renaud Guigue	Wigan	Feb-11	Aimé-Giral	W 38-30
2006	17	Alex Chan	Wigan	Feb-11	AiméGiral	W 38-30
2006	18	Bruno Vergès	Salford	Feb-17	The Willows	L 0-16
2006	19	Julien Touxagas	Salford	Feb-17	The Willows	L 0-16
2006	20	Thomas Bosc	Castleford	Feb-26	Wheldon Road	L 28-34
2006	21	Michael Dobson	Leeds	Mar-11	Aimé-Giral	L10-58
2006	22	Lionel Teixido	Leeds	Mar-11	Aimé-Giral	L10-58
2006	23	David Berthezène	Warrington	Mar-18	HJ Stadium	W 28-26
2006	24	Freddie Zitter	Thornhill	Apr-02	St. Jean Laffon	W 66-0
2006	25	Rémi Casty	Thornhill	Apr-02	St. Jean Laffon	W 66-0
2006	26	Aurélien Cologni	St Helens	Apr-17	Aimé-Giral	L 20-34
2006	27	Sébastien Martins	St Helens	Apr-17	Aimé-Giral	L 20-34
2006	28	Younis Khattabi	Wigan	Jun-18	JJB Stadium	L 18-24
2006	29	Mathieu Griffi	Salford	Jul-22	Narbonne	W 26-6
2006	30	Cyrille Gossard	St Helens	Aug-19	Canet Village	W 26-22
2007	31	Clint Greenshields	Hull FC	Feb-11	KC Stadium	D 11-11

2007	32	Adam Mogg	Hull FC	Feb-11	KC Stadium	D 11-11
2007	33	Vincent Duport	Hull FC	Feb-11	KC Stadium	D 11-11
2007	34	Dimitri Pelo	Hull FC	Feb-11	KC Stadium	D 11-11
2007	35	Casey McGuire	Hull FC	Feb-11	KC Stadium	D 11-11
2007	36	Aaron Gorrell	Hull FC	Feb-11	KC Stadium	D 11-11
2007	37	Sébastien Raguin	Hull FC	Feb-11	KC Stadium	D 11-11
2007	38	Jason Croker	Hull FC	Feb-11	KC Stadium	D 11-11
2007	39	David Ferriol	Hull FC	Feb-11	KC Stadium	D 11-11
2007	40	Luke Quigley	Bradford	Mar-25	Odsal Stadium	W 29-22
2007	41	Andrew Bentley	Featherstone	Mar-31	Gilbert Brutus	W 70-12
2007	42	Kane Bentley	Featherstone	Mar-25	Gilbert Brutus	W 70-12
2007	43	Olivier Charles	Warrington	Apr-21	Gilbert Brutus	W 27-16
2007	44	Cyril Stacul	Bradford	Sep-09	Odsal Stadium	L 8-40
2008	45	Jean Philippe Baile	Castleford	Feb-09	Wheldon Road	W 21-14
2008	46	Dane Carlaw	Castleford	Feb-09	Wheldon Road	W 21-14
2008	47	Olivier Elima	Wigan	Apr-11	JJB Stadium	W 26-24
2008	48	Florian Quintilla	Featherstone	Apr-20	Post Office Rd	W 22-12
2009	49	Steven Bell	Huddersfield	Feb-14	Gilbert Brutus	L 8-30
2009	50	Shane Perry	Huddersfield	Feb-14	Gilbert Brutus	L 8-30
2009	51	Jason Ryles	Huddersfield	Feb-14	Gilbert Brutus	L 8-30
2009	52	Greg Bird	Castleford	Mar-07	Gilbert Brutus	L 22-24
2010	53	Chris Walker	Wakefield	Feb-07	Belle Vue	L20-28
2010	54	Setaimata Sa	Wakefield	Feb-07	Belle Vue	L20-28
2010	55	Dallas Johnson	Wakefield	Feb-07	Belle Vue	L20-28
2010	56	William Barthau	Harlequins	Feb-14	The Stoop	L 4-16
2010	57	David Guasch	Crusaders	Mar-19	Racecourse	L 6-14
2010	58	Tony Gigot	Crusaders	Mar-19	Racecourse	L 6-14
2010	59	Frédéric Vaccari	Huddersfield	Apr-02	Galpharm	L 6-48
2010	60	Mickael Simon	Huddersfield	Apr-02	Galpharm	L 6-48
2010	61	Brent Sherwin	Salford	Ma -22	Gilbert Brutus	L 14-22
2011	62	Damien Blanch	Harlequins	Feb-12	Cardiff	L 4-11
2011	63	Ben Farrar	Harlequins	Feb-12	Cardiff	L 4-11
2011	64	Scott Dureau	Harlequins	Feb-12	Cardiff	L 4-11
2011	65	Lopini Paea	Harlequins	Feb-12	Cardiff	L 4-11
2011	66	Ian Henderson	Harlequins	Feb-12	Cardiff	L 4-11
2011	67	Steve Menzies	Harlequins	Feb-12	Cardiff	L 4-11
2011	68	Eloi Pelissier	Wakefield	Feb-19	Gilbert Brutus	L 14-38
2011	69	Daryl Millard	Hull KR	Feb-27	Craven Park	W 31-18
2011	70	Jason Baitieri	Hull KR	Feb-27	Craven Park	W 31-18

Year	#	Player	Opponent	Date	Venue	Result
2011	71	Mathias Pala	Bradford	Apr-25	Gilbert Brutus	D 8-8
2011	72	Thibaut Ancely	Leeds	Jul-09	Gilbert Brutus	W 38-18
2011	73	Remi Marginet	St Helens	Jul-15	Widnes	L 18-40
2012	74	Louis Anderson	Bradford	Feb-05	Odsal Stadium	W 34-12
2012	75	Ben Fisher	Bradford	Feb-05	Odsal Stadium	W 34-12
2012	76	Leon Pryce	Castleford	Feb-18	Gilbert Brutus	W 28-20
2012	77	Damien Cardace	Widnes	Mar-31	Gilbert Brutus	W 76-6
2012	78	Julian Bousquet	St Helens	Jul-20	Gilbert Brutus	L 12-25
2012	79	Kevin Larroyer	Huddersfield	Au-05	Galpharm	L 18-36
2012	80	Antoni Maria	Castleford	Sep-02	Wheldon Road	W 46-26
2013	81	Brent Webb	Hull KR	Feb-03	Craven Park	W 32-24
2013	82	Zeb Taia	Hull KR	Feb-03	Craven Park	W 32-24
2013	83	Morgan Escaré	Bradford	Mar-23	Gilbert Brutus	W 30-10
2013	84	Elliott Whitehead	London	Jul-06	Gilbert Brutus	W 34-28
2013	85	Thibaut Margalet	Salford	Jul-19	Barton	L 12-16
2013	86	Benjamin Garcia	Leeds	Aug-30	Headingley	L 12-20
2014	87	Michael Oldfield	Hull FC	Feb-14	KC Stadium	L 34-36
2014	88	Ben Pomeroy	Hull FC	Feb-14	KC Stadium	L 34-36
2014	89	Jeff Lima	Hull FC	Feb-14	KC Stadium	L 34-36
2014	90	Gadwin Springer	St Helens	Mar-14	Langtree Park	L 22-40
2014	91	Joan Guasch	London	Apr-04	Gilbert Brutus	W 40-24
2014	92	Sam Williams	Hull FC	Jun-21	Gilbert Brutus	W 20-16
2015	93	Willie Tonga	St Helens	Feb-06	Langtree Park	L 7-18
2015	94	Todd Carney	Warrington	Feb-28	Gilbert Brutus	W 38-18
2015	95	Stan Robin	Wakefield	Apr-02	Belle Vue	W 40-4
2015	96	Fouad Yaha	Hull KR	Apr-25	Gilbert Brutus	W 32-24
2015	97	Krisnan Inu	Wakefield	Jun-20	Gilbert Brutus	W 32-12
2015	98	Jordan Sigismeau	Widnes	Jul-12	Halton Stadium	L 22-29
2015	99	Lucas Albert	Widnes	Jul-12	Halton Stadium	L 22-29
2015	100	Ugo Perez	Warrington	Sep-19	HJ Stadium	L 6-48

50 + APPEARANCES IN THE SANG-ET-OR 2006-15

GAMES	PLAYER	CAREER
251	Grégory Mounis	2006-2015
210	Thomas Bosc	2006-2015
210	Rémi Casty	2006-2013+2015
171	Jamal Fakir	2006-2014
146	Clint Greenshields	2007-2012
144	David Ferriol	2007-2012
141	Jérôme Guisset	2006-2010
137	Sébastien Raguin	2007-2012
136	Vincent Duport	2007-2009, 2011-15
135	Ian Henderson	2011-2015
134	Olivier Elima	2008-2010, 2013-2015
126	Eloi Pelissier	2011-2015
126	Jason Baitieri	2011-2015
99	Casey McGuire	2007-2010
99	Daryl Millard	2011-2014
96	Scott Dureau	2011-2015
94	Cyrille Gossard	2006-2012
88	Lopini Paea	2011-2014
87	Dimitri Pelo	2007-2010
86	Alex Chan	2006-2008
85	Jean-Philippe Baile	2008-2014
83	Adam Mogg	2007-2010
81	Louis Anderson	2012-2015
81	Leon Pryce	2012-2014
81	Morgan Escaré	2013-2015
81	Zeb Taia	2013-2015
81	Dane Carlaw	2008-2010
77	John Wilson	2006-2008
75	Damien Blanch	2011-2013
74	Mickael Simon	2010-2014
71	Steve Menzies	2011-2013
69	Setaimata Sa	2010-2012
68	Elliott Whitehead	2013-2015

67	Cyril Stacul	2007-2012
66	Justin Murphy	2006-2008
66	Julien Touxagas	2006-2011
62	Jason Croker	2007-2009
61	Julian Bousquet	2012-2015
58	Frédéric Vaccari	2010-2014

MOST POINTS 2006-15

MOST POINTS	PLAYER	CAREER
1,343	Thomas Bosc	2006-2015
792	Scott Dureau	2011-2015
340	Clint Greenshields	2007-2012
252	Vincent Duport	2007-09, 2011-15
243	Morgan Escaré	2013-2015
212	Justin Murphy	2006-2008
184	Damien Blanch	2011-2013
166	Daryl Millard	2011-2014
152	Olivier Elima	2008-10, 2013-15
150	Grégory Mounis	2006-2015

MOST TRIES 2006-15

TOTAL TRIES	PLAYER	CAREER
85	Clint Greenshields	2007-2012
63	Vincent Duport	2007-09, 2011-15
60	Morgan Escaré	2013-2015
58	Thomas Bosc	2006-2015
53	Justin Murphy	2006-2008
46	Damien Blanch	2011-2013
41	Daryl Millard	2011-2014
38	Olivier Elima	2008-10, 2013-15
37	Dimitri Pelo	2007-2010
37	Zeb Taia	2013-2015
33	Elliott Whitehead	2013-2015
31	Sébastien Raguin	2007-2012

MOST TRIES IN A SEASON 2006-15

MOST TRIES IN SEASON	PLAYER	SEASON
29	Morgan Escaré	2014
27	Justin Murphy	2006
22	Michael Oldfield	2014
21	Damien Blanch	2011
19	Elliott Whitehead	2014
19	Olivier Elima	2009
19	Vincent Duport	2012
19	Morgan Escaré	2013
18	Clint Greenshields	2008

COACHING RECORDS

COACH	YR	GAMES	WINS	DRAWS	LOSSES	WIN %
Mick Potter	2006	31	10	0	21	32%
Mick Potter	2007	32	14	1	17	53%
Mick Potter	2008	31	18	2	11	58%
Kevin Walters	2009	32	16	0	16	50%
Kevin Walters	2010	31	9	0	22	29%
Trent Robinson	2011	31	17	1	13	55%
Trent Robinson	2012	32	20	0	12	63%
Laurent Frayssinous	2013	31	15	2	14	48%
Laurent Frayssinous	2014	32	17	1	14	53%
Laurent Frayssinous	2015	32	14	2	16	44%

COACH	CAREER	GAMES	WINS	DRAWS	LOSSES	WIN %
Mick Potter	2006-08	94	42	3	49	45%
Kevin Walters	2009-10	63	25	0	38	40%
Trent Robinson	2011-12	63	37	1	25	59%
Laurent Frayssinous	2013-15	95	46	5	44	48%

CATALANS HOME SUPER LEAGUE CROWDS

YEAR	NO. GAMES	SMALLEST	BIGGEST	HOME CROWDS TOTAL*
2006	15	4,197	11,122	92,794
2007	14	7,052	9,050	105,907
2008	16	6,225	9,985	135,751
2009	14	7,420	18,150	126,073
2010	14	5,055	8,884	93,818
2011	14	6,742	10,688	116,288
2012	16	7,337	13,858	140,108
2013	15	6,286	14,858	117,725
2014	14	6,488	9,864	113,017
2015	14	7,392	10,423	125,388
				1,166,869

(* Includes Challenge Cup games)

CATALANS % SUPER LEAGUE GAMES WON

SUPER LEAGUE 2006-15	PERCENTAGE OF GAMES WON
BRADFORD	50%
CASTLEFORD	57%
CELTIC CRUSADERS	67%
HARLEQUINS/LONDON BRONCOS	69%
HUDDERSFIELD	38%
HULL FC	38%
HULL KR	58%
LEEDS	24%
SALFORD	47%
ST HELENS	44%
WAKEFIELD	52%
WARRINGTON	44%
WIDNES	63%
WIGAN	31%

– POT-POURRI –

CATALANS DRAGONS V USAP

For the first time in fifteen years the Chairmen of USAP (François Rivière) and the Dragons (Bernard Guasch) agreed to discuss through the *L'Indépendant* newspaper the competition between the two rival clubs. And to answer the question: How to cohabit? (How to reconcile the two codes?)

How do you view the other code?

Bernard Guasch: "My father played for USAP in the Championship Final back in 1952 (they lost against Lourdes 20-11), then at the age of twenty signed for XIII Catalan and gave his life to rugby league. I grew up at the Stade Gilbert Brutus, my DNA is league, my passion oval-shaped. A nice try, a well-adjusted pass, a big tackle personify both codes."

François Rivière: " Without paraphrasing, this is the land of both codes. The Dragons are achieving an excellent season (2014), we must be delighted at their success even though I don't follow them very closely because USAP takes up all my time. The basic question is: can top-level sport belong to the future of our region? I believe it can."

Are both codes irreconcilable from the viewpoint of history?

BG: " Basically in every family of Roussillon, people were either pro-USAP or pro-XIII Catalan. There will always be the old divides and that's a fine thing because our difference is a blessing. Rugby league was born in 1934 here thanks to a Catalan named Jean Galia. From then on, our sport has started disturbing the normal order of things. We were despoiled by the Vichy government in 1944 (it forbade the code, NDLR), then we underwent as a traumatic event the 1981 Final (free-for-all scuffle live on state television that led to decades of boycott from all the state television channels). Even today, we suffer from a poor national media coverage whereas we play in the English Super League. We feel the sporting world don't like us. We had to fight in order to get some recognition. Nowadays, rugby league has become entertainment and businesslike, like union. We must move beyond the squabbles of the past and be less sectarian. A real fan should support both Dragons and USAP intelligently."

FR: "It's not history that will seal the reconciliation between the two codes, but the future. If we look back, the exacerbation of the quarrels and of the key personalities means that there will always be divides. My lack of experience in these circles(he has been chairman since 2013, NDLR) and my weak knowledge of history are indeed an asset because I'm not a prisoner of the past. What is sure is that, in France, union is given a lot more TV coverage. And yet, media coverage and TV ratings give rhythm to our daily life."

Renovation work at Aimé-Giral and Gilbert-Brutus: Why does each code keep to itself?

GB: "Ten years ago, we might have brought about some changes in people's attitudes. But now, considering the amount spent on the renovation of the two stadia and the present economic crisis, it's too late to contemplate a shared stadium. Fortunately, there is room for the two codes. We're lucky not to have a top-level football club in our region. We are the land of the two codes to quote Christian Bourquin (former chairman of the Languedoc-Roussillon Regional Council who died in 2013)."

FR: "It's complicated. Only one stadium is a really good idea even if it's a cause for dissension, but politically and economically speaking, it's too early to talk about this today. Let's take the example of the Toulouse area: in 20 years time, will there be room for clubs such as Blagnac, Colomiers, Castres, Albi and Montauban? Likewise, with the increasing importance of money, will Perpignan, Narbonne and Carcassonne still be alive? The future of rugby union belongs to big cities. Our future maybe linked with the Dragons. I'm not closed to any proposals".

Synergy or competition: which one is the right model?

BG: "François Rivière's recent initiative came as a pleasant surprise (operation '1 ticket for 2 matches' NDLR) and it appealed to nearly 2000 spectators. It was a clever approach for the beginnings of the reconciliation. That day, a taboo was broken, it helped to rid some sponsors of their complexes because some of them didn't dare to say openly that they were committed to both clubs. That was a real conciliatory overture, because we convey the same colours and the same Catalan values. I prefer a healthy competition to the ostracism that we have been suffering for so long".

FR: "There is still plenty of synergy to think up. First towards the spectators: the complicity between them and us must be beneficial to the fans. Then, with regard to the sponsors, our region is fairly small, so it's necessary to adapt our respective commercial policies in order to make them complementary. Thirdly, and this is the main point, the future of the 2 clubs, at least the one of USAP, is linked to the grooming of youngsters because it is not expensive. It's the only way for us to stand up to the clubs from the big cities in tomorrow's world. Why not dream up a shared training centre? If a young player does his basic training in both codes, he will obviously be a better player. Consequently, I prefer synergy to competition. To hate the others is pointless."

Who is the number 1 in the region?

BG: "This question is justified. We have remained in the shadow of USAP for long periods, but we have also enjoyed our periods of domination, mainly in the 1950's and until the 1980's when we recruited the best union players. This is something Paul Goze (former chairman of USAP) could never tolerate. We must remember that, in his days, there were 500 spectators at the Amié-Giral stadium and 5000 at Gilbert-Brutus. In 2000, when USAP became professional, we had reached rock bottom. Then, I convinced XIII Catalan and St Estève to patch things up and achieve a united front. That's why the RFL chose us. I will just say that now the league people over here deserve a lot of credit for the hard work done in the last fifteen years. Perhaps the next 10 years will be a decade of rugby league. This is in no way offensive to USAP. In 2015 we'll celebrate our tenth anniversary and we intend to take the leadership of the region and to try and snatch a trophy from the English."

FR: "Since we have been relegated to the second division (Pro 2), our values of re-conquest have been mainly based on humility. In 2014 I wish we could be acknowledged for these values. If we talk about figures (budgets, season tickets) USAP is slightly above. As far as sporting results are concerned, the Dragons are above, but the requirements and the pressure in the first two divisions (Top 14 and Pro2) have always been stronger because two clubs are relegated at the end of every season. To be honest, I don't think anybody can claim that one club is above the other one."

"So who really is number 1?" asks Bernard Guasch with a mischievous smile. The Chairman of the Dragons has a knowing look, sitting behind his flashy desk in the

American style, at the office of his business where he greeted us on the eve of their first ever win at Headingley in the first round of the play-offs in 2014 against Leeds.

"Nobody can claim that one club is above the other", answers cautiously François Rivière, his union counterpart, sitting at a table outside Quai 66, the pub owned by USAP, four days after a good win against Agen.

One is a history buff and he has been suffering for fifteen years from the condescension of USAP; the other one is a late addition, without any quarrelsome prejudice towards the Dragons. Together Guasch and Rivière are thinking today of a smooth cohabitation, a topic that mixes historical, economical and sporting rivalries in a climte of populism. But if we (*L'Indépendant*) give priority to the sporting field, we feel that the Catalans Dragons are clearly in front in the Roussillon region at this moment in time.

Translation by Jean Nohet.

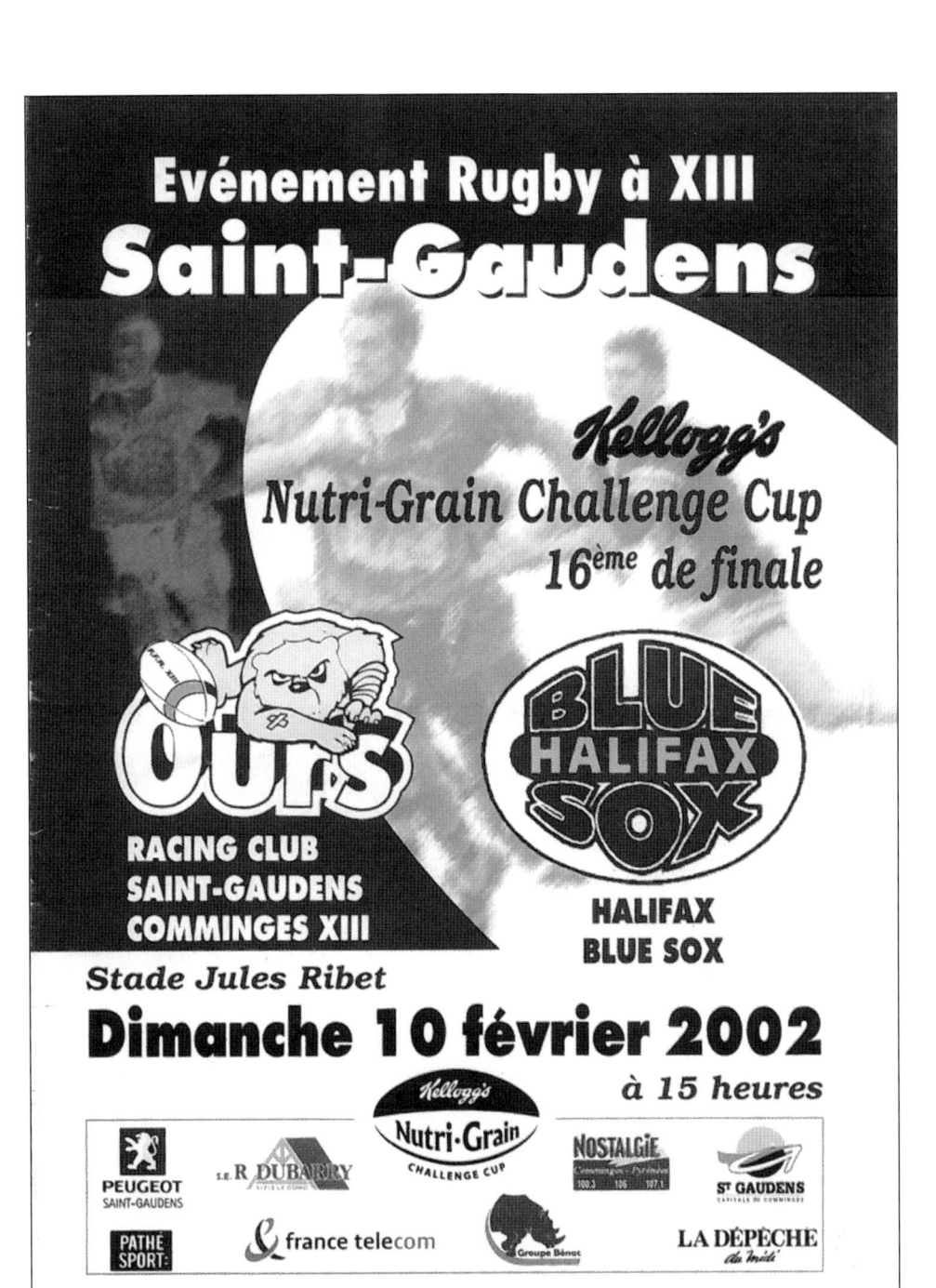

Under Richard Lewis's stewardship the Challenge Cup crossed national boundaries like never before as the 21st century came into view with France leading the way. An historic day was 10th February 2002 in the 'petite' town of St. Gaudens below the snow covered Pyrenean peaks when the hosts entertained Halifax in the first ever Cup tie played across the Channel.

SAINT HELENS - DRAGONS CATALANS : 30-8

Trop fort, Saint Helens

Battus en finale de la Cup à Wembley, les Dragons Catalans sont tombés avec les honneurs.

SAINT HELENS - DRAGONS CATALANS : 30-8 (12-4)

À Wembley, Londres. 84 241 spectateurs. Très beau temps. Excellente pelouse. Arbitre : M. Klein. SAINT HELENS : 5 E, Roby (34e), Gardner (40e, 77e), Wellens (46e), Clough (52e), 1 B, Long (67e), 4 T, Long (34e, 40e, 46e, 77e). DRAGONS CATALANS : 2 E, Khattabi (38e), Murphy (57e).
Évolution du score : 6-0, 6-4, 12-4 (mi-temps), 18-4, 22-4, 22-8, 24-8, 30-8.
SAINT HELENS : Wellens -A. Gardner, Gidley, Talau, Meli - (o) Pryce, (m) **Long** - Wilkin - Bennett, Gilmour - Fozzard, Cunningham (cap.), J. Cayless. **Entraineur** : D. Anderson. **Entrés en jeu** : Roby, Graham, Fa'asavalu, Clough.
DRAGONS CATALANS : Greenshields - Murphy, Wilson, Raguin, Y. Khattabi - (o) Mogg, (m) Jones (cap) - Mounis - Croker, Gossard - Guisset, Quigley, Chan. **Entraineur** : M. Potter. **Entrés en jeu** : Ferriol, Casty, Duport, K. Bentley.

LONDRES –
de notre envoyé spécial

LE MIRACLE n'a pas eu lieu. Hier, les Dragons Catalans, première équipe non anglaise à disputer une finale de la Coupe d'Angleterre depuis sa création, en 1896, n'ont pas réussi à battre la meilleure équipe du monde, Saint Helens, qui a ajouté une nouvelle pièce à sa collection de titres (11e Coupe). Cependant, les Catalans ont mérité leur tour d'honneur, acclamés par les 4 000 supporters roussillonnais qui avaient fait le déplacement. « On a tout donné, reconnaît le pilier Jérôme Guisset. À la fin du match, il faut reconnaître que Saint Helens est une meilleure équipe que nous. Ils jouent avec beaucoup de classe. Mais on n'a pas fait un match de figurants et le score est lourd à la sortie. » En première mi-temps, le match mettait du temps à se débrider. L'arbitre vidéo refusait un essai à Croker (28e). Un essai de funambule de Roby permettait à Saint Helens d'ouvrir le score (4-0, 34e), avant que les Dragons ne répliquent quasi instantanément par Khattabi après une belle combinaison de trois-quarts (6-4, 38e). Mais, sur la dernière action, l'arbitre accordait un essai à Gardner, malgré un en-avant évident, qui a fait gronder le stade de Wembley de mécontentement. « Se prendre un essai entaché d'un large en-avant, ça nous a fait mal, peste le pilier Casty. Car on n'était pas loin (12-4 à la mi-temps au lieu de 6-4). » Plus forts physiquement, les Saints, portés par leurs 25 000 supporters venus de cette ville de 170 000 habitants située non loin de Liverpool, inscrivaient à la reprise deux essais et mettaient un terme au suspense (52e, 22-4). Les Dragons tentaient de combler leur retard, mais commettaient trop de maladresses. Un essai de Murphy chez les Dragons (57e, 22-8) et un dernier de Gardner après un superbe travail de Wellens – archifavori pour le titre de « man of steel » (meilleur joueur de l'année) – scellaient le match. Le capitaine du jour, Keiron Cunningham, pouvait soulever la coupe dans un charivari.
En dépit de la défaite, Bernard Guasch, le président des Dragons Catalans, ne perdait pas son large sourire. « Cela restera comme une journée historique et mémorable pour le rugby à XIII français. Pour tous les treizistes, voir les Dragons Catalans pénétrer sur la pelouse de Wembley fut un moment émouvant. Nous avons désormais le record de public pour un club sportif français (84 241 spectateurs). On peut en être fiers. » Aujourd'hui, une fête est prévue à 18 heures à Perpignan, au pied du Castillet, pour rendre hommage à l'épopée des Dragons. « On va avoir une belle réception, promet Guisset. Même si on a perdu, on peut revenir la tête haute. »

BENJAMIN MASSOT

LONDRES. – Les Saints, logiques vainqueurs des Dragons, brandissent la coupe une fois de plus. (Photo Marc Francotte)

L'Équipe's Wembley coverage in 2007 for the Final of the 'Coupe d'Angleterre' underwhelming but at least they dispatched their reporter for the occasion!

Laurent Frayssinous and Aurélien Cologni go head-to-head in this Championship Final of 2002 played in Béziers. Frayssinous still in his home town colours of Villeneuve and Cologni a Catalan in the sang-et-or of UTC. Both would be Dragons by 2006 and later both successful coaches. Crowd was no great shakes that day either struggling to reach 4,000.

Si tu (Rémi Casty) devais envoyer un fax au Président Guasch ?

« Un grand bravo pour tout ce que vous avez fait, et merci de m'avoir embarqué dans cette aventure. »

"It involves matters much greater than drafting the new rules… the original and existing games have their own powerful appeal to their players and public and have the sentiments which history inspires."
Harold 'Jersey' Flegg 1933

« Écrire est un acte
    D'amour
        S'il ne l'est pas,
            Il n'est qu'écriture. »
Jean Cocteau